PORTUGUESE STUDIES

VOLUME 29 NUMBER 1
2013

Founding Editor
HELDER MACEDO

Editors
FRANCISCO BETHENCOURT
RICARDO SOARES DE OLIVEIRA
JULIET PERKINS
LÚCIA SÁ
DAVID TREECE
ABDOOLKARIM VAKIL

Editorial Assistant
RICHARD CORRELL

Production Editor
GRAHAM NELSON

MODERN HUMANITIES RESEARCH ASSOCIATION

PORTUGUESE STUDIES

A biannual multi-disciplinary journal devoted to research on the cultures, societies, and history of the Lusophone world

International Advisory Board

David Brookshaw
João de Pina Cabral
Ivo José de Castro
Thomas F. Earle
John Gledson
Anna Klobucka

Maria Manuel Lisboa
Kenneth Maxwell
Paulo de Medeiros
Laura de Mello e Souza
Maria Irene Ramalho
Silviano Santiago

Articles to be considered for publication may be on any subject within the field but should not exceed 7,500 words and should be written in English. The Editorial Assistant is willing to undertake translations of texts from Portuguese if required; there will be a charge for this service. Contributions should be submitted in a form ready for publication in English and sent as an email attachment to the Editorial Assistant at richard.correll@kcl.ac.uk. The text should conform precisely to the conventions of the *MHRA Style Guide*, 3rd edn, 2013 (978-1-78188-009-8), obtainable from www.style.mhra.org.uk, price £6.50, US $13, €8; an online version is also available from the same address. Quotations and references should be carefully checked. Any quotations in Portuguese must be accompanied by an English translation. *Portuguese Studies* regrets that it must charge contributors with the cost of corrections in proof which the Editors in their discretion think excessive. Copies of books for review should be sent to The Reviews Editor, *Portuguese Studies*, Department of Spanish, Portuguese and Latin American Studies, King's College London, Strand, London WC2R 2LS, UK.

Portuguese Studies and other journals published by the MHRA may be ordered from JSTOR (http://about.jstor.org/csp). The journal is also available to individual members of the Modern Humanities Research Association in return for a composite membership subscription payable in advance. Further information about the activities of the MHRA and individual membership can be obtained from the Honorary Secretary, Dr Barbara Burns, School of Modern Languages and Cultures, University of Glasgow, Bute Gardens, Glasgow G12 8RS, or from the website at www.mhra.org.uk.

Disclaimer: Statements of fact and opinion in the content of *Portuguese Studies* are those of the respective authors and contributors and not of the journal editors or of the Modern Humanities Research Association (MHRA). MHRA makes no representation, express or implied, in respect of the accuracy of the material in this journal and cannot accept any legal responsibility or liability for any errors or omissions that may be made.

Parts of this work may be reproduced as permitted under legal provisions for fair dealing (or fair use) for the purposes of research, private study, criticism, or review, or when a relevant collective licensing agreement is in place. All other reproduction requires the written permission of the copyright holder who may be contacted at rights@mhra.org.uk.

ISSN 0267–5315 (print)   ISSN 2222-4270 (online)   ISBN 978-1-78188-037-1

© 2013 THE MODERN HUMANITIES RESEARCH ASSOCIATION

Portuguese Studies vol. 29 no. 1

CONTENTS

Preface	4
Revisiting the Anglo-Norman Crusaders' Failed Attempt to Conquer Lisbon *c*. 1142 Lucas Villegas-Aristizábal	7
'The lyceums work in silence, they do not advertise, and have no time for envy or rivalry': A Case Study of the *Liceu Rodrigues de Freitas/ D. Manuel II* during the Portuguese Estado Novo Luís Grosso Correia	21
An Ethics of Displaying Affection: Hélio Oiticica's Expressions of Joy and Togetherness Karl Posso	44
Afro-Brazilian Culture in London: Images and Discourses in Transnational Movements Simone Frangella	78
Courting Death in Hélia Correia's *Adoecer* Isabel Fernandes	94
The Novels of Valter Hugo Mãe Carlos Nogueira	106
Abstracts	127

Preface

This issue of *Portuguese Studies* showcases once more the diverse nature of our constantly growing subject area. History, education, art, sociology and literature are represented by six articles on topics new to the journal, by contributors who are, with one exception, equally new to it. They take us from the twelfth to the twenty-first century, three of them intersecting in some way with Anglophone history, people and *loci*.

Lucas Villegas-Aristizábal undertakes a contextualized reading of the 1142 attempt to conquer Lisbon from the departure point of two Latin texts. He assesses the historical and political forces behind Anglo-Norman participation in the Iberian expedition, the ambiguous cooperation with D. Afonso Henriques, and the siege's value as a trial run for a later attempt at reconquest. **Luís Grosso Correia**'s substantially documented article analyses the socio-political *desiderata* of the Estado Novo's educational reforms and, through an illuminating case study, the specifics and extent of their realization.

Karl Posso's revelatory article on Hélio Oiticica, accompanied by striking illustrations, grounds the experimental artist in Brazilian counter-culturalism before probing his aesthetic evolution in respect of audience participation, of an art of togetherness and encounter, demonstrating the artist's use of sensation, affect and emotion for political and ethical ends. Another dimension of Brazil is the subject of **Simone Frangella**'s research. Examining, first, the insertion of a largely commodified Brazilian culture into London, she then focuses on its specifically Afro-Brazilian manifestations. Whilst demonstrating their different connotations for the community itself, for the producers and consumers, she raises important questions about cultural transpositions within the capital city's multi-ethnic environment.

Finally, two articles on important contemporary Portuguese writers turn up unexpected resonances between their aesthetics of contrary desires, morbidity and the fantastic. In her overview of the novel, *Adoecer*, **Isabel Fernandes** examines Hélia Correia's favoured canvas of biography and anglophilia, and the narrative, stylistic and psychological resources by which the novelist embroiders the ambiguities of illness, death and sexuality, archetypal to the Pre-Raphaelites and germane to the love affair between Dante Gabriel Rossetti and his model, Elizabeth Siddal. **Carlos Nogueira** presents a useful survey of the novels of Valter Hugo Mãe (valter hugo mãe, in the author's preferred spelling). He identifies the tensions and divisions, sexual and otherwise, within families and society, reveals the tonic note of violence, repression and suffering and foregrounds the conflicted homosexuality and homoeroticism of Mãe's protagonists in an early and a recent example of his work.

* * * * *

As this issue was going to press, the news was announced from Lisbon of the death on 17 January 2013 of Stephen Reckert, the distinguished Lusitanist and regular contributor to *Portuguese Studies*. Camoens Professor Emeritus of the University of London, this gifted and generous literary scholar held the Chair from 1967 until his retirement in 1982. Under his aegis, the Department of Portuguese (later to be the birthplace of this journal) expanded its teaching and research horizons to include Brazil and then Lusophone Africa. There can be no UK Lusitanist or Hispanist not in his debt for his magisterial publications on the Galician-Portuguese lyric and Gil Vicente. His readings of Camões, Cesário Verde, Pessanha, Bandeira, Drummond and Melo Neto are never less than illuminating. The original and brilliant *Beyond Chrysanthemums: Perspectives on Poetry East and West* strewed the riches of Portuguese and Brazilian poets before a wider, comparative literature readership. In teaching, research and publications, his first and best love was poetry; his human and intellectual frontiers were universal. It is a lesson in openness that we would hope to reflect in *Portuguese Studies*. We honour Stephen Reckert's memory with gratitude and affection.

THE EDITORS

Revisiting the Anglo-Norman Crusaders' Failed Attempt to Conquer Lisbon c. 1142

LUCAS VILLEGAS-ARISTIZÁBAL

Richmond, The American International University in London

The main narrative source for the Christian conquest of Lisbon in 1147 is the English chronicle known as *De expugnatione Lyxbonensi* that is kept in Corpus Christi College, Cambridge.[1] This is an important text that has been heavily researched by crusader historians for both its innovative theological approach to crusading and its detailed description of a military venture in the mid-twelfth century.[2] Describing, as it does, the sack of Lisbon by an international detachment of the Second Crusade, the best-known event of that venture outside the Latin East, it has attracted plenty of attention. Furthermore, *De expugnatione Lyxbonensi* has a little known section that says: *Inter quos Willelmus Vitulus, adhuc spirans minarum cedisque piraticae, et Radulfus frater eius et omnes fere Hamtunenses et Hastingenses, cum hiis qui ante hoc quinquennium urbem Ulyxibonam obsidendam conuenerant, omnes uno ore regis [s]ponsionem accipere nichil aliud quam proditionem aiebant* [...] [Among whom William Viel, yet breathing out threatenings and piratical slaughter, and his brother Ralph and almost all the men of Southampton and Hastings, together with those who had come to besiege Lisbon five years before this, all

---

[1] Corpus Christ College, Cambridge, Archbishop Matthew Parker Collection, Ms. 470, fls. 125ʳ–146ʳ.

[2] *História de Portugal: Edição Monumental*, ed. by Damião António Peres (Lisbon: Portucalense, 1929), II, 17–18; Augusto Vieira da Silva, *A cerca moura de Lisboa* (Lisbon: Publicações Culturais da Câmara Municipal de Lisboa, 1939); Harold V. Livermore, *A History of Portugal* (Cambridge: Cambridge University Press, 1947), pp. 61–62; Costa Brochado, *A conquista de Lisboa aos mouros* (Lisbon: Empresa Nacional de Publicidade, 1952); Giles Constable, 'A Note on the Route of the Anglo-Flemish Crusaders of 1147', *Speculum*, 28 (1954), 525–26; António H. de Oliveira Marques, *History of Portugal*, 2 vols (New York: Columbia University Press, 1972), I, 34–38; António Sérgio, *Breve interpretação da história de Portugal* (Lisbon: Livraria Sá da Costa Editora, 1981), p. 13; Bernard F. Reilly, *The Kingdom of León-Castilla under Alfonso VI* (Princeton, NJ: Princeton University Press, 1988), pp. 253–56; Jonathan Phillips, 'St Bernard of Clairvaux, the Low Countries and the Lisbon Letter of the Second Crusade', *Journal of Ecclesiastical History*, 48 (1997), 485–97; Maria João Branco, 'A conquista de Lisboa revisitada', *Arqueologia Medieval*, 7 (2001), 217–34; Matthew Bennet, 'Military Aspects of the Conquest of Lisbon, 1147', in *The Second Crusade: Scope and Consequences*, ed. by Jonathan Phillips and Martin Hoch (Manchester: Manchester University Press, 2001), pp. 71–89; *A Conquista de Lisboa aos mouros: Relato de um cruzado*, ed. by Aires A. Nascimento (Lisbon: Vega, 2007); Giles Constable, 'A Further Note on the Conquest of Lisbon', in *The Experience of Crusading*, ed. by Marcus Bull, Norman Housley, Peter Edbury and Jonathan Phillips, 2 vols (Cambridge: Cambridge University Press, 2003), I, 39–44; Helen J. Nicholson, *The Crusades* (London: Greenwood Publishing Group, 2004), p. 26.

with one voice declared that they took the king's promise to be nothing but treachery [...]].³ Here the Chronicle is referring to an earlier expedition in which a group of Anglo-Norman crusaders attempted to conquer Lisbon. Charles W. David has claimed that this expedition, which perhaps took place in 1142, was the same expedition mentioned in a Portuguese annal that is known as the *Chronicle* or *History of the Goths*. The purpose of this article is to translate and analyse the relevant section of these annals and compare it to the relevant references in *De expugnatione Lyxbonensi* and other sources. It is hoped that this will then produce a better understanding of this expedition by placing it within the context of the crusades, as a preamble to the somewhat later conquest of Lisbon in 1147.⁴ Since this is the first maritime expedition known to the historical record in which the participants, despite having taken a vow of crusade with the intention of reaching the Holy Land, had instead, or at least temporarily, taken part in an Iberian Reconquista, it is of particular interest to crusader historians.

Unfortunately for medieval historians, the *History of the Goths* only exists in two seventeenth-century copies which were published in a book edited by António Brandão and printed at the monastery of Saint Bernard in Lisbon.⁵ Nothing is known about what happened to the original manuscript from which the seventeenth-century cleric copied this text. It is likely, as is the case for many medieval manuscripts registering the history of Lisbon, that it was lost during one of the many earthquakes and fires that hit the Portuguese capital from the fourteenth to the eighteenth centuries.⁶ As Francisco Bautista has pointed out, the *Chronicon Gothorum*, as it was named by Brandão, is neither a Chronicle nor it is about the Goths — a better title might be *Annales Lusitani*, as he has suggested more recently.⁷ However, for the sake of consistency with earlier works, this article will refer to it as the *History of the Goths*.

Pierre David, who wrote extensively on early Portuguese sources from the

---

³ *The Conquest of Lisbon*, trans. by Charles W. David and ed. by Jonathan Phillips (New York: Columbia University Press, 2001), pp. 100–03; *A Conquista de Lisboa aos mouros*, ed. by Nascimento, pp. 84–85.

⁴ This expedition was not the first maritime venture by northern Europeans to the Holy Land, as it is well known that many groups of galleys from northern Europe were present during the sieges and campaigns of the First Crusade. Moreover, Vikings had raided the coasts of the Iberian Peninsula since the ninth century. John H. Pryor, 'A View from a Masthead: The First Crusade from the Sea', *Crusades*, 7 (2008), 106–15; Jaime Ferreiro Alemparte, *Arribadas de normandos y cruzados a las costas de la península ibérica* (Madrid: Sociedad española de estudios medievales, 1999), pp. 19–70.

⁵ Brandão edn, 'Historia Gothorum', in *Terceira parte da monarchia lusitana*, fols 271–76ᵛ; Lisbon, Biblioteca Nacional de Portugal, Códices Alcobacenses CDXLIX/116 (Seventeenth century), fols 319(311)ʳ–327(319)ᵛ; Enrique Florez, 'Chronicon Lusitanum', in *España Sagrada* (Madrid, 1786), xiv, 415–32; Luiz Gonzaga de Azevedo, *História de Portugal* (Lisbon: Bíblion, 1942), iv, 174; 'História dos Godos', in *Fontes Medievais da História de Portugal*, ed. by Alfredo Pimenta (Lisbon: Livraria Sá da Costa, 1948), i, 35–36.

⁶ Branco, pp. 217–18.

⁷ Francisco Bautista, 'Breve historiografía: Listas regias y anales en la Península Ibérica', *Talia dixit*, 4 (2009), 113–90 (p. 176). Stephen Lay, 'Escribiendo la Reconquista: La consolidación de la memoria histórica en el Portugal del siglo XII', *Studia historica: Historia medieval*, 29 (2011), 121–43.

twelfth century, believed that the text was part of a collection of sources that he called the *Annales Portugalenses veteres.*[8] He believed that their origin lay in a lost Chronicle composed mostly in the eleventh century, in Guimarães. This thesis, however, has been disputed more recently by Bautista and Lay, who claim that they were produced in Coimbra in a more linear way.[9]

There are two versions of the text, a longer and a shorter one, published by Brandão and subsequent editors, over which some historiographical disputes have taken place.[10] Herculano, for example, was convinced that the shorter text was the more accurate copy of the original, claiming that the longer one contained extra passages gathered from other sources at a later date.[11] Pierre David and Luiz Gonzaga de Azevedo believed that the shorter version was a seventeenth-century edition because of the prolific use of anachronistic terms.[12] However, the longer text is not exempt from anachronistic terms, such as the use of Matilda for Mafalda. On the other hand, the language used in the section describing the failed attempt to conquer Lisbon does indeed fit in with the supposition that the original is from the late twelfth or early thirteenth century. In addition, in the case of the passage under discussion here, both versions are identical. Moreover, as has been noted, these annals are based on the *Annales Conimbrigenses* I and II, although they expand the section on the reign of Afonso Henriques extensively. Their relation to the *Annales Conimbrigenses* does suggest that perhaps the chronicle comes originally from Coimbra. However, the fact that the text contains sections such as the part here discussed does suggest that the author used other sources which have been lost from the historical record.[13]

Although the original manuscript does not exist, there is a logical clue to its origins in the text itself. The second and most original part of the annals starts in 1109 and ends in 1185, years that coincide exactly with the lifespan of Afonso Henriques, the first king of Portugal. This suggests that the text was intended as either a posthumous tribute to his deeds or a compilation of earlier records.[14] This, however, does not guarantee that the text was produced during or soon after the reign of the Portuguese monarch, since Afonso Henriques as the founder of the Portuguese kingdom remained an important hero of the Portuguese nation long after his death. However, Pierre David believed that the structure of the text, in the form of annals, along with its content, dated it to the late twelfth century. He did, however, suggest that it contained some alterations from the fourteenth century. He also claimed that the text was composed of

---

[8] Pierre David, *Études Historiques sur la Galice et le Portugal du VIe au XIIIe siècle* (Lisbon: Livraria Portugália, 1947), pp. 261–90.
[9] Lay, 'Escribiendo la Reconquista', p. 123.
[10] Gonzaga de Azevedo, *História de Portugal*, IV, 174.
[11] Alexandre Herculano, *Portugalliæ Monumenta Historica*, 4 vols (Lisbon: Academia das Ciências de Lisboa, 1860), I, 5–7
[12] Gonzaga de Azevedo, *História de Portugal*, IV, 174–93; Pierre David, pp. 282–83; Bautista, p. 176.
[13] Bautista, p. 176; Lay, pp. 123.
[14] Brandão edn, 'Historia Gothorum', fols 271–76^v. 'História dos Godos', pp. 22–47.

two independent parts, with the second part (which is the one discussed in this article) being composed in the early thirteenth century.[15] Moreover, other Portuguese specialists like Joaquim Veríssimo Serrão have dated the chronicle not later than the mid thirteenth century.[16] More recently, Francisco Bautista, in his work on Iberian sources, has been very dismissive of Pierre David's assertion that the text was constructed in two independent sections.[17] He argues that the whole text was written by a single author, perhaps as a nostalgic tribute to the golden age of Afonso Henriques' reign. Bautista concludes that because the text does not include later legends about the first Portuguese monarch, and because of its writing style, that it must be from the reign of Sancho II (1223–47).[18]

Its use of the Spanish era (i.e. the era of Caesar) as the dating mechanism suggests that the text was originally from no later than the early fifteenth century. However, Bautista does point out that although the text does have some earlier phrases, it also contains some anachronisms. This suggests that Brandão — or his source — might have edited the original.[19] On the other hand, for the section explored in this article, as mentioned earlier, it appears from the language used by the copyist that he did not bother to modernize the Latin terms. Therefore, for at least this section, it is reasonable to assume that the document was not seriously altered. For example, in the first line of the text we can see that the author refers to the participants from northern Europe as men of war who had made a vow to go to Jerusalem instead of *crusignati*, as was the case in later chronicles of the thirteenth and fourteenth centuries.[20] Unlike other chronicles from the twelfth century it does not describe the participants as pilgrims, but instead treats their aims as being military.[21] In this way it is making a differentiation between peaceful pilgrims and crusaders, in the later acceptance of the word.[22]

This could, in fact, be one of the first references to this differentiation in the narrative evidence of the crusades in general. It is also the first reference to crusaders going to the Holy Land participating in the Portuguese *Reconquista*, an important event in the ever growing interest paid by foreign crusaders to

---

[15] David, pp. 257–59; Bautista, p. 177.
[16] Joaquim Veríssimo Serrão, *A Historiografia Portuguesa*, 3 vols (Lisbon: Editorial Verbo, 1971), I, 14–15.
[17] Bautista, pp. 176–77.
[18] Ibid. p. 181.
[19] Ibid. pp. 176–77.
[20] Christopher Tyerman, 'Were there any Crusades in the twelfth century?' *English Historical Review*, 110 (1995), 553–77 (p. 575); Christopher Tyerman, *Fighting for Christendom: Holy War and the Crusades* (Oxford: Oxford University Press, 2004), pp. 4, 27–32; Norman Housley, *Contesting the Crusades* (Oxford: Oxford University Press, 2006), pp. 13–23.
[21] The wording used is similar to a reference made by Ralph of Coggeshall to the sack of Constantinople in 1204, while writing in the first quarter of the thirteenth century referred to crusaders as follows: *Si quis autem plenius nosse desiderat qualiter urbs Constantinopolis semel et iterum ab exercitu latinorum hierusalem tendentium capta sit* [...] [If anyone wishes to know more fully how the city of Constantinople was captured once and again by an army of Latin Christians on their way to Jerusalem [...]]. Ralph of Coggeshall, *Chronicon Anglicanum*, ed. by Joseph Stevenson (London, 1875), p. 151.
[22] '*plenæ armatis uiris uotum habentes ire in Ieruſalem*', Brandão edn, fol. 274.

the Iberian variant of the crusades.²³ Moreover, the differentiation of these armed pilgrims from those who were unarmed is significant in understanding the perception of the crusades in the mind of their contemporaries. The fact that this Portuguese observer was able to distinguish this endeavour from a peaceful pilgrimage is of vital importance to the debate on the wording and meaning of the crusades, which is still a matter of dispute among historians.²⁴ Furthermore, as Lay has shown, the *History of the Goths* is very precise in its use of language in defining the Muslims as enemies of Christianity, which further shows the author's interest in describing the Portuguese struggle as a religious one.²⁵

The description of the crusader as *uiris uotum habentes ire in Ierufalem* is certainly relevant to the historiographical discussion between the traditionalists and the pluralists, as defined by Constable.²⁶ Of course, this reference could be used to argue that the concept of 'crusade' was not always the same throughout its history, and was not formed at a specific period of time, i.e. the First Crusade — or the Third, as Tyerman argues — but was a changing idea that had a different meaning to different people in time and space, as Chevedden has suggested.²⁷ Perhaps the idea of crusade was not invented by a single individual Pope (i.e. Urban II) but was the result of the transformation of Christian holy war from the early days of Christianity.²⁸ However, the reference can also be used by the most ardent modern traditionalist historians to argue that the fact that the chronicler refers to these warriors as 'men of war with a vow to go to Jerusalem' does imply that the Holy City had a primary significance in the formation of the idea of the crusades while the Iberian theatre of war with Islam was not considered fully equal to that of the Holy Land.²⁹ If so, this expedition was perceived not as a crusade but a simple raid on an important port on the Atlantic Iberian coast. Even so, the fact that this expedition did not receive papal

---

²³ In reference to the use of the word *Reconquista* see Francisco García Fitz, 'La Reconquista: Un estado de la cuestión', *Clio & Crimen*, 6 (2009), 142–215.
²⁴ Elizabeth Siberry, *Criticism of Crusading, 1095–1274* (Oxford: Oxford University Press, 1985), pp. vii–viii; Jonathan Riley-Smith, *What were the Crusades?* (Basingstoke: Macmillan, 1992), pp. 86–89; Norman Housley, *The Later Crusades from Lyons to Alcazar, 1274–1580* (Oxford: Oxford University Press, 1992), pp. 1–4; Jonathan Riley-Smith, *The Crusades* (London: Continuum, 2001), pp. xxvii–xxx.
²⁵ Lay, p. 127.
²⁶ Giles Constable, 'The Historiography of the Crusades', in *The Crusades from the Perspective of Byzantium and the Muslim World*, ed. by Angeliki E. Laiou and Roy Parviz Mottahedeh (Washington, DC: Dumbarton Oaks Research Library and Collection, 2001), pp. 1–22.
²⁷ Jonathan Riley-Smith, *The Crusades: A Short History* (London: Yale University Press, 1990), pp. xxviii–xxix; Tyerman, 'Were there any Crusades in the twelfth century?' pp. 533–77; Housley, *Contesting the Crusades*, pp. 18–23; Paul E. Chevedden, 'Islamic and Christian Views of the Crusades', *History*, 93 (2008), 181–200; Paul E. Chevedden, 'Session 133: The Holy War and the Origins of the Crusades', *45th International Medieval Congress* (Kalamazoo, MI, 13 May 2010).
²⁸ Paul E. Chevedden, 'Canon 2 of the Council of Clermont (1095) and the Crusade Indulgence', *Annuarium historiae conciliorum*, 37.2 (2005), 254–72.
²⁹ Brandão edn, 'Historia Gothorum', fol. 274; 'História dos Godos', pp. 35–36; Christopher Tyerman, *The Invention of the Crusades* (Basingstoke: Macmillan, 1998), pp. 4–5, 49–55; Housley, *Contesting the Crusades*, pp. 3–13; Riley-Smith, *The Crusades*, pp. xxviii–xxix.

approval and that the chronicler does not seem to emphasize its religious nature does not necessarily mean that those who took part in the attack did not feel that they were fulfilling their vows by fighting the Muslims in Iberia. Certainly, the existence of this reference is of great importance to the understanding of the evolution of the idea of Christian holy war or crusade in the eyes of those who took part. Regardless of which camp or position historians might take in the arguments regarding the origins of the crusades and their definition, the fact that this chronicler referred to these soldiers as men of war with a vow to go to Jerusalem should not be ignored, especially since it is well known that the concept was not named as a 'crusade' until much later, and even now there is no consensus among historians.

In reference to the date given by the *History of the Goths* and by the chronicle of the conquest of Lisbon (1140/42), the crusaders were not part of a large expedition, like the Second Crusade, but were a smaller force, whose trip to Jerusalem was not inspired by any general call for crusade by the papacy, but was an act of private enterprise, perhaps with a different set of motives, as we shall discuss further later. There is some discrepancy in the way the *De expugnatione Lyxbonensi* and the *History of the Goths* date this expedition. According to *De expugnatione*, this first attempt to take the city took place five years before the definitive conquest, placing it in 1142. On the other hand, the *History of the Goths* explains that the expedition to Lisbon took place around the same time that the King of Portugal made a truce with the King of Castile and Leon, and places both events in the year 1140. It is known from other sources, however, that the Treaty of Zamora was signed in 1143.[30] It is clear from the language used by the chronicler that the date of this expedition is somewhere in the vicinity of 1140 and therefore one could claim that 1142 should be the date of the expedition. It seems logical to assume that *De expugnatione Lyxbonensi* is more accurate with regard to this date, as it was written by a participant in the 1147 expedition.[31] Moreover, as explained above, the *History of the Goths* is very vague as an annal by virtue of its dating system, placed in the margin. However, with regard to the final conquest of Lisbon, it does date the event correctly to 1147.[32] Even with regard to the month of the beginning of the siege of the

---

[30] Oliveira Marques, I, 53.
[31] *The Conquest of Lisbon*, pp. 40–51; Harold V. Livermore, 'The "Conquest of Lisbon" and its Author', *Portuguese Studies*, 6 (1990), 1–16.
[32] *Era 1185 [1147]. Idem Rex Portugallis D. Alfonſus decimo nono anno regni ſui nimia audacia & animoſitate ſuccinctus noctu inuaſit caſtellum de Sanctarem viriliter cum paucis ſuorũ, fretus Dei auxilio, & vendicauit cum ſibi, & Chriſtianitati, Interfectis & excluſis inde sarracenis habitantibus in eo. Hoc autem factum eſt per voluntatem Dei quinto Idus Maij ad galli cantum, illuceſcente die Sabbati. Et in eodem anno menſe Iulio Vlixbonam obſedit, cui prouidente ex alto diuina clementia multitudo nauium de Galliarũ partibus cælitus tranſmiſſa ſubito ex inſperato aduenit in auxilium, quorũ auxilio valde fretus obſedit Ciuitatem per quinq' menſes, fortiter vexans & oppugnas eam terra & Mari, nullum permittens eggredi, vel ingredi. Tandem vero nono Calendas Nouembris feria 6. Sexta diei hora cepit Ciuitatem in manu valida & in brachio Extenſo cooperante Domini pietate, & adjuvante Domino Jeſu Chriſto, excluſis inde Sarracenis* [In the year 1185 of the Spanish Era [AD 1147] this same king of Portugal Dom Alfonso, in the nineteenth year of his reign, armed with excessive daring and enthusiasm entered

conquest of Lisbon both chronicles agreed that it was in July.[33] Of course, the importance of the final fall of Lisbon overshadowed the earlier failed expedition and the authors of both chronicles could have had better access to either written or oral sources for that expedition in particular.

Regarding the origins of the crusaders involved in this expedition, the *History of the Goths* does not provide us with much information about them, apart from claiming that they came from Gaul.[34] As was the case with the charter of allegiance quoted by the author of the *De expugnatione Lyxbonensi*, the author of the *History of the Goths* used 'Gaul' as a generic term for foreigners from northern Europe.[35] However, it does mention the names of at least some of the participants, when it explains that the crusaders were mistrustful of the Portuguese as a result of their earlier experiences in an attempt to conquer this city.[36] Moreover, as has been explained, this first group of crusaders who had attempted to conquer Lisbon in 1142 were not responding to a general call for crusade, as was the case with their more successful successors of 1147.[37]

As in the case of the conquest of Lisbon of 1147, the Anglo-Norman and Norman crusaders were coming from an area that had been suffering a period of relative political instability.[38] It is within this context that our group of

the castle of Santarém at night in manly fashion, with a few of his own men, and with the help of God, and claimed it for himself and for Christendom, having killed the Saracens that were living in it. This was done according to the will of God on the fifth ides of May at cock crow on Saturday as it was getting light. And in the month of July in the same year he besieged Lisbon; to his aid, thanks to the care of divine clemency from above, came a great number of ships, sent by Heaven from parts of Gaul suddenly and unexpectedly; much supported by their help he besieged the city for five months, strongly harrying and attacking it by land and sea, not allowing anyone to leave or enter. Finally truly on Friday 6 November at the sixth hour he took the city with a strong hand and a long-reaching arm, the Saracens having been cast out, with the aid of the Lord's compassion and the help of Our Lord Jesus Christ]. Brandão edn, fol. 274ᵛ.

[33] *The Conquest of Lisbon*, pp. 96–97.
[34] Brandão edn, fol. 274ʳ.; 'História dos Godos', pp. 35–36.
[35] *The Conquest of Lisbon*, pp. 111; The use of the word *Galliorum* or G in both chronicles in reference to foreigners of multiple origins is a further proof that both chronicles date from *before* the fourteenth century, as by then the Portuguese chroniclers had dropped the use of this generic term and started to delineate the nationalities individually, as is the case in the chronicle of Fernão Lopes. Moreover, even if the text was copied at a later date the term was not modernized. Derek Lomax and Robert J. Oakley, *Fernão Lopes: The English in Portugal, 1367–87* (Warminster: Aris & Phillips, 1988).
[36] *The Conquest of Lisbon*, pp. 100–03; Nascimento edn, pp. 84–85.
[37] Henry of Huntingdon, *Historia Anglorum*, ed. by Diana Greenway (Oxford: Oxford University Press, 1996), pp. 724–39; *Gesta Stephani*, ed. by Kenneth R. Potter and Ralph H. C. Davies (Oxford: Clarendon Press, 1976), pp. 112–37; William of Malmesbury, *De gestis regum Anglorum* 2, ed. by William Stubbs (London, 1889), pp. 569–71; John T. Appleby, *The Troubled Reign of King Stephen* (London: Harper Collins, 1969), pp. 97–102; David Crouch, *The Reign of King Stephen, 1135–1154* (Harlow: Longman, 2000), pp. 133–43; Donald Matthew, *King Stephen* (London: Hambledon Continuum, 2002), pp. 83–112.
[38] As a result of Henry I's death without leaving a male heir, England and Normandy suffered a struggle for power between Henry's daughter, Matilda, and his nephew, Stephen. This period is known in English historiography as the 'Anarchy of King Stephen'. The general debate as to whether the whole period was one of general warfare and instability, as portrayed by the clerical authors of the contemporary narratives, has been reviewed in recent decades by historians such as King and Matthews. However, it is still agreed that although the warfare was far more intermittent than sometimes claimed, there were short periods of time in which the political struggle for power increased

crusaders decided to travel to the Holy Land by sea.[39] Furthermore, it is easy to speculate that these Anglo-Normans had a variety of motives for leaving their homeland to embark on a crusade that had not been officially endorsed by the papacy. The *De expugnatione Lyxbonensi*, being an Anglo-Norman source, is naturally better informed than the *History*, and it is in the former that we find the only references to the crusaders who took part. We might think that it would also be more interested in recording the names of the leading contingents, but the only participants that have been recorded by name were William and Ralph Vitalus.[40] However, there are some clues in *De expugnatione* about the professions of those who took part. In particular, the clerical author of that chronicle describes the Vitalus brothers as pirates (*piraticae*).[41] Whether this is a clerical slander directed at opponents to Harvey of Glanville's leadership or some form of regional rivalry, it is well known that during this period English traders alternated between piracy and legitimate merchant enterprises on both sides of the English Channel.[42] Moreover, as John Pryor explains in his article on the sea voyages of the First Crusade, northern European pilgrims had already established long sea routes from northern Europe to the Mediterranean.[43]

Charles W. David, on the other hand, has asserted that William and his brother Ralph belonged to a family that had a long historical connection with the Norman ruling dynasty in England and Normandy. Judging by multiple references in the Pipe Rolls, cited by David, members of this family seem to have been involved in the transportation of horses and supplies for the Anglo-Norman monarchs since the reign of William I and continued to be involved in this kind of venture during the reign of Henry II.[44] This, together with further evidence from the early thirteenth century, shows that the Vitalus family

---

in intensity, bringing devastation to some areas of England, especially in the midlands and the south. Edmund King, 'The Anarchy of King Stephen's Reign', *Transactions of the Royal Historical Society*, 34 (1984), 133–53.

[39] At the beginning of 1141, Stephen had been captured by forces allied to Empress Matilda at the Battle of Lincoln. Empress Matilda imprisoned him at Bristol while she tried to establish her new rule over the country. Despite her early success in encouraging a great number of prelates and nobles to join her cause, she still managed to antagonize the commune of the city of London by her apparent lack of political tact. During the summer of that year, the forces loyal to Stephen under the leadership of his queen (who was also named Matilda) managed to force the Empress out of London and routed her forces at Winchester. By a stroke of luck the forces loyal to Stephen captured Roger of Gloucester, who was the Empress's half-brother and her main supporter and therefore of vital importance to her cause. So by Christmas of 1141 the English dynastic dispute had reached a stalemate that made both leading figures too weak to control the local nobility in their private squabbles. Matthew, pp. 106–11.

[40] *The Conquest of Lisbon*, pp. 100–03, n. 1.

[41] Ibid.

[42] Antonio Ortega Villoslada, 'Viajes a Flandes e Inglaterra ¿Cabotaje o *recta via*?' *Espacio, Tiempo y Forma, Serie III, Historia Medieval*, 16 (2003), 229–49 (pp. 231–34).

[43] Pryor, pp. 106–15.

[44] *The Conquest of Lisbon*, pp. 100–03, n. 1.

had some social standing in the local community in Hampshire long after the events discussed in this article.[45]

From the evidence provided by David, it is unclear which side this family took, if any, in the struggle for the throne between Stephen and the Empress Matilda, known as the Anarchy.[46] However, it seems likely that on account of their business ventures across the English Channel the Vitalus family were eager to remove themselves from the current situation within England in order to avoid being drawn into the struggle for power. In this way they would be able to wait and see who would finally be victorious. Meanwhile they were able to profit spiritually and financially from a crusade to the Holy Land. This, of course, according to some clerical chroniclers, was the main motivation of some crusaders during the Second Crusade.[47] However, it also possible that since Empress Matilda's spouse, Geoffrey Plantagenet, Count of Anjou, had taken control of Normandy they had sided with the Empress during her failed attempt to take control. Because of this they were forced to use their crusader venture as a way to protect their properties in England from the wrath of Stephen or his local supporters. In fact, Nascimento, in his edition of *De expugnatione*, claims that the Vitalis whom he calls 'Calf' had been aligned with the Empress Matilda and against Stephen.[48] Whatever the ulterior motives of the Vitalus brothers and their followers, they were certainly expecting to capture Lisbon in 1142 and were disappointed by Afonso Henriques' decision to quit the siege. From the Portuguese annals we grasp that the aim of the expedition was to reach Jerusalem, but what exactly the Anglo-Normans had planned after reaching the Holy Land on this earlier expedition remains unknown.

It is also unknown how well this group was aware of the situation there at the time. The reign of King Fulk of Jerusalem was characterized by a conflict between the old nobility of the kingdom and newcomers who had attracted the attention of the Angevin monarch.[49] On the other hand, being merchants, it is likely that — like their clerical contemporary Orderic Vitalis — they were indeed well informed about the situation in the Holy Land.[50] It is not unlikely

---

[45] A Geoffrey Vitalus, a probable descendent of the Vitalus family, appears in a local charter from Canford listing him as one of the witnesses. *The Christchurch Priory Cartulary*, ed. by Katherine A. Hanna (Winchester: Hampshire Record Society, 2007), doc. 527.
[46] *The Conquest of Lisbon*, pp. 100–03, n. 1.
[47] *ubi oportunum videretur dimicaturi pro paupertate relevanda alii qui premebantur ere alieno, vel qui debita dominorum cogitabant relinquere servitia* [They were to fight where there seemed to be the opportunity, for the sake of relieving their poverty; others, who were oppressed by money owed to others, or who thought to cast off the service which they owed to their lords]. 'Annales Herbipolenses', in *Monumenta Germaniæ Historica*, ed. by Georg Heinrich Pertz (Stuttgart: Kraus, 1963), XVI, 3.
[48] Nascimento edn, p. 164 n. 100.
[49] Hans Eberhard Mayer, 'Angevins versus Normans: The New Men of King Fulk of Jerusalem', *Proceedings of the American Philosophical Society*, 133.1 (1989), 1–25; Andrew Jotischky, *Crusading and the Crusader States* (Oxford: Oxford University Press, 2004), pp. 75–76.
[50] Orderic Vitalis finished his great work in 1141 and he was well aware of the situation in the Latin East, even though he was writing in Normandy at the time. So it is not too far-fetched to speculate that a trading family might be quite well informed about the events in the Levant. Marjorie Chibnall, *The World of Orderic Vitalis* (Oxford: Oxford University Press, 1984).

that they were intending to find a fortune and perhaps salvation in the struggle between King Fulk and Queen Melisande.

On the other hand, as described in the chronicle of William of Tyre, King Fulk endeavoured in the later years of the 1140s to fortify the position of the Latin Kingdom of Jerusalem with regard to its enemies both in the north and in the south.[51] However, none of the chronicles of the Latin East mentions the arrival of any crusader fleet in 1142. Although the documentation of this period before the Second Crusade in the Latin East is not very detailed, it is possible that the crusaders did arrive in the Holy Land as suggested by the Portuguese source.[52] A detachment might have arrived in Jerusalem sometime in the year 1143 and might have stayed in the Holy Land until the end of the year 1144. In this way, they might have brought the news of the fall of Edessa to the Anglo-Norman domains. This would explain the quick reaction of the Anglo-Normans to 'take the cross' and travel by sea to the Holy Land as part of the Second Crusade. Of course, this is speculative, since the evidence is lacking, and it is more likely that the fiasco at Lisbon simply made it impossible for this group of Anglo-Normans to continue on their way to Jerusalem as they might originally have planned.

It is likely that these Anglo-Normans were aware that since the beginning of the twelfth century the papacy had declared the Iberian campaigns against the Moors equal with those in the Holy Land, making them therefore crusades in the eyes of the Church.[53] Moreover, although this was the first known maritime expedition to get involved in a campaign against the Moors in the Peninsula, it was not the first time that a group of crusaders or adventurers from the Anglo-Norman domains was involved in the *Reconquista*. They might have known about the involvement of certain Norman nobles like Roger of Tosny and Robert Crispin in the eleventh century and later of Robert Burdet and Rotrou of Perche.[54] These last two had been involved in Iberia very recently. Moreover,

---

[51] Willelmi Tyrensis archiepiscopi, *Chronicon*, ed. by R. B. C. Huygens (Turnhout: Brepols, 1986), pp. 705–10; Joshua Prawer, *The Crusaders' Kingdom: European Colonialism in the Middle Ages* (London: Phoenix Press, 2001), pp. 83, 133; Jonathan Phillips, *Defenders of the Holy Land* (Oxford: Oxford University Press, 1996), pp. 57–72.

[52] Mayer, pp. 1–5.

[53] José Goñi Gaztambide, *Historia de la bula de cruzada en España* (Vitoria: Editorial del Seminario, 1958), pp. 43–66; Derek W. Lomax, *The Reconquest of Spain* (London: Longman, 1978), pp. 59–63; Joseph F. O'Callaghan, *Reconquest and Crusade in Medieval Spain* (Philadelphia: University of Pennsylvania Press, 2003), pp. 38–41; Lucas Villegas-Aristizábal, 'Norman and Anglo-Norman Participation in the Iberian Reconquista, c.1018–c.1248' (unpublished PhD Thesis, University of Nottingham, 2007), pp. 107–45.

[54] Joan Miret i Sans, 'La familia de Robert Burdet, el restaurador de Tarragona', in *Segundo congreso de historia de la corona de Aragón: Actas y memorias*, 3 vols (Huesca: Iusto Martinez, 1922), I, 53–74; Lawrence J. McCrank, 'Norman Crusaders in the Catalan Reconquest: Robert Burdet and the Principality of Tarragona', *Journal of Medieval History*, 7 (1981), 67–82; Eloy Benito Ruano, 'El principado de Tarragona', in *Misel·lània Ramon d'Abadal* (Barcelona: Estudis Universitaris Catalans, 1994), pp. 107–19; A. Jordà Fernández, 'Terminologia jurídica i dret comù: A propòsit de Robert Bordet, "Princeps" de Tarragona (s.XII)', *El Temps Sota Control: Homenatge a E. Xavier Ricomà Vendrell* (Tarragona: Diputación Provincial de Tarragona, 1997), pp. 355–62; Villegas-Aristizábal, 'Norman

just a few years earlier the Norman chronicler Orderic Vitalis had included the adventures of these two Normans in his chronicle.[55] It is therefore conceivable that William and his brother Ralph might have been aware that Robert had managed to get a lordship for himself in Iberia, which at the time had seemed to be in a secure position.[56] It is possible to speculate that this family of merchants, with connections both in south-east England and Normandy, might have been invited by Robert Burdet, or at least had heard of his successes directly from the Norman adventurer himself, while he was in Normandy gathering supporters; alternatively they might have heard of it from someone else.[57]

In the *History of the Goths* we can see examples of the first contacts between northern European crusaders and an Iberian monarch concerning a planned expedition against the Moors in Iberia. It is clear that the crusaders were prepared to sign an agreement with the Portuguese monarch in order to avoid any future confrontations over the siege and conquest of the city.[58] However, it is clear from the references in the *De expugnatione* that some of them were less than happy about their relationship.[59] Unfortunately the *History of the Goths*, from the Portuguese side, does not mention any falling out between the Anglo-Normans and the Portuguese over the failure of the siege of Lisbon. Instead it refers to the fact that the city was well protected and well supplied, and that therefore the Anglo-Normans had decided that any further attempt to take the city at that point was futile. It seems, though, from what *De expugnatione* claims, that they felt betrayed by the Portuguese monarch because the siege had been abandoned.[60] Now it would be logical to assume that the Portuguese chronicler who reported the events would have tried to explain why Afonso Henriques had not taken the city on this occasion, by taking into account the fact that the city was well supplied and ready to sustain a long siege.[61] On the other hand, the Anglo-Norman crusaders were, perhaps, misinformed by an over optimistic Portuguese monarch beforehand in the attempt to conquer Lisbon and therefore when the second incursion happened the crusaders from England were less than happy to cooperate in this endeavour, as they believed that it was going to end the same way.[62] These types of misunderstanding seemed to have continued in the relations between the Portuguese monarchs

---

and Anglo-Norman Participation in the Iberian Reconquista', pp. 108–45; Lucas Villegas-Aristizábal, 'Roger of Tosny's Adventures in the County of Barcelona', *Nottingham Medieval Studies*, 52 (2008), 5–16.
[55] Orderic Vitalis, VI, 402–05.
[56] Villegas-Aristizábal, 'Norman and Anglo-Norman Participation in the Iberian Reconquista', pp. 130–35.
[57] Orderic Vitalis, VI, 402–05.
[58] Brandão edn 'Historia Gothorum', fol. 274ʳ; 'História dos Godos', pp. 35–36.
[59] *The Conquest of Lisbon*, pp. 100–03; Nascimento edn, pp. 84–85.
[60] Ibid.
[61] Matthew Bennett, 'Military Aspects of the Conquest of Lisbon, 1147', in *The Second Crusade: Scope and Consequences*, ed. by Jonathan Phillips and Martin Hoch (Manchester: Manchester University Press, 2001), pp. 73–75.
[62] *The Conquest of Lisbon*, pp. 100–03; Nascimento edn, pp. 84–85.

and their crusading allies from northern Europe, as was evident during the Third Crusade in Portugal and later expeditions.[63]

On the other hand, the participation of these Anglo-Normans in the siege of Lisbon c. 1142 showed Afonso Henriques the possibility of using these waves of crusaders travelling to the Holy Land in later expeditions against the Moorish cities of the Algarve. This was actually the case in the more successful campaign of 1147. In that case the numbers of crusaders involved was much larger and perhaps Afonso Henriques knew that Bernard of Clairvaux was promoting a crusade to the Holy Land by sea, as Jonathan Phillips has suggested.[64] Therefore he was much better prepared for that venture. However, even if Afonso Henriques had not planned an expedition against Lisbon with the prior knowledge that some northern crusaders would help him, he could have predicted from this earlier experience that it would not be difficult to attract some of them to his new venture.[65]

Although this first expedition proved to be less successful than the Anglo-Normans had expected, it probably convinced Afonso Henriques of the need for a more sophisticated approach to taking the city — for example that he should first take Santarém and in this way close off the Tagus River as a supply line.[66] This attempt by the Portuguese to take Lisbon c. 1142 may have been a premeditated raid designed to measure the strength of the defences of Lisbon, in order to decide whether or not to organize a later siege, but to the Anglo-Norman participants the failure to take the city seems to have left a bitter taste. This left some distrust among some Anglo-Normans that would later hinder, to some degree, the cooperation with the Iberian monarchs. However, in the long run, perhaps because the majority of those involved in this earlier attempt came from a very restricted area of England, i.e. Hampshire and Kent, this experience did not seem to have had a lasting impact on the involvement of Anglo-Norman contingents in the Portuguese campaigns against the Muslims. On the contrary, it is well known that the crusaders involved in the many campaigns of conquest on the Portuguese coasts from the twelfth century to the early decades of the thirteenth century came not only from the Anglo-Norman domains

---

[63] Jaime Ferreiro Alemparte, *Incursiones de normandos y cruzados a las costas de la península ibérica* (Madrid: Sociedad Española de Estudios Medievales, 1999); Lucas Villegas Aristizábal, 'Revisión de las crónicas de Ralph de Diceto y de la *Gesta regis ricardi* sobre la participación de la flota angevina durante la tercera cruzada en Portugal', *Studia Historica: Historia Medieval*, 27 (2009), 153–70.

[64] Jonathan Phillips, 'St Bernard of Clairvaux, The Low Countries and the Lisbon letter of the Second Crusade', *Journal of Ecclesiastical History*, 48.3 (1997), 485–97.

[65] Alan Forey, 'The Conquest of Lisbon and the Second Crusade', *Portuguese Studies*, 20 (2004), 13–15.

[66] Santarém was conquered in March of the same year (1147), with the help of the Templars, and in this way the fluvial access to Lisbon was closed. Also Afonso Henriques managed to form an alliance with the ruler of Seville which helped to reduce the possibility of a Moorish army coming to relieve Lisbon when he finally laid siege to it during the Second Crusade. *Crónica de cinco reis de Portugal: Segunda parte da crónica geral de Espanha*, ed. by Artur de Magalhães Basto (Porto: Civilização, 1945), I, 80–92; 'A conquista de Santarém', in *Fontes Medievais da História de Portugal*, ed. by Alfredo Pimenta (Lisbon: Livraria Sá da Costa, 1948), pp. 93–106; Forey, pp. 3–4.

but from all parts of northern Europe.[67] On the other hand, although the *De expugnatione Lyxbonensi* tells that William Vitalus and his brother Ralph had a poor opinion of the King of Portugal, we can deduce from the *History of the Goths* that perhaps not everyone felt betrayed by the Portuguese monarch in this endeavour, as it is seems clear that the group of Anglo-Normans continued on their way to Jerusalem after the failed siege. Moreover, the latter source does point out that the Anglo-Normans destroyed and pillaged the area surrounding the city. Perhaps in this way they gathered enough resources for the remaining part of their trip to the Holy Land, meaning that their endeavour was not a complete disaster from their point of view.[68] This may explain why during the Second Crusade many Anglo-Normans were prepared to sign the agreement with the king of the Portuguese, even though many mistrusted him as a result of this earlier attempt on the Portuguese city.[69] It also makes more apparent why the Bishop of Porto was inclined to give his famous speech to persuade the crusaders of the worthiness of the second attempt on Lisbon.[70] Moreover, for the Portuguese this earlier alliance perhaps showed the potential that it had for later endeavours against the Muslims in the south. As a result, when the Second Crusade was finally proclaimed by Pope Eugene III, Afonso Henriques made all the preparations to launch a further attempt on Lisbon, expecting the arrival of a new army of crusaders that could easily be encouraged to take Lisbon, especially under the banner of the crusade.[71] Even if he did not receive direct support from either Pope Eugene III or St Bernard, as Forey has suggested, it is likely that he was well aware of the preparations that were being made for a crusade in the eastern Mediterranean.[72] Therefore, encouraged by that knowledge and his earlier experience, he could have planned his attack from his new position of strength at Santarém, to coincide with the 1147 summer journey to the Holy Land.

---

[67] Ferreiro Alemparte, pp. 77–105; Villegas-Aristizábal, 'Norman and Anglo-Norman Participation in the Iberian Reconquista', pp. 146–290.
[68] *Sed irruperunt fuburbana eius, & demoliti funt multas uineas, & fuccenderunt domos, & fecerunt plagam magnam in terra* [However, they entered the outskirts and destroyed many vineyards and burned their houses, and greatly plagued the land]. Brandão edn, fol. 274; 'História dos Godos', pp. 35–36.
[69] *Sed nostrorum maior pars, omni occasione remota, assensum remanendi prebet, Colonensibus, Flandrensibus, Bolonensibus, Britonibus, Scottis in hoc idem libentissime assentientibus* [But the greater part of our force, setting aside every objection, agreed to remain, and the men of Cologne, Flanders, and Boulogne, the Bretons and Scots very willingly gave their consent]. *The Conquest of Lisbon*, pp. 100–02; *De expugnatione Lyxbonensi*, trans. by David, pp. 102–05.
[70] Ibid. pp. 130–31; Tyerman, 'Were there any crusades in the twelfth century?' pp. 563–64.
[71] Jonathan Phillips, *The Second Crusade: Extending the Frontiers of Christendom* (London: Yale University Press, 2007), pp. 144–46.
[72] Forey, p. 15.

Appendix

Here is the section of the *History of the Goths* relevant to the failed attempt to conquer Lisbon *c.* 1142:

> *Eodem quoque tempore venerunt quædam naues ex in ſperato de partibus Galliarum, plenæ armatis uiris uotum habentes ire in Ieruſalem, cumque ueniſſent ad Portum Gaye & intraſſent Dorium, audiuit hec Rex, & gauiſus eſt cum eis, erant enim fere septuaginta, & pace initus cum eis ut irent ad Vlixbonam ipſe per mare & ipſe cum exercitu ſuo per terram, & obſiderent eam, forſitan placeret Domino ut traderet eam in manibus eorum. Conuentione itaque faćta, illi per mare, & Rex per terram cum exercitu ſuo uenerunt undique ad Vlixbonam, & circumderunt & oppugnauerunt eam, ſed non potuerunt aduerſus eam, quia nundum aduenerat tempus ut traderunt in manibus Chriſtianorum, ſed irruperunt ſuburbana eius, & demoliti ſunt multas uineas, & ſuccenderunt domos, & fecerunt plagam magnam in terra. Videntes itaque quod non cito, nec per multum temporis ſpatium non poßet capi, etiam ſi quotidie foret obſeßa, quoniam erat multum referta, & populoſa, & tunc ſatis abundabat omnibus bonis, reliquerunt eam. Rex cum exercitu ſuo regreſſus est in terram ſuã, & illi marini nautæ abierunt uiam suam, quod tenebant ire in Ieruſalem.*[73]

> [Around the same time unexpectedly some ships from parts of Gaul, filled with armed men who had taken a vow to go to Jerusalem, arrived at the Port of Gaia and entered the River Douro. The king [Afonso Henriques] heard this and rejoiced at it, for they were almost seventy [in number]. He entered an alliance with them so that they could go to Lisbon by sea and he with his army could go by land so that they could besiege the city; perhaps it would please the Lord so that He would deliver it into their hands. Having made the accord, they by sea and the King with his army by land, from all sides came to Lisbon, and surrounded it and attacked it, but they were unable to capture it, because the time had not yet come for it to be delivered into the hands of the Christians. However, they entered the outskirts and destroyed many vineyards and burned their houses, and greatly plagued the land. Seeing therefore that neither quickly nor over a long period of time could it be captured even if it was besieged daily, since it was very full and populous and had an abundance of all good things, they abandoned it. The king with his army returned to his land and those sailors went on their way to Jerusalem as they had intended.]

---

[73] Brandão edn, fol. 274; 'Chronicon Lusitanum', pp. 415–32; 'Chronica Gothorum', in *Monumenta Historica*, ed. by Herculano, I, 13–14; 'História dos Godos', pp. 35–36.

'The lyceums work in silence, they do not advertise, and have no time for envy or rivalry'

A Case Study of the *Liceu Rodrigues de Freitas/ D. Manuel II* during the Portuguese Estado Novo

Luís Grosso Correia

Universidade do Porto

The statement that provides the title to this paper was made in a speech to the students of the Lyceum Rodrigues de Freitas, Porto, by its Principal, José Dias Vieira, in the 1940/41 academic year.[1] This statement reflects the great social prestige and the official position that state-run lyceum schools enjoyed within the Portuguese education system.

The lyceum curriculum reform of 1895, the so-called Jaime Moniz reform, had meant that admission to a lyceum course involved sitting exams organized by the school, the only means by which candidates were accepted (Art. 26, Decree of 16 July 1895). However, the 1931 reform established the final primary school exam as the only requirement for admission (Art. 92, Decree no. 20.741, of 18 December 1931). Lyceum education was thus considered part of a school system that emphasized the principles of trust and of systemic, institutional and professional responsibility, namely by acknowledging primary school output.

Admissions to lyceum schools were restructured under the terms of Decree no. 25.461, of 6 June 1935, which established exams 'sob uma forma até então não intentada, de prova académica, que simultaneamente desempenhasse a função de inventariar conhecimentos e apurar aptidões intelectuais, que se reputassem indispensáveis para a regular apropriação da ordem de estudos desinteressada e geral, que constitui o currículo do curso geral' [under an approach untried until then, as a form of academic assessment that would simultaneously play the role of registering knowledge and of examining intellectual abilities, which were considered fundamental to the consistent achievement of the general and unspecific modules which make up the Lyceum's curriculum].[2]

---

[1] 'Os liceus trabalham em silêncio, não fazem reclamos, não têm invejas, nem competições'. Quoted by Alfredo Soares de Oliveira, 'O Liceu de Rodrigues de Freitas', *Liceus de Portugal*, 11 (1941), 891. The school in question was named the Liceu Rodrigues de Freitas on the formation of the Republic, in 1910, but in 1947 it reverted to its royalist name of Liceu Nacional de D. Manuel II.

[2] This information was provided by José de Oliveira Guimarães, the Director of the Instituto de Orientação Profissional and main author of the assessment instrument used at the time. His statement

This instrument, designed to assess the students' cognitive skills and abilities, proved its effectiveness in the way it gave support and method to the guiding principles set out in the report of Decree no. 20.741, of 18 December 1931, as follows: 'A normalidade [da lotação dos liceus] só será restabelecida quando as famílias compreenderem que os cursos dos liceus, de sua natureza difíceis, têm de ser reservados aos fortes e aos mais aptos e à medida que a selecção dos alunos se vá fazendo como convém que seja feita para restituir ao ensino secundário, e consequentemente ao ensino superior, aquele grau de elevação que ambos, cada um na sua esfera, devem manter' [The standard [of the lyceums' intake] will only be restored when families understand that courses offered at the lyceums, which are demanding by nature, must be reserved for the strong and the more able, and insofar as the selection of pupils is carried out as it should be, in order to restore to secondary education, and consequently to higher education, the level of distinction that both, each in its own sphere, must uphold].

Thus, from the moment students were admitted until they finished school, there was a selective understanding of education in the lyceum sub-system. Its purpose was to reward academic excellence and direct it towards higher education, which would magnify, from the social, economic and cultural point of view, the refining processes performed on students throughout their academic career. In fact, this was to be the lyceum's greatest trademark during the period in focus: academically selective schooling that strove to provide students with a broad humanistic and scientific training intended to prepare them for higher education.

Apart from the selective admission exams there were three other aspects of lyceum education that worked against equal opportunities: attendance fees,[3] the limitations of the state school network, and the *numerus clausus* limiting entry to each state school. Lyceums were usually located in cities, and the state school network generally covered the district capitals or the more populated municipalities. The development of the state school network, which had only thirty-six such schools in 1930, was rather slow until the mid-1960s. From that time on, the state network experienced an exponential boom, almost

---

makes it clear that the purpose was to provide admission to lyceums with an instrument that could assess the students' abilities in Drawing, Arithmetic, Geography and History, Dictation and Text Analysis. See José Joaquim de Oliveira Guimarães, 'Valor selectivo dos exames de admissão aos liceus', *Labor*, 106 (1940), 309–21.

[3] Fees for secondary-vocational education were substantially lower than the lyceums, as we can see in this example: as of 1947, the yearly lyceum fees for the first and second teaching phases were 300$00 (Portuguese escudos) and 375$00, respectively, and 90$00 per subject in the third phase; in vocational training, from 1948 onwards, the fee for the preparatory course was 100$00, while Business courses would cost 80$00, and Industrial courses 40$00. Moving between these two different branches of the Portuguese secondary education system — lyceum and vocational — was permitted, as long as vocational training students who wished to be admitted to a lyceum took an exam at the end of each teaching phase, so as to determine the most suitable year for them in the lyceum (Decree no 36.507, of 17 September 1947).

quadrupling in nearly ten years. It should also be noted, however, that not all lyceums presented the same standards of quality.[4]

These selective factors in state lyceum education — economic, academic, geographic, and in some cases restrictions as to the year-groups taught — would encourage families to consider alternative strategies so that their children could continue their post-primary studies. Three pathways presented themselves: i) students who passed with a good score could enrol in a state school (as an alternative to a private school); ii) students who passed the admission exam but could not find a place in a state school could apply to a private school; iii) students who failed the admission exam could not enrol in a lyceum, state or private.

Students entering a private school or being tutored at home were considered external students of the state lyceum in charge of that school area. This situation was legally framed by the nationalist education authorities, which never granted equal status to private schooling (Decree no. 22.842, of 19 July 1933 — *Status of Private Education*). They were 'considerados alunos externos, em relação ao ensino oficial a cujas habilitações aspiram, aqueles que seguirem os seus cursos' [those who took their courses were regarded as external pupils of the official teaching to whose qualifications they aspired]. This applied to primary, lyceum, technical vocational, artistic, and National Conservatory teaching (all non-higher education courses), which adopted curricula according to the state schools' study plans: 'provas de aptidão, exames ou quaisquer outros meios mediante os quais se validam as habilitações adquiridas fora dos estabelecimentos oficiais' [admission tests, exams or any other means of validating the qualifications obtained outside state schools] (Art. 18). This brief description of the relationship between the state and private lyceums is necessary since they had always been the most sought-after branch of post-primary education. Throughout this period, private schooling was the main source of its social expansion, given the restrictions on the number of places usually available in state schools (Appendix 1).

Aware of the lyceum's educational mission, it becomes clear why the lawmakers at the time always used a minimalistic, laconic and broad style to refer to the academic goals of this branch of secondary education:

---

[4] In the terms of the 1931 reform, the lyceums were divided into national and central (Art. 12, Decree no. 20.741, of 18 December 1931). In 1936, the lyceums could be national or provincial, and the creation of municipal lyceums was already envisaged (Art. 16 of Decree no 27.084, of 14 October 1936). In 1947, the lyceums were split between national and municipal lyceums, depending on the institution in charge of their maintenance, the State or the local council (Art. 8 of Decree no. 36.508, of 17 September 1947). In other words, the national lyceums of the 1936 reform and the central national lyceums of the 1931 reform were the only ones capable of providing the full seven years of secondary education; the other lyceums were authorized to teach the first two phases, from Year 1 to Year 5, according to the 1931 reform, and from the Year 1 to Year 6, according to the 1936 reform. The municipal lyceums mentioned in the 1936 reform could only provide the first teaching phase, which at that time finished in Year 3. The 1947 reform recovered the dual classification for the institution, at national or municipal level, but created two sub-categories for the national lyceums, based on whether they had permission to teach the third phase or not.

i) O ensino secundário tem por fim ministrar os elementos duma cultura geral que simultaneamente sirva de preparação para a vida social e de habilitação para estudos superiores. Esta cultura geral realiza-se pelo desenvolvimento normal do corpo e do espírito, tendente à formação da personalidade.

[The goal of secondary education is to provide the student with the elements of a general culture that serves both as a preparation for social life and as a qualification for higher education. This general culture is accomplished through the usual development of body and mind, aimed at the development of the personality.] (Art. 1, Decree no. 20.741, of 18 December 1931).

For this same reason, according to the introductory report of the same diploma, the lyceum was 'pelo seu carácter essencialmente formador da personalidade e pelo lugar que ocupa na organização geral da nossa instrução pública — colocado, como está, no caminho que vai dar ao nosso ensino superior e consequentemente às profissões de mais alta categoria social — , é bem no nosso País, como aliás em todos sucede, a pedra de toque do nosso estado de civilização' [in our Country, as in fact is the case elsewhere, [the lyceum is] the cornerstone of our state of civilization, because it focuses essentially on the development of character, and because of the place it takes in the general organization of our state education — given that it grants access to higher education and therefore to better ranked professions].

ii) O ensino liceal integra-se na missão educativa da Família e do Estado para o desenvolvimento harmónico da personalidade moral, intelectual e física dos Portugueses, nos termos da Constituição, e tem por finalidade específica dotá-los de uma cultura geral útil para a vida.

[The lyceum forms part of the educational mission of the Family and the State aimed at the balanced development of the moral, intellectual and physical personality of the Portuguese, as consecrated in the Constitution, and its specific goal is to provide them with general culture that is useful in life.] (Art. 1, Decree no. 27.084, of 14 October 1936)

iii) O ensino liceal revestirá carácter simultaneamente humanista, educativo e de preparação para a vida, pela determinação, disposição e conteúdo das disciplinas, pela selecção dos métodos e pela utilização de outros meios adequados.

[Lyceum education will take on a character simultaneously humanist, educational and preparatory for life, through its choice, presentation and content of subjects taught, through the selection of methodologies used, and the adoption of other appropriate means.] (Art. 1, Decree no. 36.507, of 17 September 1947)

The lyceum's structure from the 1894/95 reform by Jaime Moniz was retained: a seven-year curriculum, divided into three phases with different lengths and purposes of training, the last of which featured a programme that functioned as an introduction to higher education (Figure 1). An analysis of the curriculum

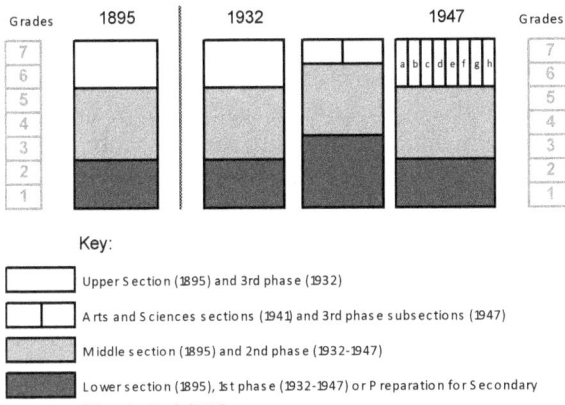

Key:

    Upper Section (1895) and 3rd phase (1932)

    Arts and Sciences sections (1941) and 3rd phase subsections (1947)

    Middle section (1895) and 2nd phase (1932-1947)

    Lower section (1895), 1st phase (1932-1947) or Preparation for Secondary Education Cycle (1968)

FIG. 1. Organization of lyceum education, between 1895 and 1970, according to the different curricular reforms, by teaching phases.
Source: Decree of 14.08.1895; Decree no. 20.741, of 18.12.1931; Decree no. 27.084, of 14.10.1936; Decree no. 31.544, of 30.09.1941; Decree no. 36.507, of 17.09.1947; Decree-Law no. 47.430, of 02.01.1967.

approved for lyceum education in 1931, 1936-1941,[5] and 1947 shows that the areas of knowledge considered fundamental in each teaching phase followed a stable, organized pattern. There were no disagreements or tensions regarding the organization of the modules included in the lyceum's curriculum, in terms of their design, length and sequence.

Across the period analysed, it is the curricular goals of the 1936 reform that reveal the most markedly fascist nature, clearly establishing a plan for the lyceum's curricula aimed at the overall shaping of personality, which the State was then interested in promoting. This overall personality should cover different dimensions: the socio-affective (moral), the cognitive (intellectual) and the motor (physical).[6]

The 1947 reform sustained the same curricular aims as the 1931 and 1936 reforms, but seemed more specific and restricted with regard to the students' academic training, particularly in the third teaching phase. An analysis of the

---

[5] The 1936 curricular reform was reviewed in terms of the study plans for the third phase by Decree no. 31.544, of 30 September 1941. The traditional areas of the Arts and Sciences were then revived.

[6] In a diploma that strategically appointed the *Mocidade Portuguesa* [Portuguese Youth] as the organization in charge of complementary curricular activities, three basic aspects of human behaviour were thus focused upon: thinking, feeling and acting. At the level of the lyceum, this meant contributing 'ao desenvolvimento da capacidade física, à formação do carácter e à devoção à Pátria, no sentido da ordem, no gosto da disciplina e no culto do dever militar' [to the development of physical capacity, to the formation of character and to the devotion to the Fatherland, in the sense of order, in the taste for discipline and in the respect for military duty] (Art. 3 of the same diploma). Thus, the *Mocidade Portuguesa* was in charge of nationalist-based sentiment and behaviour, included in the lyceum's goals, while the lyceum itself focused on academic training.

structure of the curriculum for the third phase, now organized in eight different sections as part of a greater investment in higher education, and introduced in 1947,[7] confirms that 'o currículo escrito é o testemunho público e visível das racionalidades escolhidas e da retórica legitimadora das práticas escolares' [the written curriculum is the public and visible testimony of the chosen aims and of the legitimizing rhetoric of scholastic practices].[8] However, this was not exclusive to the third phase, since the structure of the curriculum for the first two phases grew in complexity with the 1931, 1936–1941 and 1947 reforms, as it was aimed at the acquisition of more skills and knowledge. These early phases were intended to prepare and select the most proficient students to move on to the third phase and from there to higher education, as we will see later on. Thus, the lyceums are seen as the only branch of post-primary education capable of granting the training and certification needed for admission to higher education institutions, without exception.

Lyceum Education in the Portuguese Education System

Throughout this period, the widening of the social classes in the education system is an inescapable fact. However, this expansion was carried out under the socio-political concept of *educability* sustained by the regime's authorities: compulsory primary education marked the limit of school life expectancy for most of the Portuguese population (Figure 2).

Based on this data, it is possible to say that the expansion of the Portuguese education system followed a single pattern and principle on the part of the nationalist authorities: horizontal development, but only at the base of the social pyramid. However, this process was followed as a pragmatic management of socio-demographic pressures on the education market, rather than being an overarching project with socio-political intentions (with the exception of the 1973 reform, which never came into force). This pragmatic management and apparent lack of coordination of the students moving on to different levels must, however, be considered in light of the concept of social technology,[9] applied to educational policy and the legal and organizational instruments known at the time. In this sense, it can be said that the education system 'contribui largamente

---

[7] The curricular organization of the third phase in 1947, based on the logic and sequence followed, served as an answer to three critical points raised by João Camoesas, in 1923, concerning preparatory courses for the lyceum. These three points have to do, firstly, with the lack of 'ligações nem relações orgânicas com as faculdades e escolas superiores' [organic links or relations with faculties and schools of higher education]; secondly, that faculties and higher education schools did not intervene 'como deviam, na confecção dos programas do curso complementar' [as they ought, in the drawing up of the preparatory course curricula]; and thirdly, that the classic divide between two vocational sections was incompatible with the 'a natureza e extensão especializada dos conhecimentos indispensáveis para frequentar as diversas faculdades e escolas superiores' [the specialized nature and length of the required skills to have access to the different faculties and higher education schools]. See Ministério da Instrução Pública, *Reforma da Educação: Proposta de Lei* (Lisbon, 1923), p. 8.
[8] Ivor F. Goodson, *A construção social do currículo* (Lisbon: Educa, 1997), p. 20.
[9] Sérgio Grácio, *Política educativa como tecnologia social: As reformas do Ensino Técnico de 1948 e 1983* (Lisbon: Horizonte, 1986).

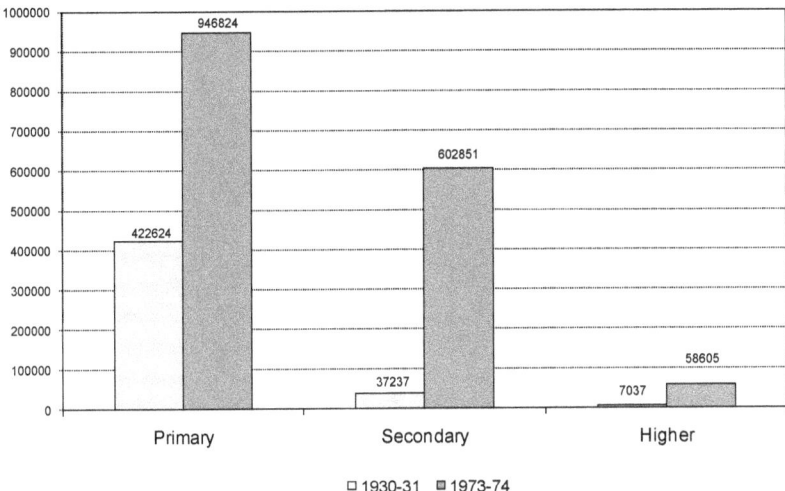

FIG. 2. Students enrolled in primary, secondary and higher education in 1930/31 and 1973/74. Source. Portugal, *Statistics Yearbook - 1931*; Portugal, *Education Statistics - 1974*.

para a interiorização de um modelo de sociedade, que traduz projectos unificadores no plano político, simbólico e cultural' [contributes largely to the internalization of a societal model, which expresses unifying projects at the political, symbolic and cultural level].[10] The institutional authorities thought of education not as a fundamental right but as a *donation* from the State.

A quantitative analysis of the structure and morphology of the education system set up by the Estado Novo reveals that, despite its demographic expansion, the same principle was maintained from the beginning: the 'reserva de princípio quanto à extensão do ensino popular para além dos parâmetros tradicionais' [restriction, as a principle, when it came to extending mass education beyond the traditional parameters].[11] This attitude becomes more noticeable when analysing the relation between the distribution of students in teaching phases and the reference age groups of these phases in the early 1970s (Figure 3).

Up to the mid-1970s, pre-school education during the Estado Novo mostly depended on private initiatives.[12] According to UNESCO,[13] the deficient

[10] António Nóvoa, 'A Educação Nacional', in *Nova História de Portugal*, ed. by Joel Serrão and A. H. de Oliveira Marques, *Vol XII: Portugal e o Estado Novo (1930–1960)*, ed. by Fernando Rosas (Lisbon: Presença, 1992), pp. 455–519 (pp. 456–57).
[11] Sérgio Grácio, *Ensinos técnicos e política em Portugal, 1910/1990* (Lisbon: Instituto Piaget, 1998), p. 127.
[12] In the 1973/74 school year, there were 54 state schools providing for the education of 3,625 children and 652 private schools with 37,445 students enrolled.
[13] UNESCO, *Para uma política de educação em Portugal* (Lisbon, 1982).

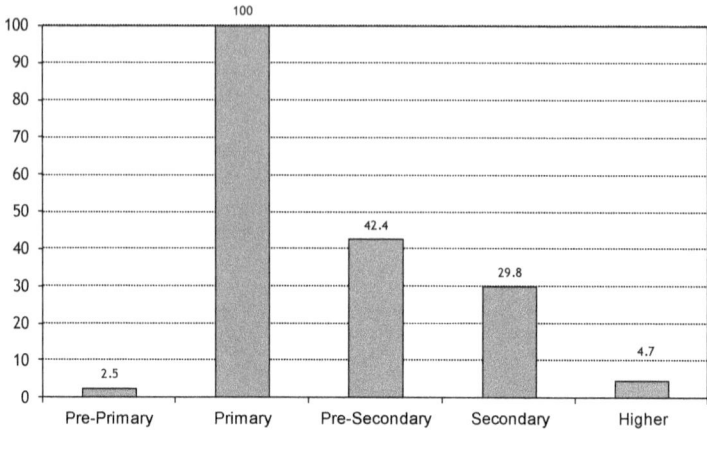

Fig. 3. Proportion of students enrolled in pre-primary school, primary school, preparation for secondary school, secondary and higher education, in relation to the corresponding school-going age groups in 1970/71 (%).
Source. Portugal, *Education Statistics – 1971*; Portugal, *Population Census – 1970*.

provision of pre-school education was one of the most serious failings of the Portuguese education system, because it reduced efficiency in its elementary stage. Socially, this meant significant delay for the most deprived children when it came to learning the codes and skills of school education.

Based on the results of post-primary education, it is clear that secondary education, and lyceums in particular, was protected from social expansion pressures if we consider that, generally speaking, the numbers attending higher education resulted mainly from lyceum *output*. At a time when there was a positive relationship between the academic certification obtained and the labour market, the nationalist authorities seemed to be primarily concerned with the possible pressure on the ruling intellectual elite trained at lyceums.[14] Thus, the definition of the lyceum's mission and goals did not seem to require any major explanations, given its crucial position within the educational structure of the Estado Novo: to provide training for social life, to prepare for higher education and provide general culture useful in life. Or, in other words, to train the future middle- and higher-ranking workers in society, through the

[14] Nevertheless, as from 1931, the nationalist authorities granted total or partial fee exemption to state lyceums and also awarded scholarships with the purpose of 'a defesa dos mais pobres no concurso à assistência e o aproveitamento social dos melhores valores das Escolas' [defending the most deprived in the competition for assistance and putting to social use the best values of schools] (cf. Decree no. 20.065, of 13 July 1931). This social assistance was given to the most deprived students with a proven record of academic excellence, which was assessed on a yearly basis. According to the most optimistic legal projections (cf. Decree no. 34.118), it never exceeded one tenth of the enrolled students.

transmission of knowledge, abilities and cognitive skills, adaptable to any area of scientific knowledge or human interaction.

The main purpose of this case study was to dissect the social market of the education provided in lyceums, based on a case study of the *Liceu Rodrigues de Freitas/D. Manuel II*, an exceptional school located in Porto, and also an exceptional urban context (boosted by the dynamics of its industrial, commercial and banking structures). The methodological approach was guided by a principle of *interiority*, moving from the interior towards the exterior, and not the principle of *exteriority*, which moves in the opposite direction, and could describe any lyceum of the period in analysis.

Putting the Lyceum in the Spotlight

The study focuses on the *Liceu Rodrigues de Freitas*, later called *Liceu Nacional de D. Manuel II* (henceforth, the Lyceum), a boys' school located in the second most populated city of Portugal, between 1933 and 1974.

From its beginnings in 1840, the Lyceum was consistently considered one of the most prestigious institutions in the country. However, when in 1930 the Lyceums Pedro Nunes, in Lisbon, and D. João III, in Coimbra, acceded to the category of *Escola normal* (a teacher training school) the lyceum in question was left out of that restricted group. Later, though, in 1957, it recovered part of the prestige it had lost, when it too became an *Escola normal*.[15]

In September 1932, the Lyceum moved from a rundown building in the Rua São Bento da Vitória, in the central parish of Vitória in Porto, to new facilities located in the street then known as Rua da Paz, in the nearby parish of Cedofeita. Changing to larger facilities meant, in terms of registrations/enrolments and attendance, a slight increase in the number of students in the first three school years (Figure 4).

Between the 1932/33 and 1972/73 school years, the number of enrolments at the Lyceum totalled 52,477. In this period, three phases stand out in terms of number of students: 1) the first twenty years (1932/33 to 1951/52) represent only a quarter of the total; 2) the following eleven years represent another quarter; 3) the last ten years (1963/64 to 1972/73) make up fully half of the enrolments.

If we omit the 1938/39 and 1946/47 peaks, the years immediately before

---

[15] From the foundation of Porto's National Lyceum through to 1974, the Lyceum had six different designations, with as many political and/or educational situations: Liceu Nacional do Porto: the Decree of 17 November 1836, called the National Lyceums Plan, stipulated that one lyceum should be built in every district capital (Art. 40). This Lyceum would only start running in 1840. Liceu Nacional da 2ª Zona Escolar do Porto, 1906. Liceu Nacional de D. Manuel II, 1908. Liceu Rodrigues de Freitas, 1910. Liceu Nacional de D. Manuel II, 1947. Liceu Normal de D. Manuel II: with the Decree-Law no. 41.273, of 17 September 1957, the Lyceum was upgraded to the category of *Escola normal* (a school providing professional teacher training). Then, together with the D. João III (Coimbra) and Pedro Nunes (Lisbon) Lyceums, it offered the *Estágio pedagógico* [Teaching Internship], the last selective stage of professionalization for lyceum teaching staff. It thus became the main training centre for teachers in the northern region of the country.

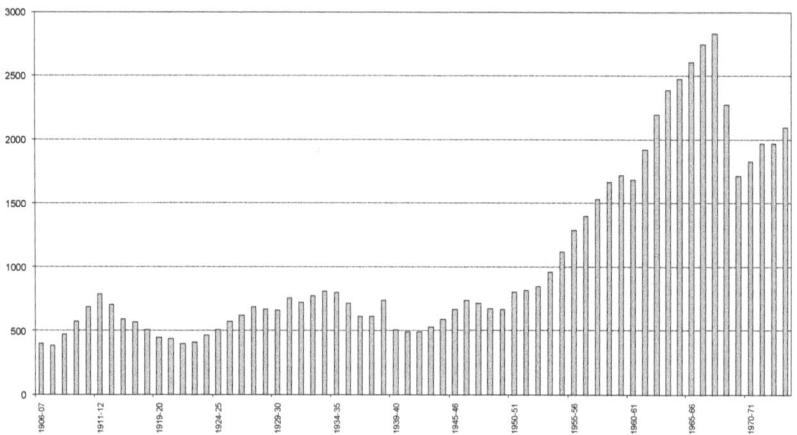

FIG. 4. Students enrolled at the Lyceum between 1906 and 1974, by school years. Source. Arquivo da Escola Secundária Rodrigues de Freitas (AESRF) [Rodrigues de Freitas High School Archive], *Termos de matrículas e frequência dos alunos internos [Internal students enrolment and attendance]*, 34 folders. Arquivo Histórico do Ministério da Educação (AHME) [Ministry of Education Historical Archive], *Relatórios dos Liceus [Lyceums Annual Reports]*, 15 folders. Lyceu Central do Porto, *Relatório do ano 1906 a 1907* (Porto, 1907).

and after World War II show a declining trend in terms of school population between 1935 and 1950. The results reveal a reversal in this decline in the early 1950s, due to the continuous rise in internal students enrolling at the Lyceum until 1967/68.[16] The boom in the Lyceum's school population, noticeable in the early 1950s, occurred before the growing trend in the national lyceums' sub-system, which did not take place until the mid-1960s, as shown in Appendix 1.

The number of students taking the Lyceum's admission exams during the summer of 1940 falls within the average of the four state lyceums in Porto, but stands out when compared to the other national lyceums, in Lisbon and Coimbra (Table 1). However, only two thirds of the applicants obtained a place, meaning that the Lyceum's failure rates were higher than either the national average or the average for Porto's state lyceums, and for that matter for *normal* lyceums in Coimbra and Lisbon. It seems, therefore, that this Lyceum had stricter criteria than the others when it came to assessing the cognitive abilities

---

[16] The 1968/69 school year does not represent the end of an increasing attendance rate in the Lyceum. It only means that the school population was no longer registered according to the Lyceum's curricular organization as defined by the 1947 reform. From 1968/69 the *Ciclo preparatório do ensino secundário* (CPES; Preparatory Cycle for Secondary Education) came into effect. This was a compulsory year of secondary education, resulting from a curricular merging between the Lyceum's first teaching phase and the preparation phase for vocational training. The Lyceum kept an independent working section of CPES until 1974. For this reason, we have omitted the number of enrolled students attending CPES at the Lyceum.

Lyceums	Applicants			Examined			Passed		
	BG	B	G	BG	B	G	BG	B	G
Total (national)	7.867	4.343	3.524	7.823	4.326	3.497	6.178	3.288	2.890
%				100	100	100	79.0	76.9	82.6
Lyceums of Porto	1.144	572	572	1.141	572	569	839	386	453
%				100	100	100	73.5	67.5	79.6
Rodrigues de Freitas	251	251	-	251	251	-	166	166	-
%				100	100		66.1	66.1	
D. João III (Coimbra)	233	233	-	232	232	-	175	175	-
%				100	100		75.4	75.4	
Pedro Nunes (Lisbon)	126	81	45	124	80	44	104	68	36
%				100	100	100	83.8	85.0	81.8

TABLE 1. Admission exams to the Lyceum's 1st year, in 1940/41, by state schools. Source. Portugal, *Education Statistics* 1940-41.

of the students who had already passed the final primary school exam and wished to be admitted to this branch of secondary education.

In order to analyse the students' social background, a sampling study was conducted, focusing on the admission exams and the students enrolled in Year 1 at the Lyceum in three different school years (Appendix 2).[17] According to the socio-occupational ranking adopted, in 1936/37 most of the Lyceum's applicants, admitted and enrolled students belonged to upper-class families.[18] By 1951/52, students with this same background came second, after the middle classes, and in 1966/67 they came third, immediately below the working classes. Likewise, in 1936/37 most of the applicants belonged to *Proprietor* families; in 1951/52, the leading professional backgrounds were *Merchants and Industrialists*, and in 1966/67, the *Independent Professions* led the number of students at the Lyceum.

The middle classes were the mainstay of the Lyceum's social structure throughout the period analysed, strengthening their leading position during the 1950s and the 1960s. Children from families running *Small and Medium-Sized Established Businesses* were predominant in 1936/37 and 1951/52, but in the 1960s, they were overtaken by the *Private Sector Middle-Ranking Skilled Workers*, and the period also witnessed the dynamic growth of *Office Staff* and other professions related to business and administration.

The number of working-class students who passed the admission exams and enrolled as internal students at the Lyceum steadily increased, both absolutely and proportionately. This evolution shows that the working classes had, on the

---
[17] These years were chosen for their political and educational symbolism (1936/37), their importance/relevance to this study (1951/52) and the fact that they represent the last generation/cohort of students to be taught, assessed and certified by the Lyceum's classic curriculum (1966/67) before the Revolution in April 1974.
[18] This study was based on the profession of the student's lawful parent or guardian, as declared in the student's personal file, and, on the professions' line up and systematic structure, their organization in terms of different professional statuses and of socio-economic prestige.

one hand, achieved greater prospects for social mobility and, on the other, the higher economic capacity needed to be able to afford lyceum education. At this stage it should be emphasized that an important structural change was taking place internally, in terms of the socio-professional backgrounds that most contributed to the rise in working-class students at the Lyceum. In 1936/37, *Shop Assistants* were bringing the highest number of such students to the Lyceum, whereas in 1951/52, the unskilled civil servants took the lead, while in 1966/67 this place was taken by yet another class, the *Skilled Workers*.

The socio-professional backgrounds that sent the highest number of students to the Lyceum were as follows:

* In 1936/37, in decreasing order, *Proprietors* and *Small and Medium-Sized Established Businesses, Shop Assistants* and *Independent Professions*;
* In 1951/52, in the same order, *Small and Medium-Sized Established Businesses, Merchants and Industrialists, Independent Professions* and *Civil Servants, Council and Administrative Workers*;
* In 1966/67, a significant change in terms of quality takes place, namely in terms of the leading socio-professional occupations: *Industry, Trade and Administration Skilled Workers, Skilled Workers, Small and Medium-Sized Established Businesses* and *Independent Professions*.

The admission exams[19] conducted in the summer of 1966 can be the key to understanding the Lyceum's autonomy and authority when organizing the classes of Year 1 students. The contrasting results obtained by the applicant students according to the different exams taken reveal difficulties in Dictation and Essay Writing,[20] whereas the highest marks were achieved in Arithmetic and Geometry. It seems the applicants were better trained during primary education in mathematics than in the use of their mother tongue (Table 2). The purpose of the admission exam, with a maximum score of 35 points, was to determine, differentiate and rank the students' cognitive abilities with respect to all the learning processes they were to accomplish at school. However, at the time, this general principle of Portuguese lyceum education was equally applied when organizing students into classes (Figure 5).

This method was typical of the Lyceum: the alphabetical ordering of the classes corresponded to the ranking of academic excellence, in decreasing order, which was assessed in the first exam taken as Lyceum *input*. This standard for class organization had been used by the Lyceum at least since 1937/38: 'Para a distribuição dos alunos do 1º ano por turmas atendeu-se principalmente ao valor das provas prestadas no exame de admissão; foram colocados na turma A os que haviam sido seriados nos primeiros grupos [pelo júri dos exames de admissão], na turma B os que se lhes seguiam e na turma C os dos últimos grupos' [to distribute Year 1 students in classes, we focused mainly on the results obtained

---

[19] As in Articles 258 to 270 in Decree no. 36.508, of 17 September 1947.
[20] Students failed straight away if they scored *Mau* (E) in any part of the exam, or if they scored *Medíocre* (D) in two different parts and did not score *Bom* (B) or above in the other parts.

Exams	Marks										Total
	A	%	B	%	C	%	D	%	E	%	
Written											
Dictation	241	27.6	188	13.2	300	10.3	181	17.0	59	39.3	969
Essay writing	23	2.6	116	8.2	632	21.6	173	16.3	26	17.3	970
Arithmetic and Geometry	338	38.8	290	20.4	227	7.8	100	9.4	15	10.0	970
Drawing	1	0.1	132	9.3	575	19.7	262	24.7	-	-	970
Oral											
Reading and Analysis	63	7.2	204	14.4	421	14.4	143	13.5	20	13.3	851
History and Geography of Port	86	9.9	232	16.3	437	14.9	91	8.6	4	2.7	850
Arithmetic and Geometry	120	13.8	258	18.2	334	11.4	112	10.5	26	17.3	850
Total	**872**	100	**1.420**	100	**2.926**	100	**1.062**	100	**150**	100	**6.430**
%	13.6		22.1		45.5		16.5		2.3		100

TABLE 2. Admission exams taken at the Lyceum in 1966/67 by results obtained.
Source. AESRF, *Admission exams 1965–1967*, Folders no. 2334 and 2335.
Key: A – Muito Bom (Very Good); B – Bom (Good); C – Suficiente (Satisfactory); D – Medíocre (Mediocre); E – Mau (Bad).

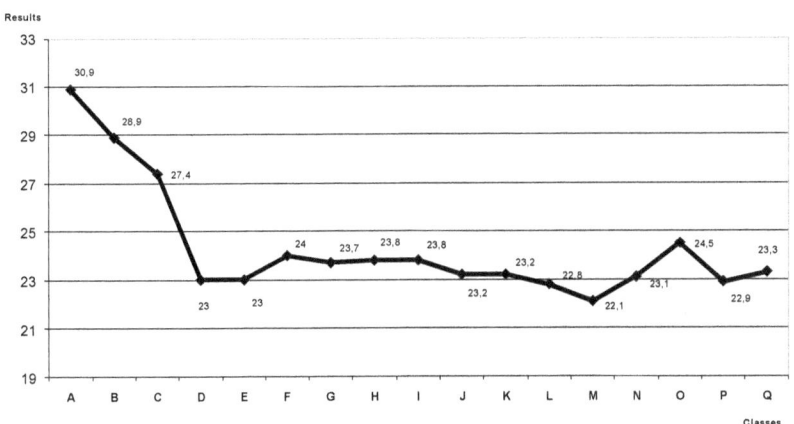

FIG. 5. Students enrolled in Year 1 for the first time according to the average results obtained in the admission exams to the Lyceum, in 1966/67, by classes.
Source. AESRF, *Admission exams 1965-1967*, Folders no. 2334 and 2335; *Internal students enrolment and attendance*, Folder no. 2380; *Students' personal files*, 82 folders.

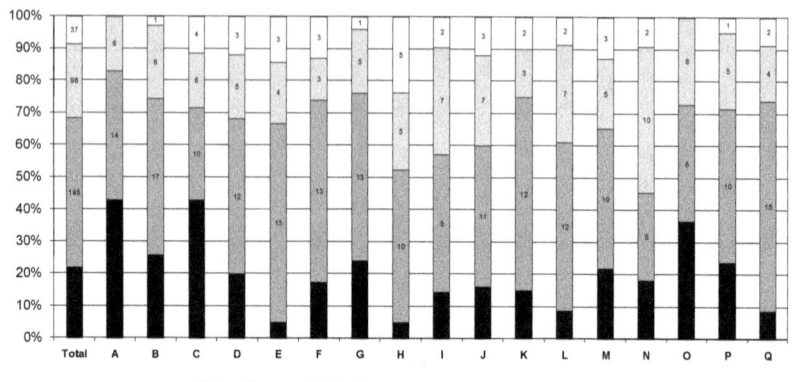

Fig. 6. Lyceum's internal students admitted to Year 1 in 1966/67 according to their families' socio-professional status, by classes (A to Q). *Source.* See Figure 5.

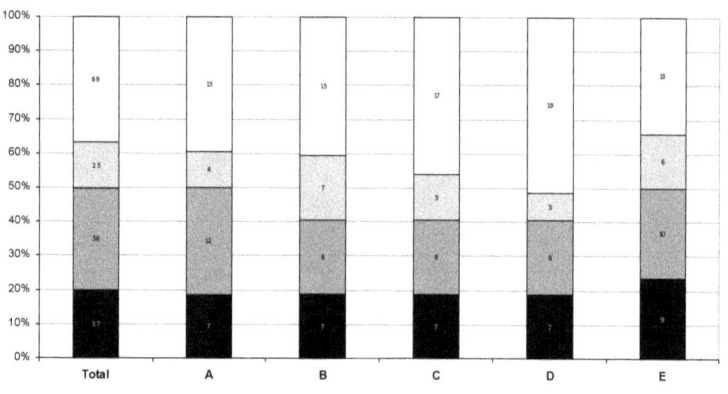

Fig. 7. Students enrolled in the Lyceum's Year 1 in 1951/52, according to their families' socio-professional status, by classes (A to E). Source. AESRF, *Admission exams 1948-1952*, Folder no. 1644; *Students admitted in 1951/52*, 4 folders.

in the admission exam; the students with the best classifications [according to the admission exam panel] were put in class A, those who came next in class B, and the last groups in class C].[21] Between 1950/51 and 1958/59, this standard of class organization was suspended following negative feedback from the Lyceum Inspection Board about the 'critério selectivo que presidiu à organização das turmas do 1º ano' [selection criterion that governed the organization of Year 1 classes].[22]

From the 1958/59 school year onwards, the selective method of organizing Year 1 students according to the results obtained in the admission exams was partially restored and the official authorities were informed of this decision. The arguments presented were based on the need for the Lyceum to provide the Teaching Internship tutors and their interns with the best working conditions possible, now that it was a *Liceu normal*: 'No 1º ano organizou-se uma turma, para ser distribuída aos metodólogos, com os alunos mais classificados no exame de admissão. As outras turmas do 1º ano foram organizadas sem se atender a qualquer princípio de escolaridade, isto é, sem obediência a nenhum critério' [In the first year, we gathered the students who scored the highest marks in the admission exams in one class intended to work with the teaching internship tutors. The other first-year classes were not organized according to any particular academic principle, in other words, without following any criterion].[23] This procedure of organizing students into classes and assigning them to teachers was governed by the students' academic excellence throughout their school career, from their admission to the moment they left the Lyceum, and it did not seem to take the students' social status into account (Figure 6).

If we consider the high numbers of upper-class students in classes A, B and C, it seems they performed better in the admission exams than the other social backgrounds. However, these assumptions should be considered bearing in mind factors which are external to the Lyceum itself. Moreover, the key aspects for an overall understanding can perhaps be found in the connection between the concepts of cultural capital, as defined by Pierre Bourdieu and Jean-Claude Passeron,[24] and of elaborate linguistic code, by Basil Bernstein.[25] Despite this remark, it seems that, generally speaking, the grouping of Year 1 students into classes obeyed mainly an internal technical and pedagogical organization, based on the students' academic excellence. Therefore, the nature of the students' stratification within the Lyceum was academic, being based on pedagogical, not social, criteria.

---

[21] AESRF, Sent Mail 1939, Folder no. 1070, 'Relatório do Liceu de 1937/38' (Letter no. 35, of 25 January 1939).
[22] See AHME, Lyceum Reports of 1950/51, Box no. 38, Report no. 304. There was a mention to be annexed to the official report of the Lyceum's activities in 1948/49.
[23] AHME, Lyceum Reports of 1957/58, Box no. 55, Report no. 499, p. 7.
[24] Pierre Bourdieu and Jean-Claude Passeron, *A reprodução: Elementos para uma teoria do sistema de ensino*, trans. by C. Perdigão Gomes da Silva (Lisbon: Vega Editora, 1970).
[25] Basil Bernstein, *La estructura del discurso pedagógico*, trans. by Pablo Manzano (Madrid: Morata, 1994).

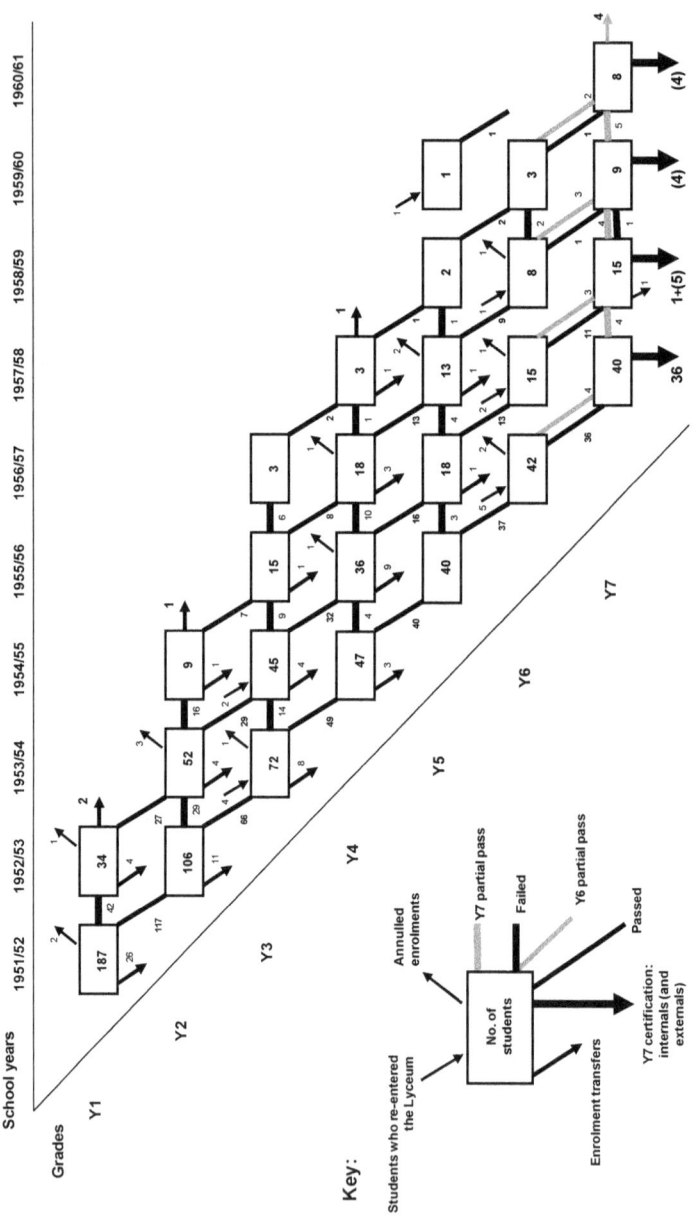

Fig. 8. The 1951/52 student cohort according to their school progress as internal students, by school years and curricular grades (1951/52 to 1960/61).
Source. AESRF, *Admission exams 1948-1952*, Folder no. 1644; *Students admitted in 1951/52*, 4 folders; *Internal student enrolment and attendance*, 13 folders; *Students' personal files*, 3 folders; *Exams proceedings*, 14 folders.

The students applying to the Lyceum's Year 1, taking exams in the summer of 1951, were analysed using the longitudinal cohort method. All the other students who enrolled in Year 1 in 1951/52 were then added, so as to provide support to the situated statistical analysis (focused on a particular moment of our observation). We intended thus to determine the progress through school of the Year 1 student cohort in the 1951/52 school year. This student *cohort*, here seen as a sample, was studied over ten school years, until 1960/61.[26] As seen previously, the process of setting up Year 1 classes in 1951/52 did not comply with the traditional standard of academic ranking based on admission exam results. This may thus be a possible exception to the Lyceum's traditional pedagogical organization. This exception is confirmed by the social structure found in the different classes when the students' social background is used as a reference, inferred from their parents' professions (Figure 7). From a formal point of view, the students in these five classes shared the same social, academic and pedagogical opportunities at the beginning of their careers in the Lyceum.

Based on the academic records of the 187 students enrolled in Year 1 in 1951/52, we intended to establish a clear framework for reference and analysis, which would enable the required overview (Figure 8). Analysing the academic records of the 187 first-year students in 1951/1952 yielded several findings on the school years between 1951/52 and 1960/61 that are worth mentioning:

* Principal reasons for withdrawal: 15 (8.0%) annulled enrolments (because students stopped paying their tuition fees or requested their annulment); 78 (41.7%) transfers to private tuition (of which a third — 26 cases — took place in Year 1); 50 cases (26.7%) of non-renewal of registration for the following school year.

* The three kinds of withdrawal mentioned above are so significant (76.4% of all who withdrew) that they overshadow the 14 cases (7.5%) of re-entry or re-enrolment at the Lyceum, by students who had requested to be transferred to private tuition. Thus, the Lyceum's approximate net withdrawal rate is 68.9%, which shows the highly selective academic mechanisms used internally.

* The overall cases of failure rose to 142. Most of them (29.6%) occurred in the first school year of the period in focus.

* It is possible to conclude from the results analysed thus far that the Lyceum's first year worked as a trial year, par excellence, of the students' academic abilities and skills. It was also seen as the most critical year for the students' school life expectancy at the Lyceum, marked by the drop-out rate (1.5%), the transfer rate (13.9%), the failure rate (22.6%) and the non-renewal rate of students admitted to the next school year (5.9%). All in all, these rates increased selectivity in the first year to 43.5%,[27] and were definitely higher

---

[26] In this study, we analyse each student's academic career, based on processes such as assessment, certification, passing, failing, school selection or elimination, annulment, transfer or re-registration, among others. For this purpose, we had to organize the database with 353 fields available for each case/student.

[27] This selective attitude towards the students registered for the first time in Year 1 would remain throughout the 1960s, as we could see, amongst the 1966/67 generation (35.0% of all the cases). Cf.

than the rate recorded in the Lyceum's admission exams (22.4%) taken in the summer of 1951.

* The pass rates were compared across the Lyceum's different levels, based on the results obtained by students enrolled in the seven year-groups, between the 1951/52 and 1957/58 school years. These rates are as follows: Year 1, 62.6%; Year 2, 62.3%; Year 3, 66.7%; Year 4, 85.1%; Year 5, 92.5%; Year 6, 95.2%; and Year 7, 90.0%. The figures reveal some discrepancy between the first three years and the last three years, setting hence the borderline at Year 4. In other words, academic selectivity was more intense from Years 1 to 3, whereas after passing Year 4 students could almost take for granted a more successful academic career, right through to Year 7.

As can be seen from what has been said previously, the Lyceum's internal efficiency in terms of students completing the full course is rather low. Of the 187 students who began their studies at the Lyceum in 1951/52, only 37 passed the third phase as internal students. This equates to a 19.3% graduation rate, after seven school years, or 21.9% after eight school years. Even if we add the 13 graduates who attended private schooling, the Lyceum's graduation efficiency rate still remains rather low: 26.7% in ten school years.

From a socially differentiated perspective, we analysed the students of the 1951/52 cohort according to the maximum attendance (not certification) achieved at the Lyceum in order to understand the representations, expectations and possibilities of the different social classes (Table 3). The results reveal that the main goal of the different social classes attending the Lyceum was to achieve the Year 7 certification. Therefore, the most sought-after diploma amongst the students was certification of the third phase of studies. However, this goal, when measured against the number of students registered in 1951/52 according to their families' social status, was achieved in waves that follow the social stratification: first, the upper-class students, followed by the middle class, and finally the working class.

Despite the efforts shown by some students to pass all three phases, obtaining the certificate for Year 5 seems to have been more appealing to working-class students than the other social backgrounds. Thus, certification in the Lyceum's traditional general course — that is, the first and second phases — shows greater relevance in terms of educational representations and strategies for social mobility by the lower strata. This is due to their limited economic resources to support longer study periods and to the fact that this certification in itself granted access to middle-ranking positions in services and administration. This is how we should also interpret the working classes' preference for attending and possible certification in the Lyceum's second year (first teaching phase).

If Year 7 is the main goal for the different social classes in terms of school career, the very opposite — in other words, failure, withdrawal or transfer

Luís Grosso Correia, 'Récita do Liceu Rodrigues de Freitas/D. Manuel II', 3 vols (unpublished PhD dissertation, University of Porto, 2002), I, 203–26.

during the very first year of studies (> Y1) — stands out as the second most relevant trend in statistical terms. However, it is almost impossible to put forward the data for their social distribution since these aspects surface mainly among students coming from the 'undeclared occupations' category — where information was either not provided by parents, or is unavailable to researchers — with an overwhelming weight of 90.6%. More generally, students for the 'undeclared occupations' tended to have a short career in the school, especially when considering the fact that only two-thirds of such students make it to Year 2 as their highest level. Curiously, the proportion of students attending or passing Year 2, or getting the certificate for the Lyceum's first phase, is lower than in Year 1, which highlights this year's role in the Lyceum's socio-educational organization, already discussed previously: acting as a filter for the students' academic abilities and skills and as a trial year for the strategies used by the different social backgrounds in view of their children's secondary education. The remaining school years between the final teaching phases, Years 3, 4 and 6, are not seen as goals for school output, from either a social or an educational point of view, because they do not provide any sort of relevant certification.

Concluding Remarks

Throughout the period in focus, the Lyceum's socio-educational purpose was clear in its prescriptive and official discourse, in the mechanisms of admission exams, and the teachers' professional attitude, which was internalized by society: it was an academically selective kind of education, intended to train the Portuguese elites.

The Lyceum's working method was marked by the uniformity, regularity and repetition of its pedagogical activities: admission exams, selection of applicants, *numerus clausus*, enrolments, educational activities dominated by cognitive content, relationship between teacher and class (the student was not the centre of attention), written and oral exams, exams at the end of each phase. If we analyse the school phenomena from a perspective of cyclic time, removed from its organizational contexts, we will not be able to grasp the uniqueness and depth of the senses imbedded in the silence of its daily life.

The Lyceum's student *input* shows quantitative evolution and social diversification throughout the period analysed. In the 1930s, the students' social profile was predominantly middle and upper class. By the 1960s, this profile had changed: the proportional weight of working-class students was now quite similar to the upper classes, while most of the students admitted belonged to the middle class. From a macro-social perspective, the social profile of the students admitted in the 1960s coincides with the growing relevance of the tertiary sector in the economy, in terms of occupation and income, and with the emergence of a more structured middle class in Portugal over the same decade. These findings bring an external phenomenon to the core of our discussion, which is nevertheless part of this study's backdrop: the economic and financial sustainability of lower-strata families which enabled their children to attend a lyceum. If we assume that this was a social environment in which most working-class families felt they were excluded from lyceum education from the outset, not even considering putting their children forward for this branch of secondary education, then a sharper approach to the Lyceum's pedagogical, curricular and school *processus* is possible, in terms of social stratification, dropping-out and an education market based on the results obtained.

From admission and enrolment through to school-leaving (as *output* or *drop-out*), the Lyceum employed highly selective assessment procedures. This socially acknowledged procedure was typical of its specific technical and pedagogical role and legal competence. The Lyceum was, therefore, meant to train elites, as seen in the analysis of the *output* provided by the 1951/52 cohort in Year 7. These elites had an academic or cultural origin, being taught, assessed and certified by the Lyceum's teachers/examiners.

After overcoming the trial of the three first years, the students' main goal seemed to be passing Year 7, i.e., the certification of all grades of lyceum education. However, working-class students were not as ambitious, given that a significant number believed that finishing Year 5 (with the final exam of the second teaching phase) fulfilled their expectations and offered real possibilities for educational and social mobility. The upper and middle classes, nevertheless, showed greater ability to survive by using more pedagogical and organizational resources throughout their careers at school — for example, by making a strategic transfer to private tuition at key stages (Years 1 or 2) and then re-applying to the Lyceum in Years 3 or 6.

The Lyceum, in its pedagogical and curricular organization, was represented by its actors as an eminently scholastic *locus*. School activities occurred outside the social sphere, guided by impersonal criteria in a relationship between student and teacher, and complied with concepts and assessment grounded strictly in the students' academic/cognitive ability. This technical and pedagogical activity, typical of the Lyceum's mission, was not directly related to the linear reproduction of social structures and relations, due to the different strategies planned and applied by each family to their children's education. Therefore, in the local education marketplace, the Lyceum came across as an institution where one could invest in and risk mobility strategies based on the students' skills, in a period dominated by the weak dynamics of social structures and agents. Ultimately, the visible, generated *output* acted as a guarantee.

APPENDIX 1. Enrolment in lyceum education in Portugal according to number of schools, students' gender, educational initiative and teachers' gender (1930-1973)

Years	Lyceum Education					
	Schools	Students			Teachers	
		BG	B	G	MW	W
1930	36*	19.268	14.253	4.745	766	---
1940	305	36.467	21.862	14.605	993*	33.3%
1950	340	48.485	25.871	22.614	1158*	43.3%
1960	385	111.821	56.367	55.454	5.702	55.8%*
1970	452	137.259	68.686	68.573	7.436	58.4%*
1973	462	211.772	102.979	108.793	10.307	63.3%*

Years	State schools				Private Schools			
	Schools	Students			Schools	Students		
		BG	B	G		BG	B	G
1930	36	14.970	11.502	3.468	---	4.298	3.021	1.277
1940	43	15.877	10.044	5.833	262	20.590	11.818	8.772
1950	43	21.962	12.399	9.563	297	26.523	13.472	13.051
1960	43	46.060	22.883	23.177	342	65.761	33.484	32.277
1970	70	65.226	30.736	34.490	382	72.033	37.950	34.083
1973	151	123.095	56.381	66.714	313	88.677	46.598	42.079

* State schools results.
Key: B - Boys; G - Girls; M - Men; W - Women.

APPENDIX 2. Admission exams to the Lyceum's 1st year according to the socio-professional ranking adopted, number of applicants, admitted and enrolled students in 1936/37, 1951/52 and 1966/67

Code	Classes and socio-professional groups	1936/37 Applicants	%	Admitted	%	Enrolled	%
1.	**Upper Classes**	44	16.9	33	17.7	17	20.2
1.1.	Proprietors	17	6.5	12	6.5	5	6.0
1.2.	Merchants and industrialists	7	2.7	4	2.2	2	2.4
1.3.	Public Administration higher ranks	-	-	-	-	-	-
1.4.	Army higher ranks	3	1.1	3	1.6	1	1.2
1.5.	Independent professions	11	4.2	10	5.4	7	8.3
1.6.	Teachers	6	2.3	2	1.1	2	2.4
1.6.1.	Primary	4	1.5	-	-	-	-
1.6.2.	Secondary	-	-	-	-	-	-
1.6.3.	Higher	1	0.4	1	0.5	1	1.2
1.6.4.	Non-specific	1	0.4	1	0.5	1	1.2
1.7.	Other	-	-	-	-	-	-
2.	**Middle Classes**	28	10.8	19	10.2	14	16.7
2.1.	Farmers	-	-	-	-	-	-
2.2.	Small and medium-sized industrialists	-	-	-	-	-	-
2.3.	Small and medium-sized established businesses	17	6.5	10	5.4	8	9.5
2.4.	Middle-ranking administration officers	3	1.1	1	0.5	1	1.2
2.5.	Industry, trade and administration skilled workers	6	2.3	6	3.2	3	3.6
2.6.	Middle-ranking Army officers	2	0.8	2	1.1	2	2.4
2.7.	Office staff	-	-	-	-	-	-
2.8.	Other	-	-	-	-	-	-
3.	**Working Classes**	30	11.5	25	13.4	14	16.7
3.1.	Skilled workers	3	1.1	3	1.6	3	3.6
3.1.1.	Food and beverage industry	-	-	-	-	-	-
3.1.2.	Carpentry	-	-	-	-	-	-
3.1.3.	Clothing and foot-wear	-	-	-	-	-	-
3.1.4.	Construction	-	-	-	-	-	-
3.1.5.	Paper industry	-	-	-	-	-	-
3.1.6.	Metallurgy	2	0.8	2	1.1	2	2.4
3.1.7.	Other	1	0.4	1	0.5	1	1.2
3.2.	Civil servants, council and administrative workers	8	3.1	6	3.2	4	4.8
3.3.	Shop assistants	14	5.4	11	5.9	5	6.0
3.4.	Officers and guards	2	0.8	2	1.1	1	1.2
3.5.	Non-specific workers	2	0.8	2	1.1	1	1.2
3.6.	Transport	1	0.4	1	0.5	-	-
3.7.	Other	-	-	-	-	-	-
4.	**Undeclared occupation**	159	60.9	109	58.6	39	46.4
Total		261	100	186	100	84	100

'The lyceums work in silence'

1951/52						1966/67					
Applicants	%	Admitted	%	Enrolled	%	Applicants	%	Admitted	%	Enrolled	%
56	18.2	51	21.3	33	24.3	152	15.6	151	19.9	92	21.9
5	1.6	5	2.1	3	2.2	17	1.7	17	2.2	4	0.9
21	6.8	21	8.8	12	8.8	48	4.9	47	6.2	26	6.2
2	0.6	2	0.8	1	0.7	2	0.2	2	0.3	1	0.2
3	1.0	2	0.8	1	0.7	5	0.5	5	0.7	3	0.7
17	5.5	14	5.9	11	8.1	65	6.7	65	8.6	47	11.2
7	2.3	6	2.5	4	2.9	13	1.3	13	1.7	11	2.6
2	0.6	2	0.8	2	1.4	6	0.6	6	0.8	5	1.2
2	0.6	1	0.4	-	-	5	0.5	5	0.7	5	1.2
2	0.6	2	0.8	2	1.4	1	0.1	1	0.1	1	0.2
1	0.3	1	0.4	-	-	1	0.1	1	0.1	-	-
1	0.3	1	0.4	1	0.7	2	0.2	2	0.3	-	-
68	22.1	61	25.5	40	29.4	301	30.9	300	39.6	195	46.4
3	1.0	3	1.3	1	0.7	21	21.6	21	2.8	5	1.2
3	1.0	3	1.3	2	1.4	7	0.7	7	0.9	1	0.2
31	10.1	29	12.1	20	14.7	75	77.0	75	9.9	44	10.5
4	1.3	2	0.8	1	0.7	12	1.2	12	1.6	9	2.1
14	4.5	13	5.4	7	5.1	92	94.5	92	12.1	70	16.7
1	0.3	-	-	-	-	6	0.6	6	0.8	4	0.9
9	2.9	8	3.3	7	5.1	42	4.3	41	5.4	29	6.9
3	1.0	3	1.3	2	1.4	46	4.7	46	6.1	33	7.9
37	12.0	30	12.6	24	17.6	225	23.2	216	28.5	96	22.9
8	2.6	8	3.3	5	3.7	86	8.8	84	11.1	31	7.4
-	-	-	-	-	-	6	0.6	6	0.8	1	0.2
2	0.6	2	0.8	1	0.7	6	0.6	6	0.8	2	0.5
1	0.3	1	0.4	1	0.7	16	1.6	16	2.1	8	1.9
3	1.0	3	1.3	1	0.7	15	1.5	14*	1.8	7	1.7
-	-	-	-	-	-	2	0.2	1	1	-	-
-	-	-	-	-	-	25	2.6	25	3.3	8	1.9
2	0.6	2	0.4	2	1.4	16	1.6	16	2.1	5	1.2
16	5.2	13	5.4	10	7.4	26	2.7	26	3.4	15	3.6
9	2.9	5	2.1	5	3.7	30	3.1	29*	3.8	17	4.0
3	1.0	3	1.3	3	2.2	20	2.2	18	2.4	7	1.7
-	-	-	-	-	-	7	0.7	7	0.9	1	0.2
1	0.3	1	0.4	1	0.7	33	3.4	29	3.8	13	3.1
-	-	-	-	-	-	23	2.4	23	3.1	12	2.9
147	47.7	97	40.6	39	28.7	295	30.0	91	12.0	37	8.8
308	100	239	100	136	100	973	100	758	100	420	100

An Ethics of Displaying Affection: Hélio Oiticica's Expressions of Joy and Togetherness

Karl Posso

University of Manchester

A arte já não é mais instrumento de domínio intelectual [...] só restará da arte passada o que puder ser apreendido como emoção direta [...] a busca do suprasensorial [...] sem transposição metafórica.[1]

[Art is no longer an instrument of intellectual domination [...] the only art of the past that will remain is that which can be apprehended as direct emotion [...] the search for the suprasensorial [...] without metaphorical transposition.][2]

Hélio Oiticica

Sensational, Emotional, Conceptual

Hélio Oiticica (1937–80), whose oeuvre has been variously branded 'avantgarde', 'conceptual' and 'Neoconcrete', is often discussed as a progenitor of the distinctive aesthetic of the late 1960s Brazilian countercultural movement, or rather, the interdisciplinary artistic concurrences, which came to be known retrospectively as Tropicália.[3] Before Tropicália, in the mid 1950s, Oiticica had belonged to Rio de Janeiro's Grupo Frente, which drew extensively on De Stijl and Concrete Art, and later to the short-lived Grupo Neoconcreto: he dedicated these years to structural explorations of chromatism.[4] From

---

[1] Hélio Oiticica, 'O aparecimento do suprasensorial na arte brasileira' (1967), *Revista GAM*, 13 (1968), 39; repr. in his *Hélio Oiticica: Aspiro ao grande labirinto*, ed. by Luciano Figueiredo, Lygia Pape and Waly Salomão (Rio de Janeiro: Rocco, 1986), pp. 102–05 (p. 105).

[2] Hélio Oiticica, 'Appearance of the Supra-Sensorial' (1967), in *Hélio Oiticica*, ed. by Mat Verberkt, trans. by Stephen Berg et al. (Rotterdam: Witte de With/Galerie Nationale du Jeu de Paume, 1992), pp. 127–30 (p. 130).

[3] Brazilian counterculture, with its agenda of civil and political rights, was clearly primed by similar movements in the United States and Europe during the 1960s. See Olavo Ramalho Marques, 'Do tropicalismo sob o prisma da cultura: Memórias de juventude e ação sobre o mundo', in *Tropicália: Gêneros, identidades, repertórios e linguagens*, ed. by Ana Mery Sehbe de Carli and Flávia Brocchetto Ramos (Caixas do Sul: EDUCS, 2008), pp. 231–49.

[4] Ronaldo Brito, *Neoconcretismo: Vértice e ruptura do projeto construtivo brasileiro* (Rio de Janeiro: Funarte/Instituto Nacional de Artes Plásticas, 1985), pp. 106–13; Fernando Cochiarale and Anna Bella Geiger, *Abstracionismo geométrico e informal: A vanguarda brasileira nos anos cinqüenta* (Rio de

gouaches of buckling grids and blocks, *Metaesquemas* [Metaschemes] (1957–58), he moved onto creating navigable structures, *Núcleos* [nuclei] (1960–63), and haptically provocative objects, *Bólides* [meteors] (1963–69), all of which shunned representation in favour of producing space and time (rhythm) through colour. During the 1960s — in line with international, avant-garde 'conceptual' reconsiderations of the 'object of art' — Oiticica's abiding interest in expanding audience perception matured into a fully-fledged art of participation, notably, through his acclaimed *Parangolé* banner, tent and cape sculptures (produced between 1964 and 1974 approximately), which he also called 'estruturas-côr no espaço' [colour-structures in space].[5] Designating Oiticica a 'conceptual artist' may seem problematic given that his formative years were caught up in the debate between Concrete and Neoconcrete notions of art's materiality, and that his subsequent work, which dialogues openly with popular culture, may be seen to extend from Neoconcretism's (Merleau-Pontian) engrossment with 'the phenomenological affect of the artwork as an "almost body"', to wit, a quasi-body or centre of indetermination which engages several of the audience's or participants' senses and their intuition or emotions rather than just their 'disembodied gaze' and intellect.[6]

Janeiro: Funarte/Instituto Nacional de Artes Plásticas, 1987), p. 11; Ferreira Gullar, 'Cor e estrutura-cor', in his *Etapas da arte contemporânea: Do Cubismo ao Neoconcretismo* (São Paulo: Nobel, 1985), pp. 254–57 (first publ. in *Jornal do Brasil*, 26 November 1960); Hélio Oiticica, 'Cor, Tempo e estrutura', in his *Hélio Oiticica: Aspiro ao grande labirinto*, ed. by Luciano Figueiredo, Lygia Pape and Waly Salomão (Rio de Janeiro: Rocco, 1986), pp. 44–49 (first publ. in *Jornal do Brasil*, 24 November 1960); trans. by Stephen Berg *et al.* as 'Colour, Time and Structure', in *Hélio Oiticica*, ed. by Mat Verberkt (Rotterdam: Witte de With/Galerie Nationale du Jeu de Paume, 1992), pp. 34–37; Mário Pedrosa, 'A bienal de cá para lá', in *Arte brasileira hoje (situação e perspectivas)*, ed. by Ferreira Gullar (Rio de Janeiro: Paz e Terra, 1973), pp. 1–64 (p. 61); Mário Pedrosa, 'Arte ambiental, arte pós-moderna, Hélio Oiticica', in his *Dos murais de Portinari aos espaços de Brasília*, ed. by Aracy A. Amaral (São Paulo: Perspectiva, 1981), pp. 205–09 (first publ. in *Correio da Manhã*, 26 June 1966); Mário Pedrosa, 'Um passeio pelas caixas no passado' (1967), in his *Mundo, homem, arte em crise*, ed. by Aracy Amaral, 2nd edn (São Paulo: Editora Perspectiva, 2007), pp. 153–57 (p. 154).
[5] Hélio Oiticica, 'Bases fundamentais para uma definição do "Parangolé"' (1964), in his *Hélio Oiticica: Aspiro ao grande labirinto*, ed. by Luciano Figueiredo, Lygia Pape and Waly Salomão (Rio de Janeiro: Rocco, 1986), pp. 65–69 (p. 65); trans. by Stephen A. Berg and Héctor Olea as 'Cornerstones for a Definition of "Parangolé"', in *Hélio Oiticica: The Body of Colour*, ed. by Mari Carmen Ramírez (London: Tate, 2007), pp. 296–97 (p. 296). See also Ariane Figueiredo — Projeto Hélio Oiticica, 'Hélio Oiticica: Cronologia (1937–80)', in *Fios soltos: A arte de Hélio Oiticica*, ed. by Paula Braga (São Paulo: Perspectiva, 2008), pp. 291–303 (p. 301); Boris Groys, 'The Mimesis of Thinking', in *Open Systems: Rethinking Art c.1970*, ed. by Donna de Salvo (London: Tate, 2005), pp. 50–63 (p. 63).
[6] Peter Osborne, 'Survey', in *Conceptual Art*, ed. by Peter Osborne (London and New York: Phaidon, 2002), pp. 12–51 (p. 38). See also Lygia Clark, 'Bêtes/Bichos' (1960), in *Lygia Clark*, ed. by Manuel J. Borja-Villel, Corinne Diserens, Vicente Todolí and Piet Coessens (Paris: Réunion des Musées Nationaux/Fundació Antoni Tàpies, 1998), pp. 119–45 (pp. 139–42); Ferreira Gullar, 'Teoria do não-objeto', in *Projeto construtivo brasileiro na arte, 1950–1962*, ed. by Aracy A. Amaral (Rio de Janeiro: Museu de Arte Moderna/Pinacoteca de São Paulo, 1977), pp. 85–94 (first publ. in *Jornal do Brasil*, 19 December 1959); Ferreira Gullar, Amilcar de Castro, Franz Weissmann *et al.*, 'Manifesto Neoconcreto', in Ronaldo Brito, *Neoconcretismo: Vértice e ruptura do projeto construtivo brasileiro* (Rio de Janeiro: Funarte/Instituto Nacional de Artes Plásticas, 1985), pp. 12–13 (first publ. in *Jornal do Brasil*, 22 March 1959). For comprehensive accounts of the distinct tenets of Concretism and Neoconcretism and the taxonomical challenges presented by Oiticica's work see Michael Asbury, 'Hélio Oiticica: Politics and Ambivalence in 20th Century Brazilian Art' (unpublished doctoral thesis, University of the Arts,

In Torquato Neto's 'Geléia geral' [General jam] column for *Última Hora* in September 1971, Oiticica takes exception to being labelled 'conceptual'; he considers his formulation of ideas for or about art quite different from the practice of proposing ideas as forms of art, namely, the professed 'dematerialization' of art objects, which was arguably the common drive behind the neo-avant-garde movements in the Americas, Europe, Asia and Australia in the 1960s and early 1970s.[7] Broadly speaking, in conceptual art, ideas, aesthetic or otherwise, and their transmission are privileged over their execution (their base properties); by making concepts the fundamental objects of the artistic experiences on offer, it follows that audiences are primarily engaged intellectually.[8] If all conceptual art of the 1960s and 1970s has its roots in the crisis of formalist modernism, then, according to Luis Camnitzer and Peter Osborne, what makes Latin American 'conceptualism' of the period distinctive is a more pronounced preoccupation with societal needs, politics and pedagogy.[9] That said, by repudiating traditional art objects and withdrawing from the commercial gallery circuit, conceptual art, whether from Latin America or elsewhere, often attempts to realize its sundry aspirations through defamiliarizing interventions and by dwelling on activity or process and on bodily experience. Clearly, this all

London, Camberwell College of Arts, 2003), pp. 59–159; Anna Dezeuze, 'Tactile Dematerialization, Sensory Politics: Hélio Oiticica's *Parangolés*', *Art Journal*, 63.2 (2004), 58–71 (pp. 62–64).

[7] Hélio Oiticica, 'Quero esclarecer que não vou expor em galeria', Projeto Hélio Oiticica, fol. 0239/70, in *Programa Hélio Oiticica* <http://www.itaucultural.org.br/aplicexternas/enciclopedia/ho/index.cfm?fuseaction=documentos&cd_verbete=4523&cod=346&tipo=2> [accessed 1 September 2012] (publ. as 'Exposição? Eu não!' in *Última Hora*, 29 September 1971). See also Aracy A. Amaral, 'Hélio Oiticica', in *Arte e meio artístico: Entre a feijoada e o x-burger* (São Paulo: Nobel, 1982), pp. 192–93; Hélio Oiticica, letter to Torquato Neto, in Torquato Neto, *Os últimos dias de paupéria*, ed. by Ana Maria Silva de Araújo Duarte and Waly Salomão, 2nd edn (São Paulo: M. Limonad, 1982), p. 82. It was not uncommon in the early 1970s for artists branded 'conceptualists' to reject such categorization; like Oiticica, they insisted on the need for artworks to be materially available to experience. See Carl Andre, Jan Dibbets, Dan Graham and Douglas Huebler quoted in Tony Godfrey, *Conceptual Art* (London: Phaidon, 1998), pp. 157–60; Derek Matravers, 'The Dematerialization of the Object', in *Philosophy and Conceptual Art*, ed. by Peter Goldie and Elisabeth Schellekens (Oxford: Clarendon Press, 2007), pp. 18–32.

[8] 'Conceptual art' itself is a disputed term inasmuch as it implies the existence of art which is purely non-conceptual. Central to debates about conceptual art is the question of the ineliminability of the aesthetic as a necessary element of the artwork, that is, despite its insufficiency when it comes to the artwork's meaning-producing capacity. See Art & Language (Terry Atkinson, David Bainbridge, Michael Baldwin and Harold Hurrell), 'Introduction', *Art–Language*, 1.1 (May 1969), 10; Sol LeWitt, 'Paragraphs on Conceptual Art' (1967), in *Six Years: The Dematerialization of the Art Object from 1966 to 1972*, ed. by Lucy Lippard (New York: Praeger, 1973), pp. 28–39; Lucy Lippard and John Chandler, 'The Dematerialization of Art', *Art International*, 12.2 (1968), 31–36. See also Gregory Currie, 'Visual Conceptual Art', in *Philosophy and Conceptual Art*, ed. by Peter Goldie and Elisabeth Schellekens (Oxford: Clarendon Press, 2007), pp. 33–50; Godfrey, *Conceptual Art*, p. 88, p. 111, pp. 142–44; Joseph Kosuth, 'Art After Philosophy', in his *Art After Philosophy and After: Collected Writings, 1966–1990*, ed. by Gabriele Guercio (Cambridge, MA: MIT Press, 1991), pp. 13–32 (pp. 18–21, p. 26); Peter Osborne, 'Conceptual Art and/as Philosophy', in *Rewriting Conceptual Art*, ed. by Michael Newman and Jon Bird (London: Reaktion Books, 1999), pp. 47–65 (pp. 48–49, pp. 53–58); Osborne, 'Survey', pp. 15–18, pp. 29–30.

[9] Luis Camnitzer, *Conceptualism in Latin American Art: Didactics of Liberation* (Austin: University of Texas Press, 2007), p. 60, pp. 111–13, pp. 165–69; Osborne, 'Survey', pp. 37–39.

resonates with many of Oiticica's own creative endeavours.[10] Furthermore, as Oiticica's extensive writings on the theoretical or philosophical underpinnings of his projects bear out, by eliciting participation, his emotive, collaborative art is ultimately designed to generate specific cognitive values phenomenologically; he deems such experiential knowledge more important than the objects which serve as their vehicular medium. These cognitive values are often described by abstract neologisms such as 'crelazer' [creleisure] and 'o suprasensorial' [the suprasensorial]; even his fascination with 'pure' colour is sustained by the intellectual ambition of facilitating an intuition of 'côr-tempo' [colour-time], a heightened awareness of Bergsonian 'duration' in the viewer.[11] As Mari Carmen Ramírez states, 'Oiticica began the gradual dematerialization of color into pure sensory stimuli, which would reach a climax with the *Parangolés*'.[12] This is not to say that he ever dismissed the medium as immaterial; the materiality of these conceptual artworks qualifies how they are perceived and thus how they, or their embodied concepts, come to be understood.[13] As the vibrant, wearable *Parangolés* in particular show, the conventional aesthetic concerns which conceptual art ostensibly challenges remain central to Oiticica's mission to attract and involve his audience. His work's transformational social objectives and its incorporation of popular — 'low' — art forms, though, chime with the neo-avant-gardes of the 1960s and early 1970s, which appear to have been consecrated as a complex, far-reaching, if controversial and terminologically

[10] Hélio Oiticica, 'Esquema geral da nova objetividade', in his *Hélio Oiticica: Aspiro ao grande labirinto*, ed. by Luciano Figueiredo, Lygia Pape and Waly Salomão (Rio de Janeiro: Rocco, 1986), pp. 84-98 (p. 84); trans. by Stephen Berg *et al.* as 'General Scheme of the New Objectivity' (1967), in *Hélio Oiticica*, ed. by Mat Verberkt (Rotterdam: Witte de With/Galerie Nationale du Jeu de Paume, 1992), pp. 110-20 (p. 110).
[11] The portmanteau term 'crelazer', made up of 'crer' [to believe] and 'lazer' [leisure], but which also alludes to the English verb 'to create' and the notion of 'laziness', is inspired by Herbert Marcuse's discussion of a non-alienated leisure time countering capitalist and Marxist conceptions of work. Oiticica's 'environmental' installations such as *Eden* at the Whitechapel Gallery, London (1969) are correlates of 'crelazer'. Hélio Oiticica, 'Crelazer', in his *Hélio Oiticica: Aspiro ao grande labirinto*, ed. by Luciano Figueiredo, Lygia Pape and Waly Salomão (Rio de Janeiro: Rocco, 1986), pp. 113-17; trans. by Stephen Berg *et al.* as 'Creleisure' (1968-69), in *Hélio Oiticica*, ed. by Mat Verberkt (Rotterdam: Witte de With/Galerie Nationale du Jeu de Paume, 1992), pp. 132-38. See Lygia Clark and Hélio Oiticica, *Lygia Clark/Hélio Oiticica: Cartas, 1964-1974*, ed. by Luciano Figueiredo (Rio de Janeiro: UFRJ, 1996), pp. 41-54, pp. 118-25; Waly Salomão, *Hélio Oiticica: Qual é o Parangolé e outros escritos* (Rio de Janeiro: Rocco, 2003), p. 72. See also Herbert Marcuse, *Eros and Civilization: A Philosophical Inquiry into Freud* (Boston, MA: Beacon Press, 1966), pp. 45-48. On 'colour-time' and 'the suprasensorial' see Hélio Oiticica, 'Côr Tempo' (December 1959), Projeto Hélio Oiticica, fol. 0017/59, in *Programa Hélio Oiticica* <http://www.itaucultural.org.br/aplicexternas/enciclopedia/ho/index.cfm?fuseaction=documentos&cd_verbete=4523&cod=28&tipo=2> [accessed 1 September 2012]; Oiticica, 'Appearance of the Supra-Sensorial', pp. 127-30; Oiticica, *Hélio Oiticica: Aspiro ao grande labirinto*, pp. 44-49, pp. 102-05. See also Gullar, de Castro, Weissmann *et al.*, 'Manifesto Neoconcreto', pp. 12-13.
[12] Mari Carmen Ramírez, 'Hélio's Double-Edged Challenge', in *Hélio Oiticica: The Body of Colour*, ed. by Mari Carmen Ramírez (London: Tate, 2007), pp. 17-24 (p. 20).
[13] Hélio Oiticica, 'Carta' (25 September 1962), Projeto Hélio Oiticica, fol. 0022/62, in *Programa Hélio Oiticica* <http://www.itaucultural.org.br/aplicexternas/enciclopedia/ho/index.cfm?fuseaction=documentos&cd_verbete=4523&cod=35&tipo=2> [accessed 1 September 2012]; Oiticica, *Hélio Oiticica: Aspiro ao grande labirinto*, pp. 21-23.

unsettled, 'conceptual' movement by 'Information', the large international group show curated by Kynaston McShine at New York's Museum of Modern Art (MoMA) in 1970. 'Information' featured some of Oiticica's *Ninhos* [nests], also known as *Babylonests*, which are referred to later.[14] Although arguable, therefore, it is certainly possible to admit Oiticica under the 'conceptual' label, and there are several well-reasoned precedents which do so, in particular, studies by Frederico Coelho, Catherine David and Celso Favaretto.[15] Furthermore, the contention that the emotions engendered by these artworks are as conceptual — or conceptualized — as any ideas or questions they may be said to embody is central to this paper which looks at how participants experience some of Oiticica's art.

The *Parangolés*, and works associated with them, are partly coextensive with the socio-political upheaval that gave rise to Tropicália in the late 1960s. (Internationally, the *Parangolés* gained prominence much later, when they were exhibited in the politically oriented 'documenta X', in 1997.) Oiticica's non-dogmatic and questioning approaches to art during this period, eagerly commandeered by Tropicália's ringleaders, have been described at length, but they remain curiously under-analysed. Whilst there appears to be critical consensus that when it comes to his oeuvre 'o que sobressai é a exposição sensorial' [what stands out is sensorial exhibition], few critics expand on what this purported visual art of sensation might actually be or how it operates.[16] Oiticica's own feverish writings on the subject often do obeisance

---

[14] Kynaston McShine, 'Information' Exhibition Research, Series IV, folders 64a and 64b. The Museum of Modern Art Archives, New York. See also Camnitzer, *Conceptualism in Latin American Art*, pp. 189–90; Esther Gabara, 'Perspectives on Scale: From the Atomic to the Universal', in *Art and Globalization*, ed. by James Elkins, Zhivka Valiavicharska and Alice Kim (University Park: Pennsylvania State University Press, 2010), pp. 200–08 (pp. 200–01).

[15] As Frederico Coelho points out with regard to the fragmentary theoretical corpus in particular, Oiticica was more prolific textually than 'visually'; in *Livro ou livro-me: Os escritos babilônicos de Hélio Oiticica (1971–1978)* (Rio de Janeiro: EdUERJ, 2010), pp. 13–14. Catherine David, 'Hélio Oiticica: Brazil Experiment', in *The Experimental Exercise of Freedom: Lygia Clark, Gego, Mathias Goeritz, Hélio Oiticica, and Mira Schendel*, ed. by Rina Carvajal and Alma Ruiz (Los Angeles, CA: Museum of Contemporary Art, Los Angeles, 1999), pp. 169–201; Celso Favaretto, *A invenção de Hélio Oiticica*, rev. edn (São Paulo: EDUSP, 2000), pp. 182–85. See also Alex Alberro, 'A Media Art: Conceptualism in Latin America in the 1960s', in *Rewriting Conceptual Art*, ed. by Michael Newman and Jon Bird (London: Reaktion Books, 1999), pp. 140–51 (pp. 146–47, p. 151); *Conceptual Art*, ed. by Peter Osborne (London and New York: Phaidon, 2002), pp. 148–49; Luciano Figueiredo, '"The World is the Museum": Appropriation and Transformation in the Work of Hélio Oiticica', trans. by Stephen A. Berg and Héctor Olea, in *Hélio Oiticica: The Body of Colour*, ed. by Mari Carmen Ramírez (London: Tate, 2007), pp. 105–25 (pp. 117–18); Godfrey, *Conceptual Art*, pp. 118–20, p. 431; Osborne, 'Survey', p. 39; Mari Carmen Ramírez, 'Tactics for Thriving on Adversity: Conceptualism in Latin America, 1960–1980', in *Global Conceptualism: Points of Origin, 1950s–1980s*, ed. by Luis Camnitzer, Jane Farver and Rachel Weiss (New York: Queens Museum of Art, 1999), pp. 53–71; Donna de Salvo, 'Where We Begin: Opening the System, c.1970', in *Open Systems: Rethinking Art c.1970*, ed. by Donna de Salvo (London: Tate, 2005), pp. 10–23 (pp. 16–17, p. 22).

[16] Favaretto, *A invenção de Hélio Oiticica*, p. 149. See also Jacqueline Barnitz, *Twentieth-Century Art of Latin America* (Austin: University of Texas Press, 2001), p. 225; Silviano Santiago, 'É proibido proibir', in his *Ora (direis) puxar conversa!* (Belo Horizonte: UFMG, 2006), pp. 209–14 (p. 213); David Sperling, 'Body + Art = Architecture: Propositions by Hélio Oiticica and Lygia

AN ETHICS OF DISPLAYING AFFECTION   49

to the scholarship of Mário Pedrosa which was committed to the pursuit of Gestaltian and, more generally, phenomenological lines of aesthetic enquiry, tempered at times by Bergsonian and Wittgensteinian thought.[17] Pedrosa wrote a professorial thesis entitled 'Da natureza afetiva da forma na obra de arte' [On the affective nature of the work of art's form] (Universidade do Brasil, Rio de Janeiro, 1949); a stalwart of the Concrete movement, he went on to assert that art which eschews representation can reveal 'virtualidades irrealizáveis pelo nexo causal simples' [potentialities which cannot be attained through simple causal relations], and that these lead us to discover 'maneiras de sentir e, portanto, de ser. Uma nova ética' [ways of feeling and, therefore, of being. A new ethics].[18] Similar statements abound in his later work.[19] Outside Brazil, Guy Brett, the linchpin of Oiticica's *Whitechapel Experiment* in 1969, has repeatedly underscored — albeit in a more cursory fashion and without recourse to Pedrosa's philosophical armoury — the role of sensation in the artist's bid to foment 'alternative life-processes'.[20] Together, Pedrosa and Brett have guided — and perhaps delimited — subsequent discussions of Oiticica's compulsion to exercise sensation though art.[21] This paper is clearly indebted

Clark', in *Fios soltos: A arte de Hélio Oiticica*, ed. by Paula Braga (São Paulo: Perspectiva, 2008), pp. 136–45.
[17] Oiticica, 'O aparecimento do suprasensorial na arte brasileira', p. 39; Oiticica, *Hélio Oiticica: Aspiro ao grande labirinto*, p. 62, pp. 80–84, p. 98, passim; Mário Pedrosa, 'Das formas significantes à lógica da expressão' (1954), in his *Mundo, homem, arte em crise*, ed. by Aracy Amaral, 2nd edn (São Paulo: Editora Perspectiva, 2007), pp. 61–71 (pp. 61–62); Mário Pedrosa, 'Especulações estéticas: O conflito entre o "dizer" e o "exprimir" — I' (1967), in his *Mundo, homem, arte em crise*, ed. by Aracy Amaral, 2nd edn (São Paulo: Editora Perspectiva, 2007), pp. 121–25; Mário Pedrosa, 'Especulações estéticas: Forma e informação — II' (1967), in his *Mundo, homem, arte em crise*, ed. by Aracy Amaral, 2nd edn (São Paulo: Editora Perspectiva, 2007), pp. 127–31 (pp. 128–29).
[18] Pedrosa, 'Das formas significantes à lógica da expressão', pp. 70–71. See also Mário Pedrosa, 'Da natureza afetiva da forma na obra de arte' (1949), in his *Arte/forma e personalidade: 3 estudos* (São Paulo: Kairós, 1979), pp. 12–82.
[19] See Pedrosa, 'Arte ambiental, arte pós-moderna, Hélio Oiticica', p. 206; Pedrosa, 'Especulações estéticas: Forma e informação — II', p. 130.
[20] Guy Brett, 'Recollection', in *Oiticica in London*, ed. by Guy Brett and Luciano Figueiredo (London: Tate, 2007), pp. 11–16 (pp. 13–16). See also Guy Brett, 'Border Crossings', in *Transcontinental: Nine Latin American Artists*, ed. by Guy Brett (London: Verso/Ikon Gallery/Cornerhouse, 1990), pp. 9–35 (pp. 27–33); Guy Brett, 'The Experimental Exercise of Liberty', in *Hélio Oiticica*, ed. by Mat Verberkt, trans. by Stephen Berg et al. (Rotterdam: Witte de With/Galerie Nationale du Jeu de Paume, 1992), pp. 222–39 (p. 227, p. 237); Guy Brett, *Kinetic Art: The Language of Movement* (London and New York: Studio Vista/Reinhold, 1968), p. 65; Guy Brett, 'Lygia Clark: In Search of the Body', *Art in America*, July 1994, pp. 56–63, p. 108 (p. 60).
[21] See, for example, Rina Carvajal, 'The Experimental Exercise of Freedom', in *The Experimental Exercise of Freedom: Lygia Clark, Gego, Mathias Goeritz, Hélio Oiticica, and Mira Schendel*, ed. by Rina Carvajal and Alma Ruiz (Los Angeles, CA: Museum of Contemporary Art, Los Angeles, 1999), pp. 33–54 (p. 35, pp. 39–42); Favaretto, *A invenção de Hélio Oiticica*, p. 30, p. 69, p. 90, p. 98, p. 103, passim; Simone Osthoff, 'Lygia Clark and Hélio Oiticica: A Legacy of Interactivity and Participation for a Telematic Future', in *Corpus Delecti: Performance Art of the Americas*, ed. by Coco Fusco (London and New York: Routledge, 2000), pp. 156–73 (pp. 157–58, p. 164); Mari Carmen Ramírez, 'The Embodiment of Color — "From the Inside Out"', in *Hélio Oiticica: The Body of Colour*, ed. by Mari Carmen Ramírez (London: Tate, 2007), pp. 27–73 (p. 46, p. 57, p. 65); Susana Vaz, 'HO|ME: Hélio Oiticica and Mircéa Eliade', in *Fios soltos: A arte de Hélio Oiticica*, ed. by Paula Braga (São Paulo: Perspectiva, 2008), pp. 93–109 (pp. 102–03).

to both critics, and to their academic legacy; notwithstanding, it seeks to think through some of the lacunae in their claims about Oiticica's work in order to provide a better understanding of what they describe as non-representational, sensorial 'potentialities' and its attendant 'life-processes' or 'new ethics'. In so doing, it examines the centrality of emotion, or more accurately, affect, to Oiticica's 'revolutionary' aesthetic practices from the mid 1960s onwards. The aim is to show how these practices make sensation or affective qualities the artistic — and manifestly conceptual — domain of politics and in particular of ethics.[22] Alighting on how Oiticica's works transmute, or forsake, varying idealized conceptions of love or togetherness through sensation, the discussion seeks to explicate how such a disfiguring process is, paradoxically, key to the achievement of ethical ends. In addition to the *Parangolé* series, which Oiticica worked on well beyond the wake of Tropicália, the paper focuses on his *Quasi-cinema* project (1971–73). Developed in New York alongside some of the final *Parangolés*, the *Quasi-cinema* sequences mark something of a midpoint between installation art and cinema; in recent years, these have become some of Oiticica's most exhibited and commercialized works.[23]

Tropical Roots: Day-Glo Disaffection

Tropicália flourished in Brazil between 1967 and 1968, but its cultural impact has been far-reaching. The so-called Tropicalists coalesced in response to growing civil unrest related to the military regime which, in the interests of suppressing President João Goulart's socialist reforms and associated 'communist threats' to social order, seized power in 1964 and thereafter set about transforming the country's economy, making it more responsive to the market and dependent on foreign loans and investment.[24] Civil protest against the regime escalated during 1967, and in June 1968 Rio de Janeiro witnessed the 'Passeata dos Cem Mil' [March of the One Hundred Thousand]; the govern-

---

[22] Oiticica, 'Esquema geral da nova objetividade', pp. 94–95; Oiticica, 'General Scheme of the New Objectivity', p. 117.

[23] Major exhibitions include: *Hélio Oiticica: Quasi-cinemas*, curated by Carlos Basualdo, Wexner Center for the Arts, Ohio; Kölnischer Kunstverein, Cologne; New Museum for Contemporary Art, New York; Whitechapel Gallery, London, 18 September 2001–5 October 2002; *Hélio Oiticica/Neville d'Almeida CC Program in Progress*, curated by César Oiticica Filho, Centro de Arte Hélio Oiticica, Rio de Janeiro; MALBA — Fundación Costantini, Buenos Aires, 10 September 2005–30 January 2006; *Suprasenorial: Experiments in Light, Color, and Space*, curated by Alma Ruiz, Museum of Contemporary Art, Los Angeles; Hirshhorn Museum and Sculpture Garden, Smithsonian Institution, Washington, DC, 12 December 2010–11 September 2011. Permanent institutional installations: *Maileryn* (*Cosmococa CC3*), Museu d'Art Contemporani de Barcelona; *Cosmococa* series *CC1* to *CC5*, Galeria Cosmococas, Instituto de Arte Contemporânea Inhotim, Brumadinho, Minas Gerais. Exhibitions in commercial galleries include: *Trashiscapes* (*Cosmococa CC1*), Galerie Lelong, New York, 5 May–17 June 2006; *Trashiscapes* (*Cosmococa CC1*), Alison Jacques Gallery, London, 6 June–7 July 2007.

[24] Boris Fausto, *A Concise History of Brazil*, trans. by Arthur Brakel (Cambridge: Cambridge University Press, 1999), pp. 277–308; Duncan Green, *Silent Revolution: The Rise and Crisis of Market Economics in Latin America*, 2nd edn (New York and London: Monthly Review Press/Latin America Bureau, 2003), pp. 23–25, pp. 28–31; Thomas E. Skidmore, *Brazil: Five Centuries of Change* (New York and Oxford: Oxford University Press, 1999), pp. 154–57, pp. 177–83.

ment responded in December that year by passing the Fifth Institutional Act (AI-5) which prohibited political opposition and suspended habeas corpus. As the designation of a movement, Tropicália is most coherent with regard to developments within popular music, challenging the latter's preoccupation with supposed national purity, but its name and proclivities stem from other fields of cultural production, namely the visual arts and theatre.[25] Tropicalist tendencies included reassessing kitsch mass culture — national, sentimental *cafonice* and North-American pop and hippy fads — duly resuscitating the 'anthropophagic' intertextual and citational strategies of the Modernists. The precipitation of dialogue between popular and high cultural forms at the time frequently advanced through allusions to stereotypes of Brazil as a tropical paradise and as a barbaric land of violence and social wretchedness. In this last respect, a considerable influence was exerted by socially and politically engaged offerings — often produced on modest budgets — of the nation's Cinema Novo *auteurs* who had risen to artistic, though not commercial, prominence in the early 1960s.[26] Tropicália's most celebrated musician, Caetano Veloso, and its leading theatre director, José Celso Martinez Corrêa (of Teatro Oficina), claim that Glauber Rocha's *Terra em transe* (translated as *Land in Anguish* and

---

[25] In some contexts, the appellation Tropicália appears to be used interchangeably with *tropicalismo*; for instance, see Celso Favaretto, *Tropicália: Alegoria, Alegria* (São Paulo: Kairós, 1979); Gilberto Gil and Augusto de Campos, in Augusto de Campos, *Balanço da bossa, e outras bossas*, 2nd edn (São Paulo: Perspectiva, 1974), p. 193; Hermano Vianna, 'Tropicália's Politics', in *Tropicália: A Revolution in Brazilian Culture (1967–1972)*, ed. by Carlos Basualdo (São Paulo: Cosac Naify, 2005), pp. 131–42. However, there are putative distinctions between these terms. As Frederico Coelho states, the '-ismo' suffix suggests an organized or coherent movement, which Tropicália, a loose congregation of artists and cultural practices, was not; he calls it 'muito mais a reunião criativa de contradições do que a confluência plácida de consensos' [much more a creative meeting of contradictions than a serene confluence of like-mindedness]; in 'Nota editorial', in *Tropicália*, ed. by Sergio Cohn and Frederico Coelho (Rio de Janeiro: Beco do Azougue, 2008), pp. 12–15 (p. 12). The issue of coherence may explain why the term *tropicalismo* appears to be used more often to designate the music of the period than in relation to all associated countercultural manifestations. The Concrete poets' promotion of Ezra Pound, which seems to have had an enduring effect on Brazilian artists of the 1960s, is also relevant here. Pound distinguishes literary 'inventors' from 'diluters' in his *ABC of Reading* (1934) — see (New York: New Directions, 1960), p. 39. The Tropicalists equated convergence under an '-ism' with artistic compromise and compliance and therefore with 'dilution'. Another reason for their rejection of the term *tropicalismo* was its ostensible derivation from *Luso-tropicalismo*, Gilberto Freyre's theory of Portuguese colonial adaptability in the tropics, appropriated at the time by right-wing discourse. See Christopher Dunn, *Brutality Garden: Tropicália and the Emergence of a Brazilian Counterculture* (Chapel Hill: University of North Carolina Press, 2001), p. 8, p. 73; Gilberto Freyre, 'Em torno de um novo conceito de tropicalismo', in *Ciência para os trópicos: I Congresso Brasileiro de Tropicologia — documentação básica*, ed. by Maria do Carmo Tavares de Miranda (Recife: Fundação Joaquim Nabuco/Editora Massangana, 1986), pp. 35–45 (first publ. in *Brasília*, 7 (1952)); Arlette Neves, 'Tropicalismo: Movimento, mito, escola ou cafajestada sob encomenda?', in *Tropicália*, ed. by Sergio Cohn and Frederico Coelho (Rio de Janeiro: Beco do Azougue, 2008), pp. 118–25 (first publ. in *O Cruzeiro*, 20 April 1968).

[26] Randal Johnson, 'The Rise and Fall of Brazilian Cinema, 1960-1990', in *New Latin American Cinema*, ed. by Michael T. Martin (Detroit, MI: Wayne State University Press, 1997), II, 365–93 (pp. 382–88); Glauber Rocha, *Revolução do Cinema Novo* (Rio de Janeiro: Alhambra/Embrafilme, 1981), p. 158, pp. 198–207; Ismail Xavier, *Allegories of Underdevelopment: Aesthetics and Politics in Modern Brazilian Cinema* (Minneapolis: University of Minnesota Press, 1999), pp. 1-2, pp. 9–10, pp. 22–28.

Entranced Earth; first screened in May 1967) alerted left-wing artists to the conditions that came to define the movement.[27] The film is an allegory of the 1964 coup as seen by a dying socialist poet who contemplates the failures of the left and the ineffectuality of *engagé* art.[28] It was also around this time that on hearing an as-yet untitled song by Veloso, cinematographer Luís Carlos Barreto pointed out its aesthetic affinities with Oiticica's *Tropicália* installation (1966–67) at the 'Nova Objetividade Brasileira' [New Brazilian Objectivity] exhibition in Rio de Janeiro's Museum of Modern Art (April 1967) [Figure 1]. Veloso's song became the installation's namesake.

Drawing on Oswald de Andrade's 'Manifesto antropófago' [Anthropophagite Manifesto] (1928), Oiticica's *Tropicália*, with its tag 'a pureza é um mito' [purity is a myth], is meant to address or actualize Brazil's 'mito de miscigenação' [myth of miscegenation].[29] *Tropicália* is a *Penetrável* [penetrable] — to be more precise, it comprises conjoined *Penetráveis* (*PN2* and *PN3*) — through which Oiticica broadened his exploration of art's habitability in the concurrent *Parangolé* series. Surrounded by tropical plants and caged parrots, *Tropicália*'s precarious *favela*-inspired wooden structures support gaudy, often floral, drapery which cloisters a television set showing brightly coloured images; it is meant to lure in and swallow observers, making them participants in the work of art. Hallowed museum space re-contextualizes the installation's effulgent triteness as all manner of native icons and external influences are absorbed to induce reflection on identities, potentially with a view to arriving at something new.[30] The structure and logic of Veloso's 'Tropicália' are entirely comparable: a *bricolage* of stock Brazilian images and national and international current and 'primitive' styles, tellingly described by Favaretto as 'montagens eisensteinianas' [Eisensteinian montage].[31] The song, together with the syncretic, cosmopolitan compositions of the 1968 collaborative concept album, *Tropicália, ou panis et circensis* [sic] — under the vanguardist direction of Rogério Duprat — became a manifesto for this piecemeal countercultural efflorescence.[32]

---

[27] Caetano Veloso, *Verdade tropical* (São Paulo: Companhia das Letras, 1997), pp. 99–106; José Celso Martinez Corrêa, 'O rei da vela' (1968), in *Tropicália*, ed. by Sergio Cohn and Frederico Coelho (Rio de Janeiro: Beco do Azougue, 2008), pp. 58–75 (p. 64, p. 74). Tropicália's other seminal work was Teatro Oficina's 1967 Artaud-inflected performance of Oswald de Andrade's *O rei da vela* (1933; publ. 1937), directed by Martinez Corrêa; the production was dedicated to Glauber Rocha.

[28] During the early 1960s, left-wing cultural production in Brazil was informed by the agitprop activities of the Centros Populares de Cultura [People's Centres for Culture]. See Carlos Zílio, 'Da antropofagia à Tropicália', in *O nacional e o popular na cultura brasileira*, ed. by Adauto Novaes (São Paulo: Brasiliense, 1982), pp. 13–53.

[29] Salomão, *Hélio Oiticica: Qual é o Parangolé e outros escritos*, p. 69.

[30] Oiticica emphasizes he is not 'representing' Brazil 'or anything else' at MoMA's 'Information' exhibition (1970). See *Information*, ed. by Kynaston L. McShine (New York: Museum of Modern Art, 1970), p. 103.

[31] Favaretto, *Tropicália: Alegoria, Alegria*, p. 9.

[32] The title of the album inaccurately cites Juvenal on what it took to placate the Roman citizenry. Veloso eventually put paid to speculation about the incorrect Latin — 'circensis' should have been 'circenses' — being intentional macaronic, and therefore anthropophagite, subversion, confirming it was just a misspelling. Favaretto, *Tropicália: Alegoria, Alegria*, p. 55; Veloso, *Verdade tropical*, p. 279.

Figure 1. Hélio Oiticica, *Tropicália (Penetráveis PN2 & PN3)* (1966–67), Rio de Janeiro. Courtesy of Projeto Hélio Oiticica, Rio de Janeiro.

Figure 2. Nildo da Mangueira wearing Hélio Oiticica's *Parangolé P04, capa 01* (1964), Rio de Janeiro. Courtesy of Projeto Hélio Oiticica, Rio de Janeiro.

(Like 'international' pop, Tropicalist music was youth-oriented and pitched against conservatism, but it commodified revolutionary desire. Although market integration was at odds with left-wing ideology, it allowed Tropicalists to disseminate their own brand of political and cultural contrariety.)[33] The use of exogenous electric instruments, often through collaborations with rock band Os Mutantes, and of outlandish *mise-en-scène* by Veloso and his fellow torchbearer Gilberto Gil, incensed supporters of traditional popular music.[34] A notorious concert at Rio's Sucata club in October 1968 was closed down by the DOPS (Department of Political and Social Order) for the brandishing of a seditious textile artwork by Oiticica, not a wearable *Parangolé* on that occasion, but a bright red banner emblazoned with the slogan 'seja marginal, seja herói' [be an outlaw, be a hero], which was made as a homage to the criminal Alcir Figueira da Silva, a bank robber, who committed suicide in 1966 whilst being pursued by police. (The silk-screened cadaver is often mistakenly thought to be that of an altogether more infamous transgressor, Manoel Moreira, known as Cara de Cavalo [Horse Face], an acquaintance of Oiticica who police gunned down in 1964.)[35] Due to their provocations, in December that year, shortly

---

[33] José Ramos Tinhorão argues that this linked Tropicalist musicians to the military regime's economic mission vis-à-vis foreign capital investment. Christopher Dunn's riposte highlights how said musicians foregrounded social contradictions and the repressive mechanisms of military rule in their songs, and that they participated in anti-authoritarian protests. José Ramos Tinhorão, *Pequena história da música popular: Da modinha à lambada* (São Paulo: Art, 1991), p. 267; Dunn, *Brutality Garden*, p. 121.

[34] Christopher Dunn, 'Tropicália: Modernity, Allegory, and Counterculture', in *Tropicália: A Revolution in Brazilian Culture (1967–1972)*, ed. by Carlos Basualdo (São Paulo: Cosac Naify, 2005), pp. 59–78 (p. 76); Favaretto, *Tropicália: Alegoria, Alegria*, p. 18; Lorraine Leu, *Brazilian Popular Music: Caetano Veloso and the Regeneration of Tradition* (Aldershot: Ashgate, 2006), p. 35.

[35] Photographs of Cara de Cavalo are used by Oiticica in *Bólide B33, caixa 18, poema caixa 2, 'Homenagem a Cara de Cavalo'* [meteor B33, box 18, poem box 2, 'homage to Cara de Cavalo'] (1966) and in *Bólide B56, caixa 24, 'Caracara de Cara de Cavalo'* [meteor B56, box 24, 'Cara de Cavalo's face-to-face'] (1968). The confusion surrounding the identity of the quasi-cruciform figure in the 'seja marginal, seja herói' banner may stem from the fact that it is very similar to the newspaper image of Cara de Cavalo used in *Bólide B33, caixa 18*. The error may have been compounded by Veloso's incorrect assertion in *Verdade tropical* (pp. 306–07) and by a host of misleading associations in authoritative studies and catalogues: Celso Favaretto, 'Tropicália: The Explosion of the Obvious', in *Tropicália: A Revolution in Brazilian Culture (1967–1972)*, ed. by Carlos Basualdo (São Paulo: Cosac Naify, 2005), pp. 81–96 (p. 92); Ariane Figueiredo, María C. Gaztambide and Daniela Matera Lins, 'Chronology (1937–1980)', in *Hélio Oiticica: The Body of Colour*, ed. by Mari Carmen Ramírez (London: Tate, 2007), pp. 337–401 (p. 385); Salomão, *Hélio Oiticica: Qual é o Parangolé e outros escritos*, p. 44. At the 2010 São Paulo Bienal the figure on the banner was identified as Mineirinho (José Rosa de Miranda), another high-profile Carioca criminal; see 'Artistas: Hélio Oiticica', in *29ª São Paulo Bienal* <http://www.bienal.org.br/FBSP/pt/29Bienal/Participantes/Paginas/participante.aspx?p=87> [accessed 1 September 2012]. Mineirinho — later immortalized by Clarice Lispector in *A legião estrangeira* [*The Foreign Legion: Stories and Chronicles*] (1964) — was shot dead in 1962 by Milton Le Cocq de Oliveira, the detective and death squad leader who was himself killed by Cara de Cavalo in 1964. Oiticica discusses marginality and his artistic 'tributes' to lionized antiheros, such as Cara de Cavalo and Mineirinho, and to 'anonymous' outlaws, like Alcir Figueira da Silva, in 'O herói anti-herói e o anti-herói anônimo' (25 March 1968), Projeto Hélio Oiticica, fol. 0131/68, in *Programa Hélio Oiticica* <http://www.itaucultural.org.br/aplicexternas/enciclopedia/ho/index.cfm?fuseaction=documentos&cd_verbete=4523&cod=145&tipo=2> [accessed 1 September 2012]. The photographic sources for *B33 Bólide caixa 18* and for the 'seja marginal, seja herói' banner are reproduced in Hélio Oiticica, 'Arquivo: O herói anti-herói e o anti-herói anônimo',

after the AI-5 was issued, Veloso and Gil were arrested and imprisoned; the following year they were allowed to go into exile.³⁶ It was also at this critical point that Oiticica left to work abroad; he spent most of the 1970s away from Brazil. With this Tropicalist 'diaspora' of sorts, the movement's core aesthetic and ideological concerns continued to evolve but in relation to a duly broadened socio-political purview.

Aesthetics aside, the reclaiming of Oiticica as a cornerstone for a phase of Brazilian cultural production preoccupied with rupturing the status quo may have seemed less likely than Rocha, whose films were known precisely for their politics and comprehensive iconoclasm. The controversial 'seja marginal, seja herói' ensign is not representative of Oiticica's corpus. Commenting on *Bólide B33, caixa 18, poema caixa 2* [meteor B33, box 18, poem box 2] (1966), an earlier tribute to a criminal, this time Cara de Cavalo, Oiticica claims he was driven to screen the outlaw's body after experiencing 'um momento ético' [an ethical moment].³⁷ Gonzalo Aguilar deliberates on how this explicit 'ethical turn' in Oiticica's oeuvre cannot be dissociated from politics. He maintains that displaying the image of Cara de Cavalo's bullet-riven corpse in *Bólide B33, caixa 18* underscores the injustice of the State's spectacular transformation of a felon into a *homo sacer* as a means of flaunting its (extra-legal) omnipotence, that is, by suspending the law — in the case of Cara de Cavalo, via the Scuderie Detetive Le Cocq death squad.³⁸ The same could be said of the 'seja marginal, seja herói' banner: Figueira da Silva, an unknown bandit, took his own life, thereby fulfilling the work of the State as an outlaw; he showed, as Giorgio Agamben puts it, how 'the law is outside itself', in other words, how State sovereignty operates outside and inside the juridical order.³⁹ Figueira da Silva's embodiment of this paradox was then captured photographically and disseminated by the media. Oiticica comments on the State displaying its unique power to annihilate

---

Sopro: Panfleto político-cultural, 45 (2011), 12–16. See also Claudia Calirman, *Brazilian Art under Dictatorship: Antonio Manuel, Artur Barrio, and Cildo Meireles* (Durham, NC: Duke University Press, 2012), pp. 95–96; Irma Rizzini, 'O surgimento das instituições especializadas na internação de menores delinquentes', in *Para além das grades: Elementos para a transformação do sistema socioeducativo*, ed. by Maria Helena Zamora (Rio de Janeiro: PUC-Rio, 2005), pp. 13–34 (pp. 30–31); R. S. Rose, *The Unpast: Elite Violence and Social Control in Brazil, 1954–2000* (Athens: Ohio University Press, 2005), pp. 242–45; Beatriz Scigliano Carneiro, *Relâmpagos com claror: Lygia Clark e Hélio Oiticica, vida com arte* (São Paulo: Editora Imaginário/FAPESP, 2004), pp. 193–230.

³⁶ On 14 December 1968, a day after the promulgation of AI-5, *O Cruzeiro* magazine published Marisa Álvarez Lima's article 'Marginália — arte e cultura na idade da pedrada', which features a full-page photograph of Caetano Veloso wearing a *Parangolé*. See Marisa Álvarez Lima, *Marginália, arte e cultura na 'idade da pedrada'* (Rio de Janeiro: Aeroplano, 2002), pp. 43–46.

³⁷ Oiticica, 'O herói anti-herói e o anti-herói anônimo'; Oiticica, *Hélio Oiticica: Aspiro ao grande labirinto*, text included in plate section between p. 120 and p. 121; '*Whitechapel Experiment* catalogue, 1969: facsimile', in *Oiticica in London*, ed. by Guy Brett and Luciano Figueiredo (London: Tate, 2007), pp. 97–134 (p. 103).

³⁸ Gonzalo Aguilar, 'La ley del bandido, la ley del arte. *Bólide caixa 18, Poema caixa 2, Homenagem a Cara de Cavalo* de Hélio Oiticica', *Revista iberoamericana*, 75.227 (2009), 539–50 (p. 549).

³⁹ Giorgio Agamben, *Homo Sacer: Sovereign Power and Bare Life*, trans. by Daniel Heller-Roazen (Stanford, CA: Stanford University Press, 1998), p. 15.

all 'unsavoury' forms of life in the margins, no matter how paltry, and he extols criminal striving as a direct assertion of faith in the attainability of joy.[40] Yet the unequivocal, that is, representational, nature of his socio-political engagement in these works, which certainly endeared him to the Tropicalists, was short-lived: his ethical and political interventions became paradoxically both more direct (literally intrusive), but also more rarefied, more in tune with the non-figurative, chromatic abstraction of his earlier Neoconcrete pieces. As Waly Salomão states, the Cara de Cavalo works — and the Che Guevara *Parangolé* cape, *Parangolé P20, capa 16*, 'Guevarcália' (1968) — mark the apogee of Oiticica's representational 'romantismo desbragado' [unbridled romanticism] regarding outlawry, of his idolization of the oppositional.[41] (That said, his *Quasi-cinemas*, produced in the 1970s, share something of the representational, confrontational directness of these works, as will be discussed later.) Oiticica's overarching concern with the *Parangolé* series is not the rubrication or representation of social and political injustice, but a performative politics of inclusion — the *favela* meeting the museum: as with aesthetics, he entertains an 'ethical' anthropophagic policy of incorporation.[42] As Robert Stam says of Modernist anthropophagy, 'the cannibalism-as-critique motif contemplates the melancholy distance separating contemporary society from the imagined ideal *communitas* of the Amerindian'; it magnifies the ideal of 'togetherness'.[43] Oiticica, though, develops artistic modes for intervening in the world ethically

[40] Hélio Oiticica, 'Anotações sobre o Parangolé', in his *Hélio Oiticica: Aspiro ao grande labirinto*, ed. by Luciano Figueiredo, Lygia Pape and Waly Salomão (Rio de Janeiro: Rocco, 1986), pp. 70–83 (p. 82).
[41] Salomão, *Hélio Oiticica: Qual é o Parangolé e outros escritos*, p. 35. Oiticica later subscribes to a Deleuzian reading of Nietzsche which categorically divorces heroism from a romantic striving for greater causes and ties it to the 'creative' or 'artistic' affirmation of life in adversity; in his 'Manifesto Caju' (3 November 1979), Projeto Hélio Oiticica, fol. 0114/79, in *Programa Hélio Oiticica* <http://www.itaucultural.org.br/aplicexternas/enciclopedia/ho/index.cfm?fuseaction=documentos&cd_verbete=4523&cod=722&tipo=2> [accessed 1 September 2012]. See similar comments in Oiticica, 'Anotações sobre o Parangolé', pp. 82–83; Hélio Oiticica, 'NTBK 4/73' (25 September 1973–28 June 1974), Projeto Hélio Oiticica, fol. 0318/73, in *Programa Hélio Oiticica* <http://www.itaucultural.org.br/aplicexternas/enciclopedia/ho/index.cfm?fuseaction=documentos&cd_verbete=4523&cod=408&tipo=2> [accessed 1 September 2012]. See also Michael Asbury, 'Hélio Oiticica and the Notion of the Popular in the 1960s', *Arara: Art and Architecture of the Americas*, 3 (2000) <http://www.essex.ac.uk/arthistory/arara/99-04.archive/issue_three/paper3.html> [accessed 1 September 2012]. On the relationship between Oiticica's art and his anarchist heritage (his grandfather was activist and philologist José Rodrigues Leite e Oiticica) see Silviano Santiago, 'Hélio Oiticica e a cena americana', in *Entrefalas*, ed. by Glória Ferreira (Porto Alegre: Zouk, 2011), pp. 87–116 (pp. 92–93, p. 104).
[42] Oiticica, 'Esquema geral da nova objetividade', pp. 94–97; Oiticica, 'General Scheme of the New Objectivity', pp. 116–19. Apart from the pervasive legacy of Oswald de Andrade, crucial here is the influence of Ferreira Gullar who abandoned Neoconcretism on the grounds that the 'supervalorização dos fatores formais e estilísticos sobre os de conteúdo' [prizing of formal and stylistic factors over content] was elitist and embedded in the ideology of an oppressive bourgeoisie. Gullar, who subsequently turned to the communist Centros Populares de Cultura, advocated an artistic practice which privileged communication with 'the people'. Ferreira Gullar, *Cultura posta em questão; Vanguarda e subdesenvolvimento: Ensaios sobre arte* (Rio de Janeiro: José Olympio Editora, 2002), p. 154 (first publ. 1965).
[43] Robert Stam, *Tropical Multiculturalism: A Comprehensive History of Race in Brazilian Cinema* (Durham, NC: Duke University Press, 1997), p. 239. See also David, 'Hélio Oiticica: Brazil Experiment', p. 182.

by turning away from the representation of transcendent ideals, in the case of the works to be examined here, *communitas*, love or affection. When asked about his work during an interview in 1970, he says that his aim is to make 'uma arte que leve as pessoas a uma relação afetiva com o mundo' [art that puts people in affective relation to the world].[44] When devising his later works, Oiticica entertains affection in its two main conceptual permutations, *eros* and *agape* (*caritas*), as the ultimate integration of self and other, and therefore as panacea for all social ills. However, instead of then resorting to stock, hence readily digestible, images of amity or of things amatorial, which would have minimal impact on viewers, he prefers to affect audiences directly, making them become other in the process, even if this only means becoming aware of cognitive habits and limitations when confronted with — affected by, put in affective relation to — something new (other). In other words, Oiticica's art shuns representation of affection in favour of affection as 'violent' sensation, a means of interrupting action–reaction circuits; in this respect, it reveals itself to be an heir to Dada and a kindred spirit of Fluxus, both of which cultivated, and exalted, the 'senseless' in order to shock — to rupture socio-cultural equanimity and 'aesthetic immanence' — as a means of ushering in a change in viewers' life praxis.[45] The blustering means by which Oiticica sometimes achieves these ruptures puts his projects in conflict with a moral dialectic of considerate versus heedless, good versus bad. This paper aims to show that this affective suspension of representation, and of judgement, in or by his work, functions as a timely event of ethical intensity.

Hélio Oiticica's Agapasm: Capes, Cocaine and Joy

During the 1960s, Oiticica's interests shifted from geometric and chromatic abstraction to working with the residents of Rio de Janeiro's *favelas*.[46] Favaretto and Dan Cameron compare Oiticica's work to developments such as Italy's Arte Povera and the USA's Minimal Art, but see in Oiticica's 'New Objectivity', which furthered the concerns of late Constructivism, a more 'highly charged' and affective confrontation with social inequities in Brazil.[47] They distinguish his work from body art, where the body itself becomes 'the work', and compare his evolution from plastic artist to anthroposophic social sculptor to that of

[44] Hélio Oiticica with Norma Pereira Rêgo, 'Mangueira e Londres na rota, Hélio propõe uma arte afetiva', in *Hélio Oiticica*, ed. by César Oiticica Filho *et al.* (Rio de Janeiro: Beco do Azougue, 2009), pp. 96–101 (p. 101) (first publ. in *Última Hora*, 31 January 1970).
[45] Peter Bürger, *Theory of the Avant-Garde*, trans. by Michael Shaw (Minneapolis: University of Minnesota Press, 1984), p. 80. See also Dorothée Brill, *Shock and the Senseless in Dada and Fluxus* (Lebanon, NH: University Press of New England, 2010), pp. 2–16.
[46] Paola Berenstein Jacques, *Esthétique des favelas: Les Favelas de Rio à travers l'œuvre de Hélio Oiticica* (Paris: L'Harmattan, 2002), pp. 58–76.
[47] Favaretto, *A invenção de Hélio Oiticica*, pp. 181–84; Dan Cameron, 'Through the Glass, Darkly', in *Hélio Oiticica: Quasi-Cinemas*, ed. by Carlos Basualdo (Ostfildern: Hatje Cantz and Wexner Center for the Arts, Ohio State University, 2001), pp. 34–38.

Joseph Beuys. Inspired by the *bricoleur* exuberance of the samba school of the Mangueira *favela*, but also by Henri Bergson's *Matter and Memory* (1896–1910) and *Creative Evolution* (1907) and Maurice Merleau-Ponty's *Phenomenology of Perception* (1945), Oiticica developed the roughly stitched coloured fabric and plastic confections, *Parangolés*, which rose to prominence during the Tropicalist period [Figure 2].[48] *Parangolés* embody the Tropicalist ideal of fusing lofty conceptualism and popular appeal, using recycled materials and embracing the 'bad taste' *cafonice* of carnival (that is, prior to the uncritical, reactionary promotion of 'tropical kitsch' in the early 1970s).[49] Oiticica also claimed to have been inspired by a beggar who had scrawled the word 'parangolé', slang for 'conversa fiada' [chatter], on burlap attached to a shack.[50] Christopher Dunn maintains that 'parangolé', was also an expression 'used in Rio de Janeiro to describe a spontaneous and sudden "happening" that produces joy'.[51] Some *Parangolés* bear slogans which are revealed when they are worn and danced around with, but most do not; their *raison d'être* is art as raiment for action.[52] During the 1960s, many *Parangolés* were paraded by members of the Mangueira samba school. In more recent decades, *Parangolés* have been fated to hang lifeless in art galleries, that is, until the 1998 São Paulo Bienal and 'The Body of Color' retrospective in 2006–07 at Houston's Museum of Fine Arts which introduced replicas for public use.[53] As Johannes Birringer notes though, this initiative involving facsimiles enjoyed limited success as museum audiences proved reticent, especially in the presence of guards.[54] When not treated as a museum artefact, a *Parangolé* affects an expressive transmutation both in the person donning it and the people around the wearer, often drawing bystanders

[48] For Oiticica on Bergson and Merleau-Ponty see *Hélio Oiticica: Aspiro ao grande labirinto*, pp. 16–17; Hélio Oiticica, 'Heliotape para Augusto e Haroldo de Campos' (March 1974), transcription, ed. by Frederico Coelho, in *Hélio Oiticica*, ed. by César Oiticica Filho et al. (Rio de Janeiro: Beco do Azougue, 2009), pp. 122–39; Hélio Oiticica, 'The Sense Pointing Towards a New Transformation' (25 June 1968), Projeto Hélio Oiticica, fol. 0486/69, in *Programa Hélio Oiticica* <http://www.itaucultural.org.br/aplicexternas/enciclopedia/ho/index.cfm?fuseaction=documentos&cd_verbete=4523&cod=625&tipo=2> [accessed 1 September 2012]. See also Michael Asbury, 'O Hélio não tinha ginga (Hélio Couldn't Dance)', in *Fios soltos: A arte de Hélio Oiticica*, ed. by Paula Braga (São Paulo: Perspectiva, 2008), pp. 52–65 (pp. 55–58); Berenstein Jacques, *Esthétique des favelas*, p. 196; Ramírez, 'The Embodiment of Color — "From the Inside Out"', pp. 43–44, p. 50, p. 64.
[49] Hélio Oiticica, 'Brasil diarréia', in *Arte brasileira hoje (situação e perspectivas)*, ed. by Ferreira Gullar (Rio de Janeiro: Paz e Terra, 1973), pp. 147–52 (pp. 147–49).
[50] Hélio Oiticica with Jorge Guinle Filho, 'A última entrevista', in *Hélio Oiticica*, ed. by César Oiticica Filho et al. (Rio de Janeiro: Beco do Azougue, 2009), pp. 262–75 (p. 269) (first publ. in *Interview*, April 1980).
[51] Dunn, *Brutality Garden*, p. 84. The term 'parangolé' has also been linked to the *malandro* figure (petty crook, dandy, idler, pimp), a somewhat romanticized Carioca antihero; see the translator's note in Oiticica, 'Cornerstones for a Definition of "Parangolé"', p. 296.
[52] Oiticica, *Hélio Oiticica: Aspiro ao grande labirinto*, pp. 16–17. See also Favaretto, *A invenção de Hélio Oiticica*, pp. 42–43; Ramírez, 'The Embodiment of Color — "From the Inside Out"', pp. 46–47, p. 64.
[53] The London leg of 'The Body of Color' exhibition at Tate Modern, between June and September 2007, did not include replica *Parangolés*.
[54] Johannes H. Birringer, 'Bodies of Color', *PAJ: A Journal of Performance and Art*, 87 (2007), 35–45 (p. 44).

into participation, hence re-codifying the environment — gallery visitors' inhibition also attests to this. *Parangolés* constitute a case of art as entropic performance rather than commodified object, and this is something which photographs of their wearers and admirers cannot really capture.[55]

Perhaps lending substance to Dunn's etymology, Haroldo de Campos describes the *Parangolé* as a catalyst for joy, an 'asa-delta para o êxtase' [hang-glider for ecstasy].[56] For Oiticica, this ecstasy of *Parangolé* happenings — or as he preferred to call them, 'manifestações ambientais' [environmental events] — which stimulate others, not spectators but 'fruidores, desfrutadores' [enjoyers], to unite in performance, generates much-needed love, 'um amor que precisa ser inventado' [love which needs to be fabricated].[57] De Campos's and Oiticica's writings on the conception of the pieces bring them close to a Cartesian definition of love: 'an emotion of the soul caused by the movement of the spirits which incite it to join itself willingly to objects which appear to it agreeable'.[58] In a post-coup, proto-Tropicalist age of mounting oppression, and in the context of a profoundly segregated Carioca society, Oiticica conceived of his 'agreeable objects' as the means of 'colouring' inter-corporal space, of creating 'centres of indetermination', that is, experiences which violate participants' sense of being individuals in the world, differentiated yet simultaneously collective, both intimate and spectacular.[59] The *Parangolé* is sensorial extension or a form for empowerment: it expands one's consciousness, generating an extra amount of sensorial income, thus carrying transformative effects into the body-mind. Brett refers to this as a 'sensitizing process', or an 'affective interflow', between wearers and observers; a process not unlike the actor–audience interaction

---

[55] Dezeuze comments on the experience of being photographed wearing Oiticica's *Parangolé P11, capa 7* and on photographs' inability to capture or stand in for the 'temporal process of discovery' which is the crux of the *Parangolé* experience; this, she argues, explains why photographs of *Parangolés* being used cannot become 'fetishized' commodity art objects; in 'Tactile Dematerialization, Sensory Politics: Hélio Oiticica's *Parangolés*', pp. 59–60, p. 70. See also Asbury, 'Hélio Oiticica and the Notion of the Popular in the 1960s'; David, 'Hélio Oiticica: Brazil Experiment', p. 179.

[56] Haroldo de Campos, 'Hang-glider of Ecstasy', in *Hélio Oiticica*, ed. by Mat Verberkt, trans. by Stephen Berg et al. (Rotterdam: Witte de With/Galerie Nationale du Jeu de Paume, 1992), pp. 217–21 (p. 217); Salomão, *Hélio Oiticica: Qual é o Parangolé e outros escritos*, p. 33. Silviano Santiago discusses the preoccupation with joy in post-1964 Brazilian art in terms of affirmative, non-oppositional Nietzschean responses to oppression; in 'Poder e alegria' (1988), in his *Nas malhas da letra: Ensaios* (Rio de Janeiro: Rocco, 2002), pp. 13–27 (pp. 26–27).

[57] Oiticica with Guinle Filho, 'A última entrevista', pp. 268–69; Hélio Oiticica, 'Apocalipopótese no Pavilhão Japonês', Projeto Hélio Oiticica, fol. 0145/68, in *Programa Hélio Oiticica* <http://www.itaucultural.org.br/aplicexternas/enciclopedia/ho/index.cfm?fuseaction=documentos&cd_verbete=4523&cod=134&tipo=2> [accessed 1 September 2012].

[58] René Descartes, *The Passions of the Soul*, article LXXIX, in *The Philosophical Works of Descartes*, trans. by Elizabeth S. Haldane and G. R. T. Ross (Cambridge: Cambridge University Press, 1911), I, 366.

[59] Hélio Oiticica, notebook, 'Respostas para Mário Barata/Aparecimento do Suprasensorial (Para Simpósio de Brasília)/Gerchman/JOF/Notas para José Oiticica Filho/Roteiro', Projeto Hélio Oiticica, fol. 0112/67, in *Programa Hélio Oiticica* <http://www.itaucultural.org.br/aplicexternas/enciclopedia/ho/index.cfm?fuseaction=documentos&cod=123&tipo=2> [accessed 1 September 2012].

prized at the time by Martinez Corrêa and Augusto Boal.⁶⁰ This affective transformation is not metaphorical but, to use Lygia Clark's (anthropophagic) terminology, 'metabolic'.⁶¹ However, although Oiticica and de Campos saw what was being transmitted or produced metabolically by the *Parangolé* as love and ecstasy, it is clear that both men were inadvertently (perhaps) attempting to fix the objects' qualitative transformation of the environment and of bodies. At the opening of the 1965 'Opinião' [Opinion] exhibition, where the *Parangolés* were to have their official debut, the personnel of Rio's Museum of Modern Art read this same collective effervescence as incipient violence: their own emotional response to the *Parangolés* was shock or fear, so they promptly kicked everyone out of the gallery.⁶²

Oiticica arrived at 'Opinião 65' with a troupe of Mangueira *passistas* [samba dancers] who clearly did not belong to the expected gallery-visiting demographic, and who manifestly failed to comply with sartorial etiquette. The *Parangolé* tumult drew artists and visitors out into the museum gardens.⁶³ A similar 'misjudgement' took place in 1994 at the São Paulo Bienal: the perambulation of *Parangolé* wearers through the gallery led the unnerved Dutch curator Wim Beeren to yell — 'berrava assustado' [he screamed, afraid] — demanding that the dancers leave immediately.⁶⁴ Apart from highlighting the limitations of museums as space for art, or restricted expectations about the qualities of art, but also conceptual art's ability to make its point by frustrating those expectations, these incidents show that although Oiticica conceived the *Parangolés* as a means of transmitting joy and affection and a sense of communion in a city where neighbourly proximity of socially-distinct groups is often perceived as hostile, he was either being naively utopian or somewhat disingenuous. He would have known that transgression or irreverence, given its very nature and despite its conveyors' festive elation, would encounter resistance from the establishment. Whilst certain modes of generating (transformative) affection, that is, of raising — rousing — awareness of propinquity with an other (togetherness), are more likely to lead to goodwill than anger, ultimately, one has no control over how that affection is then translated emotionally by the affected party.⁶⁵ Furthermore, these events give the lie to Pedrosa's tenet in 'Da natureza afetiva da forma na obra de arte', namely, that 'a chave da emoção artística está nas propriedades

---

⁶⁰ Brett, 'The Experimental Exercise of Liberty', p. 229.
⁶¹ Lygia Clark, 'A casa é o corpo', in *Lygia Clark*, ed. by Manuel J. Borja-Villel, Corinne Diserens, Vicente Todolí and Piet Coessens (Paris: Réunion des Musées Nationaux/Fundació Antoni Tàpies, 1998), pp. 213–43 (pp. 216-33); Lygia Clark, 'L'Homme, structure vivante d'une architecture biologique et cellulaire', *Robho*, 5/6 (1971), 12.
⁶² *Opinião 65: Ciclo de exposições sobre a arte no Rio de Janeiro* (Rio de Janeiro: BANERJ, 1988); Salomão, *Hélio Oiticica: Qual é o Parangolé e outros escritos*, pp. 58–60.
⁶³ Vera Pacheco Jordão, '*Parangolé* no MAM', *O Globo*, 16 August 1965, Artes Plásticas section; Salomão, *Hélio Oiticica: Qual é o Parangolé e outros escritos*, pp. 58–59.
⁶⁴ Luciano Figueiredo, 'The Other Malady', *Third Text*, 28/29 (1994), 105-16 (p. 116); Salomão, *Hélio Oiticica: Qual é o Parangolé e outros escritos*, pp. 64–65.
⁶⁵ Elaine Fox, *Emotion Science: Cognitive and Neuroscientific Approaches to Understanding Human Emotions* (Basingstoke: Palgrave Macmillan, 2008), pp. 77–82.

intrínsecas do objeto de arte' [the key to artistic emotion lies in the work of art's intrinsic properties].[66] Clearly, what makes the *Parangolés* politically and ethically significant is precisely that such expression of expansive communion is insubordinate inasmuch as it flies in the face of segregative social mores, so collision is paradoxically implicit in Oiticica's idealized togetherness. Hence, he appears to be more accurate when he dispenses with actual joy as his project's fixed determinant, or at least recognizes such joy as utopian, and delineates his (Nietzschean) ethical proposal thus:

> o meu programa ambiental a que chamo de maneira geral *Parangolé* não pretende estabelecer uma 'nova moral' [...], mas 'derrubar todas as morais', pois que estas tendem a um conformismo estagnizante, a estereotipar opiniões e criar conceitos não criativos. A liberdade moral [...] está acima do bem, do mal etc. Deste modo estão como que justificadas todas as revoltas individuais contra valores e padrões estabelecidos [...]. São importantes tais manifestações, pois não esperam gratificações, a não ser a de uma felicidade utópica, mesmo que para isso se conduza à autodestruição.[67]

> [my environmental programme, which I refer to generally as *Parangolé*, is not meant to establish a 'new morality'; it is meant to 'raze all forms of morality' because these tend towards stagnant conformity, stereotypical opinions and uncreative concepts. Moral freedom lies beyond good and evil etc. It follows that all personal revolutions against received values and standards are justified. Any such manifestations are important because they do not expect rewards other than a utopian happiness even if this leads to self-destruction.]

At best then, Oiticica's art facilitates virtual transmission: not meaning, symbolism or interpretation, but uncoded sensation, the germ of that which may eventually unfold as new possibility, and therein rests its ethical zeal. Oiticica's work and its reception clarifies the distinction between what C. S. Peirce calls 'qualities of feeling' and 'secondary' feelings: the former are monads (uncoded sensation), whereas the latter are generalizations which group together a variety of these monads under capacious descriptive terms such as 'pain' and 'pleasure'.[68] If feeling is the undifferentiated mode of being of quality in consciousness (anoesis), once these have actualized themselves in perceptual judgements, qualities of feeling become the first premise of reasoning.[69]

---

[66] Pedrosa, 'Da natureza afetiva da forma na obra de arte', p. 60.
[67] Oiticica, 'Anotações sobre o *Parangolé*', pp. 81–82. On the *Parangolés*' utopian 'anti-repressive' aspirations see Dezeuze, 'Tactile Dematerialization, Sensory Politics: Hélio Oiticica's *Parangolés*', pp. 70–71.
[68] C. S. Peirce, 'The Basis of Pragmaticism in the Normative Sciences', in *The Essential Peirce*, ed. by Nathan Houser and Christian Kloesel (Bloomington: Indiana University Press, 1998), II, 371–98 (p. 379).
[69] In his influential 'Emotion and Feeling in Psychology and Art', Rudolf Arnheim dismisses emotion or feeling as 'the *tension or excitement level* produced by the interaction of mental forces', that is, by cognitive activity. Judgement resolves 'tension or excitement' into what Peirce calls 'secondary feelings', which is also why Arnheim calls emotion an 'effect'. By admitting for unqualified 'stress' which is induced by perception but which precedes reasoned resolution into emotion, Arnheim's

Parangolés provide intense affective experiences — qualities of feeling — for wearers and spectators, but these experiences are actualized or resolved into different 'secondary' feelings by these two groups in relation to social role and attendant rationale. (Which is why, as Brian Massumi explains, 'thought's approach cannot be phenomenological. It must be unabashedly metaphysical. It must extend to that which conditions what is appearing'.)[70] The point is that what is actually transmitted through the work of art — its ethics — is potential inventiveness, the potential for spatial and corporal re-codification: it may produce joy but also fear or anger. Rather than providing fixed emotions, morals or answers, *Parangolé* performances simply pose the problem of the body's openness towards change. This also reveals Oiticica's hoped-for 'love' or 'joyful togetherness' to be a subjective socio-linguistic fixing of an (violent) experience of intensity in which a body becomes other to itself through inter-corporality. Before turning to his more complex indagation of affect in the overtly representational context of experimentations with film, a few further considerations on love as an ideal need to be advanced.

Love is an ideal which encompasses myriad qualities of feelings which generally incline the subject towards renouncing notions of personal fullness; as such, it is an ideal founded on subjectivity's deferred plenitude, its openness or becoming. According to Peirce, when qualities of feeling 'become welded together in association, the result is a general idea'.[71] Ideals are admirable ideas, reasonable feelings or logical sentiments 'whose adoption as ideals — as a result of our habits being indefinitely attracted and harmoniously associated to them — makes us partake in the growth of concrete reasonableness in the world'.[72] (The more an ideal or habit of feeling consolidates, the more qualities of feeling are attracted to it.) Love is an ideal because it would appear to be a meliorative making-rational of the world: its aim is to reconcile the self to something other to it. If love makes us act with concern for others, it must combat self-seeking perniciousness, but altruism and self-interest are not always mutually exclusive. For Peirce, nonetheless, love, often in the theological guise of *agape*, is society's rational *summum bonum*: his romantic paragon of selfless community is underpinned by unimpeachable common sense, namely, the charitable reduction of antagonism.[73] Oiticica's art — and what was to become iconic Tropicalist or neo-anthropophagic inclusiveness — shares a certain

---

model (unwittingly) points to a distinction between affect and emotion. In *Toward a Psychology of Art: Collected Essays* (Berkeley: University of California Press, 1966), pp. 302–19 (p. 310).

[70] Brian Massumi, 'The Future Birth of the Affective Fact: The Political Ontology of Threat', in *The Affect Theory Reader*, ed. by Melissa Gregg and Gregory J. Seigworth (Durham, NC: Duke University Press, 2010), pp. 52–70 (p. 66).

[71] C. S. Peirce, *The Collected Papers of Charles Sanders Peirce*, ed. by C. Hartshorne and P. Weiss (Cambridge, MA: Harvard University Press, 1935), VI, 137.

[72] Martin Lefebvre, 'Peirce's Esthetics: A Taste for Signs in Art', *Transactions of the Charles S. Peirce Society*, 43.2 (2007), 319–44 (p. 330).

[73] C. S. Peirce, *The Collected Papers of Charles Sanders Peirce*, ed. by C. Hartshorne and P. Weiss (Cambridge, MA: Harvard University Press, 1934), V, 433.

affinity with Peirce's normative agapasm, albeit divested of its ecclesiastical associations. His aesthetics from the Tropicalist period onwards are admirable or attractive inasmuch as they appear to be concerned with transcendental (agapastic) ideals, love and togetherness, which were particularly appealing given national socio-political predicaments. Yet as reactions to the *Parangolés* at 'Opinião 65' and the 1994 São Paulo Bienal show, the relay from qualities of feeling and aesthetics to ideals relies on habits of interpretation: qualities of feeling can only be condensed into ideals through the deferral of aesthetics — attraction to the movement and colour of the *Parangolés* — to logic and deontology. The poignancy of Oiticica's work rests on the cluttered transmission of qualities of feeling rather than hackneyed representation (analogical or symbolic shorthand), and in so doing it runs the risk of not conveying any predetermined ideals. And yet ironically, although such semiotic openness clearly diverges from Peirce's sanguine assumption that a receptive disposition towards otherness inclines asymptotically towards moral 'perfectionment', it chimes with the incompleteness of being which was said to be at the heart of love as an ideal. At the time of the Tropicalists' exodus, Oiticica — partly via Rocha — escalates his artistic auscultation of ideals and affectivity. He does this by veering into film and by latching onto what Flora Süssekind — noting the military regime's integrationist and capitalist development of telecommunications and advertising — labels Tropicália's most significant innovation in terms of cultural critique: a mindfulness of the 'market forces, the entrenchment of the entertainment industry, and the star system to which artists connected to popular culture were subjected'.[74] This recasts Tropicália's much-vaunted dispelling of national essentialisms as its mere by-product.

At the height of the military dictatorship, as Veloso and Gil were ejected from Brazil, Oiticica was invited to show his *Parangolés* and *Tropicália* at London's Whitechapel Gallery (1969).[75] After a year in London, he returned home to Rio de Janeiro before travelling again to participate in McShine's 'Information' exhibition at MoMA; later in 1970, having been awarded a Guggenheim fellowship, he moved to New York, where he remained for most of the 1970s, living something of a hand-to-mouth existence. Prior to the first of these departures, Oiticica played a minor part in Rocha's *Câncer* (1968; completed in 1972) where he appears with samba dancers from the Mangueira *favela*.[76] Following the

[74] Flora Süssekind, 'Chorus, Contraries, Masses: The Tropicalist Experience and Brazil in the Late Sixties', in *Tropicália: A Revolution in Brazilian Culture (1967–1972)*, ed. by Carlos Basualdo (São Paulo: Cosac Naify, 2005), pp. 31–56 (p. 40). See also Roberto Schwarz, 'Remarques sur la culture et la politique au Brésil: 1964–1969', *Les Temps Modernes*, 288 (1970), 37–73 (p. 52).
[75] He was originally invited to exhibit at London's Signals Gallery but this closed down. See Brett, 'Recollection', p. 11.
[76] Oiticica also acted in Andreas Valentin's *One Night on Gay Street* (New York, 1975) and in Ivan Cardoso's *Dr. Dyonélio* (Rio de Janeiro, 1978) and *O segredo da múmia* (Rio de Janeiro, 1979). In 1979, Cardoso produced a short on the artist entitled *HO*. Oiticica created *Penetráveis* for Júlio Bressane's *Lágrima pantera míssil* (New York, 1973) and *O gigante da América* (Rio de Janeiro, 1978). He directed, but never finished, a few films on Super 8: *Brasil Jorge* (1971); *Agripina é Roma-Manhattan* (1972); *Helena inventa Ângela Maria* (1975) and *Norma inventa La Bengell* (1975). For a complete Oiticica-

recommendations of Jean-Marie Straub, and drawing on André Bazin's theories of the preservation of spatio-temporal integrity, *Câncer* experiments with the production of tension using improvisation during extremely drawn-out static long takes and through the wavering qualities of direct sound.[77] Rocha often includes the filming process itself within the frame in a bid to give forms of presentation an equal billing with the narratives represented. His desire to challenge the alienated passivity of the spectator appealed to Oiticica, who began driving his own artistic experimentation closer to film, resulting in his series of 'quasi-films', the *Quasi-cinemas*, halfway houses between installation-cum-performance art and film proper. But as cinema stakes communication more overtly on representation than abstract, gambolling caped performances, working with film evidently involved investigating less straightforward routes to an art of affective openness in order to challenge perceptual judgement and make semiosis itself an object of contemplation. Interest in film leads Oiticica to assume the seemingly perverse challenge of trying to overcome images (representation) through images.[78] Unsurprisingly, like Rocha, Oiticica seeks counsel in Jean-Luc Godard's pioneering work; in the process, he once again undertakes a utopian territorialization of the effects of unshackling communication from habitual signification as 'joyful':

> GODARD [...] penetra todos os meandros possíveis do cinema: joyful pela libertação gradativa do espectador numbeizado por absolutismos de linguagem e imagem: no BRASIL [...] o pessoal foi ficando cada vez mais 'sério' e com obsessiva 'preocupação quanto aos destinos do cinema brasileiro' e à busca de 'sentidos' [...] excessivo concern: muita busca!: sem joy: [...] GODARD já ia longe num passo q jamais seria possível aos q pensam demais ou preocupam-se com destinos desconhecidos: questionar a razão de ser de cinema-linguagem.[79]
>
> [Godard penetrates all of cinema's possible ins and outs: joyful at the numbed spectator's gradual release from the absolutism of language and image. In Brazil people have grown increasingly serious, worrying obsessively over

---

related filmography see *Hélio Oiticica*, ed. by Mat Verberkt, trans. by Stephen Berg et al. (Rotterdam: Witte de With/Galerie Nationale du Jeu de Paume, 1992), p. 270; *Hélio Oiticica: Quasi-Cinemas*, ed. by Carlos Basualdo (Ostfildern: Hatje Cantz and Wexner Center for the Arts, Ohio State University, 2001), p. 155. See also Irene Small, 'One Thing after Another: How We Spend Time in Hélio Oiticica's *Quasi-cinemas*', *Spectator*, 28.2 (2008), 73–89 (p. 87 n. 26).

[77] Rocha, *Revolução do Cinema Novo*, pp. 148–50; André Bazin, *What is Cinema?*, trans. by Hugh Gray (Berkeley: University of California Press, 2005), II, 43.

[78] Oiticica comments on the challenge of overcoming representation — variously meaning linear narratives, the capitalist regime of images and stock signification — through images themselves in his 'NTBK 4/73'. See also Carlos Basualdo, 'Waiting for the Internal Sun: Notes on Hélio Oiticica's *Quasi-Cinemas*', in *Hélio Oiticica: Quasi-Cinemas*, ed. by Carlos Basualdo (Ostfildern: Hatje Cantz and Wexner Center for the Arts, Ohio State University, 2001), pp. 39–53 (p. 51); Small, 'One Thing after Another: How We Spend Time in Hélio Oiticica's *Quasi-cinemas*', p. 89 n. 44.

[79] Hélio Oiticica, 'BLOCO-EXPERIÊNCIAS in COSMOCOCA — programa in progress', Projeto Hélio Oiticica, fol. 0301/74, in *Programa Hélio Oiticica* <http://www.itaucultural.org.br/aplicexternas/enciclopedia/ho/index.cfm?fuseaction=documentos&cd_verbete=4523&cod=520&tipo=2> [accessed 1 September 2012]. See also Santiago, 'Hélio Oiticica e a cena americana', pp. 109–10.

the fate of Brazilian cinema and the pursuit of meaning. Excessive concern: too much searching, without joy. Godard went far by taking a step which would have been impossible for those who think too much or worry about unknown destinations: questioning cinema-language's *raison d'être*.]

In New York in the 1970s Oiticica took to collaborating with one of Brazil's post-Cinema Novo — 'marginal' or *udigrudi* (a corruption of 'underground') — directors, Nelson d'Almeida, who shared his concerns over Brazilian cinema's mounting conservatism. Nevertheless, Oiticica's earliest drafts for cinematic installations, provisionally called *Nitro Benzol & Black Linoleum* (London, September 1969), are partly conceived as a homage to Rocha.[80] *Udigrudi* directors came to the fore during Tropicália; like Oiticica, they criticized late Cinema Novo's bourgeois intellectualism, its thematic pusillanimity in the face of tighter censorship, its financing, and its increasingly polished production values, particularly in so-called Tropicalist films such as Joaquim Pedro de Andrade's adaptation of *Macunaíma* (1969) and Nelson Pereira dos Santos's *Como era gostoso o meu francês* [*How Tasty Was My Little Frenchman*] (1971).[81] Rocha proved an exception, having continued to plough his own uncompromising furrow with *Câncer*, *O dragão da maldade contra o santo guerreiro* [The dragon of evil against the warrior saint] (1969), better known as *Antônio das Mortes* and *Der Leone Have Sept Cabeças* [*The Lion Has Seven Heads*] (1970). Notwithstanding, 'marginal' directors such as Júlio Bressane and Rogério Sganzerla criticized Rocha, but this involved citing his work in their own, which simply underscored indebtedness, what Robert Stam calls a display of 'Oedipal hostility' towards their cinematic parent.[82] For his part, Rocha

[80] In addition to long takes of daily life at the Mangueira *favela* and other Rocha-inspired footage, *Nitro Benzol & Black Linoleum* is meant to involve 'viewers' in various sex acts, drinking Coca-Cola, tasting a selection of liquids and inhaling nitrobenzol (nitro benzene). Hélio Oiticica, 'Nitro Benzol & Black Linoleum' (9 September–10 October 1969), Projeto Hélio Oiticica, fol. 0322/69, in *Programa Hélio Oiticica* <http://www.itaucultural.org.br/aplicexternas/enciclopedia/ho/index.cfm?fuseaction=documentos&cd_verbete=4523&cod=147&tipo=2> [accessed 1 September 2012]. Oiticica's drafts are reproduced in *Hélio Oiticica: Quasi-Cinemas*, ed. by Basualdo, pp. 81–88.
[81] Oiticica criticizes late Cinema Novo and praises Júlio Bressane, Rogério Sganzerla and Nelson d'Almeida in a tape-recorded at Glauber Rocha's New York apartment in 1971; see transcription: 'Héliotapes (Júlio Bressane/Glauber's Loft)', Projeto Hélio Oiticica, fol. 0502/71, in *Programa Hélio Oiticica* <http://www.itaucultural.org.br/aplicexternas/enciclopedia/ho/index.cfm?fuseaction=documentos&cd_verbete=4523&cod=667&tipo=2> [accessed 1 September 2012]. Some early Cinema Novo films were financed by the National Bank of Minas Gerais, which was owned by the Magalhães Pinto family, a leading civilian force behind the 1964 coup. In 1969, the military government founded Embrafilme, originally to distribute Brazilian films abroad; in 1973, Embrafilme became involved in film financing and co-production. Various Cinema Novo directors benefited from State funding through this enterprise, amongst them, Joaquim Pedro de Andrade, Carlos Diegues, Nelson Pereira dos Santos and Glauber Rocha. See Randal Johnson, *Cinema Novo x5: Masters of Contemporary Brazilian Film* (Austin: University of Texas Press, 1984), pp. 8–11; Glauber Rocha, *Revisão crítica do cinema brasileiro* (São Paulo: Cosac Naify, 2003), pp. 172–76 (first publ. 1963); Alex Viany, *O processo do Cinema Novo*, ed. by José Carlos Avellar (Rio de Janeiro: Aeroplano, 1999), p. 91, p. 268, pp. 461–63.
[82] Robert Stam, 'On the Margins: Brazilian Avant-Garde Cinema', in *Brazilian Cinema*, ed. by Randal Johnson and Robert Stam, rev. edn (New York: Columbia University Press, 1995), pp. 306–27 (p. 318).

claimed to have inspired *udigrudi* directors with *Câncer*, but rejected their truly low-budget films as 'um aborto restaurador do formalismo decadente' [an aberration which reinstates decadent formalism].[83] Despite this antagonism, and a different set of goals, both parties shared a commitment, which might be labelled Godardian, to finding novel ways of innerving spectators, which is where their work intersects with Oiticica's. Following the violent, improvisational *Câncer*, Oiticica approached d'Almeida with the idea for *Mangue Bangue* (1971), an improvisational film with a transgendered protagonist set in Rio de Janeiro's Mangue red-light district; d'Almeida then directed this alone as Oiticica left to work abroad. The film was banned from release and d'Almeida left Brazil; he eventually screened *Mangue Bangue* at MoMA in 1973 and this led to the *Quasi-cinema* collaborations.

Oiticica called his 'films' without action *Quasi-cinemas*; these are more accurately described as room-sized installations in which 35mm slides are projected whilst a variety of audio tapes are played and lighting is modified; the movement of participants is meant to interrupt the projection, altering the filmic event.[84] *Quasi-cinemas* are therefore a continuation of *Penetráveis* such as *Tropicália* and mass *Parangolé* happenings, *Parangolé Coletivo* (Rio de Janeiro, 1967) and *Apocalipopótese* (Rio de Janeiro, 1968). As well as being influenced by the coarsely edited, non-teleological *Câncer* and *Mangue Bangue*, the slide projections are partly inspired by the early installations of Peter Campus and by the work of underground filmmaker Jack Smith, best known for *Flaming Creatures* (1963), particularly his East Village loft slide shows which became associated with the experiments known as 'expanded cinema', and which like *Câncer*, modulated audience tension by regulating duration.[85] It is in relation to Smith, around May 1971, that Oiticica first deploys the term 'quasi-cinema', which he excitedly describes as the conflation of television, Godard and Artaud.[86] The only *Quasi-cinema* work exhibited during Oiticica's lifetime is the *Neyrótika* series.[87] The seven *Neyrótika* sequences (April–May 1973) clearly

---

[83] Rocha, *Revolução do Cinema Novo*, p. 214.
[84] See Small's excellent analysis of the projection principles of *Quasi-cinemas* in 'One Thing after Another: How We Spend Time in Hélio Oiticica's *Quasi-cinemas*', pp. 79–82.
[85] Gene Youngblood, *Expanded Cinema*, intro. by R. Buckminster Fuller (London: Studio Vista, 1970), pp. 75–77, pp. 359–64.
[86] Clark and Oiticica, *Lygia Clark/Hélio Oiticica: Cartas, 1964–1974*, p. 204. Oiticica's discussion of fragmented, 'illiterate' cinema is influenced by Marshall McLuhan's theories of television's 'para-sensoriality' and its demand for 'social completion' in *Understanding Media: The Extensions of Man* (New York: McGraw-Hill, 1964), pp. 249–55. Oiticica, 'BLOCO-EXPERIÊNCIAS in COSMOCOCA — programa in progress'; Hélio Oiticica, 'PN12 e PN16 NADA/Propor propor/Auto-teatro/"subterranean Tropicália Projects"', Projeto Hélio Oiticica, fol. 0511/71, in *Programa Hélio Oiticica* <http://www.itaucultural.org.br/aplicexternas/enciclopedia/ho/index.cfm?fuseaction=documentos&cd_verbete=4523&cod=712&tipo=2> [accessed 1 September 2012]; Hélio Oiticica and Neville d'Almeida, *Cosmococa: Programa in Progress* (Rio de Janeiro: Projeto Hélio Oiticica, 2005), pp. 307–08.
[87] *Neyrótika* was included in 'Expo-Projeção 73' (Belo Horizonte, 19 June 1973), curated by Aracy A. Amaral. See Aracy A. Amaral, *Expo-Projeção 73: Som, audio-visual, super 8, 16mm* (São Paulo: Centro de Artes Novo Mundo, 1973), p. 11; Basualdo, 'Waiting for the Internal Sun: Notes on Hélio Oiticica's *Quasi-Cinemas*', p. 50.

draw on Smith's brand of homoerotic camp, not to mention Andy Warhol's films with Mario Montez and his (Paul Morrissey's) objectification of Joe Dallesandro in *Flesh* (1968) and *Trash* (1970); they juxtapose stills of male body parts which have at times been cosmetically feminized. Reflection on Smith's and Warhol's films also had immediate consequences for Oiticica's long-standing work on the *Parangolé* series. In New York he took photographs of what appears to be the 'joyful' tumult of people wearing *Parangolé, capa 30* [cape 30] (1972) in the rather insalubrious-looking subway; these are brumal versions of photographs taken in Rio de Janeiro, specifically those in the Mangueira *favela*; but away from home, as Brett observes, he also gave freer rein to an exploration of the erotic dimension of (male) bodies exhibiting themselves through interaction with a *Parangolé*.[88] Whilst in New York, Oiticica compiled notes for a projected volume, occasionally referred to as his 'Newyorkaises'; amongst these notes are details of a scheme entitled 'Bodywise' (1973) which describes how his *Parangolé* project, inasmuch as it denaturalizes and re-contextualizes bodies, should concern corporal ornamentation and undressing in equal measure.[89] Accordingly, his photographic record of the semi-clad young men he entangled in *Parangolés* around New York documents both their preening exhibitionism and a stripping away of self-possession [Figure 3]. Their public displays of muscularity are subsumed by the performances with Oiticica's conspicuous, unlikely garments, a process which foregrounds artifice, thereby dissociating anatomical sex from assumed gender propriety; this, of course, is coupled with the fact that acquiescing to the photographer's demand for self-exposure suggests both egotistical eroticism (being confidently provocative) and depleted agency (being made to look decoratively ridiculous). The images of the New York *Parangolés* and the *Neyrótika* sequences bring to mind Georges Bataille's dictum that 'eroticism, in a sense, is laughable. ... Allusion to the erotic is always capable of arousing irony'.[90] By hovering between eroticism and irony, agency and ridicule, camp proves itself to be nettlesome.[91] Oiticica, recognizing an affinity between camp's operation though performance, appropriation and

[88] Brett, 'The Experimental Exercise of Liberty', p. 233. When Oiticica then returns to Rio de Janeiro in 1978, photographs of *Parangolés* continue in the same vein, with a greater propensity to involve partial male nudity; see, for instance, stills from Ivan Cardoso's film *HO*, included in *Hélio Oiticica: The Body of Colour*, ed. by Mari Carmen Ramírez (London: Tate, 2007), p. 318. See also 'Hélio Oiticica (1937–1980)', in *Enciclopédia Itaú Cultural de artes visuais*, ed. by Tânia Francisco Rodrigues <http://www.itaucultural.org.br/aplicexternas/enciclopedia_ic/index.cfm?fuseaction=artistas_obras&acao=mais&inicio=65&cont_acao=9&cd_verbete=4038> [accessed 1 September 2012]. Oiticica's writing during this period also takes a more explicitly homoerotic turn; see Coelho, *Livro ou livro-me*, pp. 90–93.
[89] Hélio Oiticica, 'BODYWISE/apontamentos/Newyorkaises' (June–October 1973), Projeto Hélio Oiticica, fol. 0200/73, in *Programa Hélio Oiticica* <http://www.itaucultural.org.br/aplicexternas/enciclopedia/ho/index.cfm?fuseaction=documentos&cod=493&tipo=2> [accessed 1 September 2012]. See also Coelho, *Livro ou livro-me*, pp. 148–53.
[90] Georges Bataille, *The Tears of Eros*, trans. by Peter Connor (San Francisco: City Lights Books, 1989), p. 66.
[91] Andrew Ross, 'Uses of Camp' (1988), in *Camp: Queer Aesthetics and the Performing Subject*, ed. by Fabio Cleto (Edinburgh: Edinburgh University Press, 1999), pp. 308–29 (pp. 325–27).

decoding — its annexation of semiotic surplus — and Tropicália's acquisitive and synthetic dynamic, then classifies Smith, Warhol and Montez as being 'pre- and post-Tropicalist' simultaneously; he calls their aesthetic 'Tropicamp' and begins to see his own artistic principles educing from theirs.[92]

Oiticica also indulges a Warholian — 'Tropicamp' — infatuation with celebrity and Godardian citation of pop culture in the more extensive *Cosmococas: Programs in Progress* sequences (1973), his so-called 'block-experiments', which involve close-ups of pop-cultural icons under striations or a veneer of cocaine powder.[93] The *Cosmococas* were developed in collaboration: the first five series were executed with d'Almeida; others affiliated with the project are Brett, Thomas Valentin and Silviano Santiago. Two of the better known *Cosmococa* editions were produced with d'Almeida, *Maileryn* (*Cosmococa CC3*) and *Hendrix-War* (*Cosmococa CC5*); they make use of the portraits on the cover of Norman Mailer's 1973 biography of Marilyn Monroe [Figure 4] and on the record sleeve of Jimi Hendrix's posthumous album, *War Heroes* (1972) [Figure 5]. Oiticica's icons are inescapably commodified: he selects famous images of celebrated faces used as or on packaging; but book covers and record sleeves are also clearly surfaces suitable for snorting cocaine; these are images which are also meant to be ingested — perceived, sensed — through non-optical means. (Drugs also lend the *Quasi-cinemas* the aura of irrepressible criminality cherished by Oiticica since the 1960s.) In some slides the portraits are defamiliarized through the lines and mounds of cocaine which emboss contours or redact features, and by masks of acuminate drug-taking paraphernalia. Also ineludible in these images is drug-related death: Hendrix and Monroe were long since dead when Oiticica produced the *Cosmococa* series in 1973, both having overdosed, wittingly or otherwise, on hypnotics. During the 1970s and 1980s, the *Cosmococas* were rusticated from galleries due to the photographic use of cocaine; the quantities of the drug involved established incriminating ties between the artists and suppliers.[94] This meant that its audiences were reduced to a coterie and confined to domestic redoubts — Oiticica's *Babylonests*, not unlike Kurt Schwitters's *Merzbau* (1923–43) — in downtown New York and later in Rio de Janeiro.[95] Oiticica detested the isolating 'claustrophobic' seating arrangement at the Anthology Film Archives;

[92] Oiticica also dubs this 'Tropicamp' aesthetic 'Tropicália-Subterrânea' [Underground-Tropicália] in 'Mario Montez' (12–15 October 1971), Projeto Hélio Oiticica, fol. 0275/71, in *Programa Hélio Oiticica* <http://www.itaucultural.org.br/aplicexternas/enciclopedia/ho/index.cfm?fuseaction=documentos&cd_verbete=4523&cod=505&tipo=2> [accessed 1 September 2012] (first publ. in *Presença*, 2 (December 1971)). See also Max Jorge Hinderer Cruz, 'Tropicamp: Pre- and Post-Tropicália at Once. Some Notes on Hélio Oiticica's 1971 Text', *Afterall: A Journal of Art, Context, and Enquiry*, 28 (2011), 4–15.
[93] Hélio Oiticica, 'Neville d'Almeida's *Mangue Bangue*/Bosta Get Lost/Block-Experiments in COSMOCOCA — programa in progress' (3 March–26 May 1974), Projeto Hélio Oiticica, fol. 0484/74, in *Programa Hélio Oiticica* <http://www.itaucultural.org.br/aplicexternas/enciclopedia/ho/index.cfm?fuseaction=documentos&cd_verbete=4523&cod=621&tipo=2> [accessed 1 September 2012].
[94] On Oiticica's acquisition and use of cocaine in New York and his brushes with the FBI see Santiago, 'Hélio Oiticica e a cena americana', p. 89, p. 103, p. 108.
[95] Salomão, *Hélio Oiticica: Qual é o Parangolé e outros escritos*, pp. 103–05.

Figure 3. Jeff wearing Hélio Oiticica's *Parangolé P31, capa 24* (1972), New York City. Photograph by Hélio Oiticica. Courtesy of Projeto Hélio Oiticica, Rio de Janeiro.

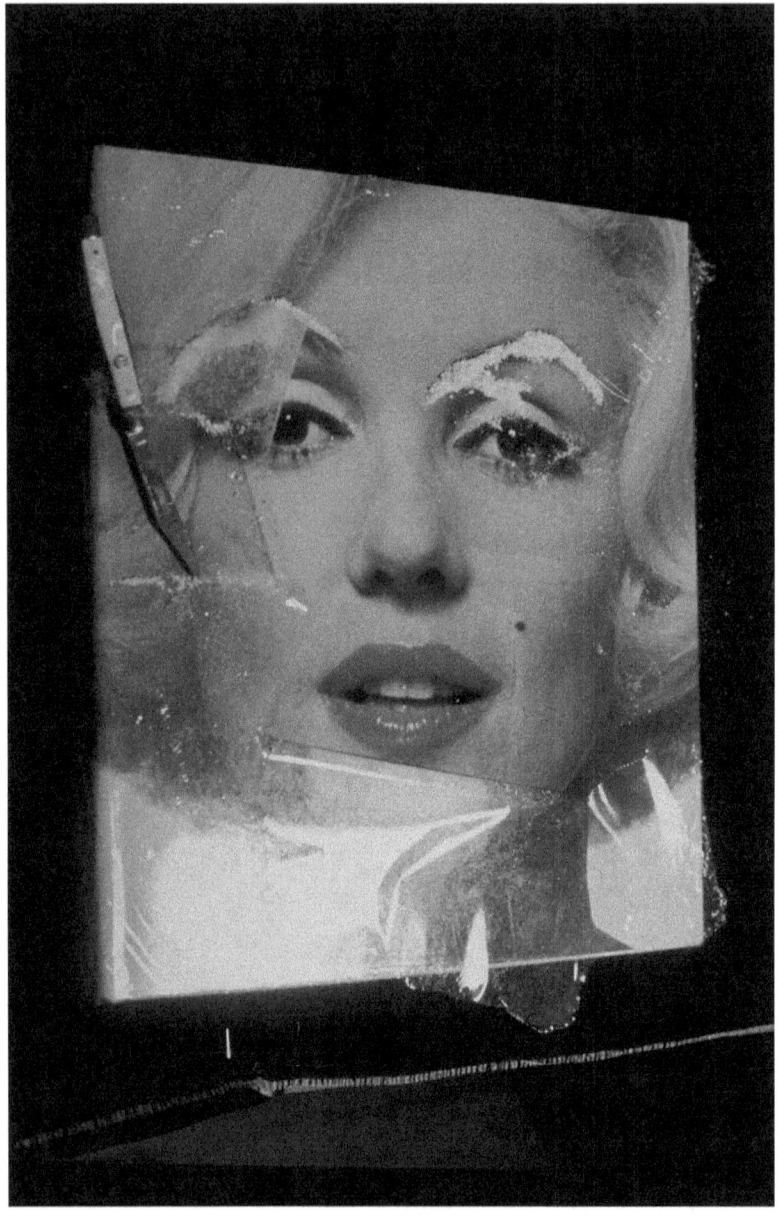

Figure 4. Hélio Oiticica and Neville d'Almeida, slide from *Cosmococa CC3, Maileryn* (1973), New York City. Courtesy of Projeto Hélio Oiticica, Rio de Janeiro.

he wanted his cinematic installations to offer something antithetical to this: an 'anti-insular' environment.[96] Although he never referred to 'expanded cinema' of the mid 1960s directly, his *Ninhos* are very much akin to Stan VanDerBeek's 'emotional Movie-Dromes' where images and sounds collide and 'each individual makes his own conclusions or realizations', thereby '[re-ordering] the levels of awareness of any person', though the *Cosmococas* are perhaps as much about digression and desire as they are about sensory assault.[97] Oiticica's copious notes detail how his 'quasi-films' should be exhibited in public; these were finally used when the works gained gallery admittance in Rotterdam's Witte de With gallery in 1992.[98] He induces homely intimacy and insouciance in gallery enclosures by inviting spectators to lie on vinyl-covered sand dunes or to soak their feet in basins during projections (*Maileryn*), to recline in hammocks (*Hendrix-War*), or to file their nails as a means of inducing rhythmic self-absorption (*Cosmococa CC1, Trashiscapes*) — clearly also a play on *se lixando* [to be completely disinterested]. This sense of nestling contiguity has not always been recreated successfully in current installations, for example, in the vast rooms of the breathtaking, but indisputably monumental, Cosmococas pavilion at Instituto Inhotim in Minas Gerais [Figure 6]. Other *Cosmococa* installations offer leisure and festivity — or opportunities for 'crelazer' — through the use of sand, swimming pools and coloured floodlights; and all the *Quasi-cinemas* involve an array of sounds or music, particularly experimental compositions by John Cage or Karlheinz Stockhausen, and, adding a narcotic counterpoint to stimulants, the Rolling Stones's version of 'Sister Morphine'.[99] Both *Maileryn* and *Hendrix-War* also intercalate images of *Parangolé*-festooned merriment. Oiticica's use of slides rather than film permits montage to remain aleatory during each projection and for the duration of frames to be altered at will, so that any emergent narrative threads are thus provisional at best. So,

[96] The Anthology Film Archives was founded by Jonas Mekas, Jerome Hill, Stan Brakhage, P. Adams Sitney and Peter Kubelka in 1969; it is described by Oiticica in a letter to Ivan Cardoso (23 February 1971), Projeto Hélio Oiticica, fol. 1096/71, in *Programa Hélio Oiticica* <http://www.itaucultural.org.br/aplicexternas/enciclopedia/ho/index.cfm?fuseaction=documentos&cd_verbete=4523&cod=635&tipo=2> [accessed 1 September 2012]. See also Small, 'One Thing after Another: How We Spend Time in Hélio Oiticica's *Quasi-cinemas*', pp. 77–78.
[97] Stan VanDerBeek, 'Culture Intercom and Expanded Cinema: A Proposal and Manifesto', *Film Culture*, 40 (1966), 15–18 (pp. 16–18). See also Liz Kotz, 'Disciplining Expanded Cinema', in *X-Screen: Film Installations and Actions in the 1960s and 1970s*, ed. by Matthias Michalka (Cologne: Walther König, 2004), pp. 44–57 (p. 53).
[98] Basualdo, 'Waiting for the Internal Sun: Notes on Hélio Oiticica's *Quasi-Cinemas*', p. 52; Brett, 'The Experimental Exercise of Liberty', p. 229. The first five *Cosmococa* sequences were exhibited at MALBA — Fundación Costantini, Buenos Aires, 10 September 2005–30 January 2006. Hélio Oiticica and Neville d'Almeida, *Cosmococa: Programa in Progress*, ed. by Paulo Herkenhoff et al. (Buenos Aires: MALBA Colección Costantini/Instituto Inhotim, 2005).
[99] The Galeria Cosmococas at the Instituto de Arte Contemporânea Inhotim includes a swimming pool for visitors. Unsurprisingly, cocaine itself, which is listed as a prop in Oiticica's *Cosmococa* instructions, has never been used in any museum installation of these works. See Hélio Oiticica, 'CC1 TRASHISCAPES – Especificações técnicas' (13 March 1973), Projeto Hélio Oiticica, fol. 0300/73, in *Programa Hélio Oiticica* <http://www.itaucultural.org.br/aplicexternas/enciclopedia/ho/index.cfm?fuseaction=documentos&cd_verbete=4523&cod=539&tipo=2> [accessed 1 September 2012].

Figure 5. Hélio Oiticica and Neville d'Almeida, slide from *Cosmococa CC5, Hendrix-War* (1973), New York City. Courtesy of Projeto Hélio Oiticica, Rio de Janeiro.

Figure 6. *Cosmococa CC3, Maileryn* (1973) installation at Galeria Cosmococas, Instituto Inhotim. *Cosmococa CC3, Maileryn*: 3 projectors, slides, sand covered with transparent vinyl, balloons, soundtrack (Yma Sumac) and audio equipment. Photograph by Eugénio Savio. Courtesy of Instituto Inhotim, Brumadinho, Minas Gerais.

whilst the configurations of cocaine adorning the surface of photographs are exhibited, the linearity of the configuring process is elided; in other words the predominant sense or awareness of duration unifying events is that of the participants' consciousness. (Fragmentation through slides and competing sounds dismembers film's mimetic illusion into its constituents; it also reminds us that all representation consists of a cut or interval: the severing of the story from the producing subject as scene for another subject's interpretation.) The *Cosmococa* assemblages are meant to endure as ludic 'works in progress'; Oiticica did not intend for them to be contemplated as completed art objects.

The *Quasi-cinemas* are bluntly self-referential, as if aspiring to supplant connotation with impossibly immediate denotation: *Onobjects* (*Cosmococa CC2*), for instance, presents conceptual art, Yoko Ono's *Grapefruit* (1964), next to a phenomenological treatise, Heidegger's *What is a Thing?* (1935–36; first publ. 1962; trans. 1967). There is an urgency here about overcoming insurmountable semiosis, and this extends to Oiticica undermining the cachet he previously attributed to outlawry, as this explicitly derives meaning 'from elsewhere', that is, through opposition. To this end, *Neyrótika* and *Cosmococas* are about exposure rather than transgression. The latter certainly derive countercultural currency through State interdiction which senselessly transfers prohibition of the referent (drugs) onto the sign (indexical policing), but such currency is accidental or secondary. Transgression adheres to the law or taboo by completing its dialectic, whereas exposure, as Michael Hardt explains, operates rather on a purely positive logic of emanation: 'it involves casting off, or really, emptying out all that is external to its material existence and then intensifying that materiality [...] a pure affirmation'.[100] *Neyrótika* gives the viewer a disjunction of male flesh: an anonymous communion of fragmented bodies intensifies erotic experience, but also leads to the undifferentiation of matter. The concatenated images of male body parts, empties homoeroticism of mystique or subversiveness, it just lays male bodies bare as flesh: the possible intensification of male eroticism is also its erasure through indifferent overexposure, what Jean Baudrillard calls an excrescential 'fatal strategy'.[101] *Cosmococa* images of knolls of cocaine present the drug in all its snowy, floury materiality: the only certainty exposed — the only unthinking leap into signification we are permitted to make — is through the denotation of the materiality of white powder; the powder's connotations waver. The underlying close-ups of famous faces bring possible connotations of youth, beauty, heedlessness, perishability and of stardom's glamorous excess, but such connotations are incidental. Here, Oiticica's drugs do not enter into dialectics: the images may inhere in the allure of analeptic or narcotic intoxication and artistic psychoactive experimentation or in the filial

---

[100] Michael Hardt, 'Exposure: Pasolini in the Flesh', in *A Shock to Thought: Expression after Deleuze and Guattari*, ed. by Brian Massumi (London and New York: Routledge, 2002), pp. 77–84 (p. 80).
[101] Jean Baudrillard, *Fatal Strategies*, trans. by Philip Beitchman and W. G. J. Niesluchowski (New York and London: Semiotext(e)/Pluto, 1990), pp. 50–70.

thrill of circumventing the constraints of a State *in loco parentis*, but only to the same extent that they apparently betoken absurdity and abjection.

Monroe's flour-like or saccharine cocaine mask strips away her siren charms: she looks like a clown. In some of the Hendrix slides, ample vermicular circuits of powder suggest self-annihilation rather than pleasure. It is also perfectly feasible, however, to infer that these sequences comment on pleasure: the chemical manipulation of dopamine and serotonin in the nucleus accumbens, but also the love of, or senseless addiction to, celebrity and popular culture.[102] The seduction and cacoethes of capitalism: its hyperbolic imperative of joyful consumption, its regulations and pathologies, but also its actual bliss. On some of the images of Hendrix there is a book of matches advertising Coca-Cola with its 'Enjoy!' slogan: Coke® 'The Real Thing' versus coke (the real thing); the absolute enjoyment which ordinary merchandise only promises to deliver juxtaposed with a forbidden product that actually delivers it.[103] The antithesis of capitalism: addictive drugs — the 'trash-image' — is the one product of consumption that ends desire for any other products; it suspends the ordered, socially-conditioned subjectivity which occurs through the misidentification of desire and the objects offered by the market, replacing it with a drive, a 'kind of vertigo of endless repetition'.[104] And yet, although drug consumers transgress the law, in the context of capitalism they are also not transgressive per se given that they are merely taking capitalism's sustaining fantasy, its ideological injunction to enjoy, literally: they abandon the symbolic for the real, so rather than transgress, they expose.[105] Any (unlikely) element of

---

[102] Jerome J. Platt, *Cocaine Addiction: Theory, Research, and Treatment* (Cambridge, MA: Harvard University Press, 1997), pp. 61–62. Freud famously lauds cocaine-induced euphoria and industriousness in *Über coca* (1884); included in Sigmund Freud, *On Cocaine* (London: Hesperus, 2011), pp. 21–26. Oiticica writes a paean to *Über coca* on 9 June 1973; see his 'Newyorkaises' (9–17 June 1973), Projeto Hélio Oiticica, fol. 0267/73, in *Programa Hélio Oiticica* <http://www.itaucultural.org.br/aplicexternas/enciclopedia/ho/index.cfm?fuseaction=documentos&cd_verbete=4523&cod=18&tipo=21> [accessed 1 September 2012]. See also Coelho, *Livro ou livro-me*, pp. 67–70.

[103] Images from *Hendrix-War* with the Coca-Cola matchbook are available online; 'Hélio Oiticica (1937–1980)', in *Enciclopédia Itaú Cultural de artes visuais*. As Ole Bjerg argues, 'compared to the enjoyment produced by sniffing a line of cocaine, it must be considered a misleading trade description when Coca-Cola is marketed under slogans such as "Enjoy" and "The Real Thing"'; in 'Drug Addiction and Capitalism: Too Close to the Body', *Body & Society*, 14.1 (2008), 1–22 (p. 16).

[104] Avital Ronell, *Crack Wars: Literature, Addiction, Mania* (Lincoln: University of Nebraska Press, 1992), p. 42. See also Michael Taussig on cocaine as fetish in his *My Cocaine Museum* (Chicago, IL: University of Chicago Press, 2004), p. xviii.

[105] Oiticica's work with cocaine roughly coincides with the Andean stimulant's glamorous ascent ascent as an illicit recreational drug in the USA, largely as the preserve of celebrities, but precedes its violent boom as a (cheaper) global black market commodity. Said boom occurred later in the 1970s and expanded with the capitalist frenzy of Reaganite yuppie culture in the 1980s. Curtis Marez outlines the ways in which the State, particularly the USA, has waged a war on drugs such as cocaine not simply to end trafficking, but also to harness it for the furthering of political and economic interests; in *Drug Wars: The Political Economy of Narcotics* (Minneapolis: University of Minnesota Press, 2004), pp. 248–50. See also Paul Gootenberg, *Andean Cocaine: The Making of a Global Drug* (Chapel Hill: University of North Carolina Press, 2008), pp. 310–12; Mary Roldán, 'Cocaine and the "Miracle" of Modernity in Medellín', in *Cocaine: Global Histories*, ed. by Paul Gootenberg (London and New York: Routledge, 1999), pp. 166–82.

AN ETHICS OF DISPLAYING AFFECTION   75

censure Oiticica may have intended is delivered in the midst of the projections' environment of *Ninhos-lazer* [leisure-nests], homely serenity, or flood-lit chromatic *divertissement*, and conversely, any purported notions of (outlaw) hedonistic abandon are underscored iconically by the photographed stars' lurid, ignominious deaths. If Oiticica sought to convey meaning iatrogenically with his disrobed or coked-up, indolently transitioning, imagery, he only ensures the connotative 'symptoms' are confounding. As Salomão states of his experience of *Hendrix-War* in a New York loft in October 1974:

> O laboratório em que a COSMOCOCA é fabricada opera com um complexo movimento simultâneo de afirmação e negação de imagens. O tubo de imagens funciona pela absorção e deformação das outras imagens do farto campo imagético. Conecta, matematiza, prolonga, completa, transforma, sublima, sublinha, desarticula, deforma. O tapete é retirado de baixo dos pés e o terreno sólido desliza em direção ao terreno virtual. [...] catatonia. Vertigem.[106]
>
> [the laboratory producing the COSMOCOCA operates through complex, simultaneous movements which affirm and cancel out images. The picture tube absorbs and disfigures images drawn from an already replete imagescape. It connects, devises, prolongs, completes, transforms, sublimates, emphasizes, dismantles and deforms. It pulls the rug from under one's feet, making solid ground veer towards the virtual. Catatonia. Vertigo.]

Oiticica creates an 'ambiência de saturação virtual, sensorial' [atmosphere of virtual, sensorial saturation]; there is a glut of signification and yet no ordering narrative.[107] As Pedrosa states, commenting on art and the Gestalt principle of perceptive totality: the accumulation or dilation of perception, exacerbated by an unfamiliar but unthreatening context, frustrates the mundane psychological reflex which impoverishes sensorial experience to produce useful 'information'.[108] The result is that during exposure to the *Quasi-cinemas*, self-enclosed, viewing subjects — masterly organizers of perception — speedball into suspension, albeit fleetingly.

Oiticica's audience gathers in 'cocoon' hammocks or 'nests' (also 'nest-cells'): passive bodies which are meant, however, to activate meaning through the installation's visual, aural and tactile stimulation, as well as in relation to the reactions of fellow audience members (co-participants).[109] The *Quasi-cinemas* show that the qualities of feeling which make up the 'secondary' feelings available to reason must be a panoply of sensings in which sight, touch and

---

[106] Salomão, *Hélio Oiticica: Qual é o Parangolé e outros escritos*, p. 104.
[107] Pedrosa, 'Arte ambiental, arte pós-moderna, Hélio Oiticica', p. 209.
[108] Pedrosa, 'Especulações estéticas: Forma e informação — II', pp. 130–31. See also Pedrosa, 'Arte ambiental, arte pós-moderna, Hélio Oiticica', pp. 207–09; Pedrosa, 'Da natureza afetiva da forma na obra de arte', pp. 15–18.
[109] On the development of the 'nest-cells' as part of the *Eden* installation (1969) at the Whitechapel Gallery, see Brett, 'Recollection', p. 13.

hearing cohere, inflecting each other's transformation; they are 'the contraction of the qualitative movement from one to the other into an immediate co-presence'.[110] All elements are in immediate relation. The *Quasi-cinemas* are what Oiticica at the height of his Tropicalist phase projected as an artistic exploration of the 'suprasensorial', that is, of the expansive, expressive interior which precedes habitual sensory capacities — he links the 'suprasensorial' to Op Art and drug use.[111] This is conceived as art which extends beyond the object to its exterior relations, between the object and perceiver-participant, offering theatricalized experience as the means of access to alternative modes of self-fashioning. *Quasi-cinemas* are *Tropicália* intensified, on a high. The sensory stimulation and resistance to narrative of Oiticica's 'quasi-films' lead to a perception of confusion; the perceivers' 'secondary' feelings of confusion, that is, their inability to resolve affection into rational coherence, may make them reflect on the (attempted) process of meaning formation, or alternatively just cause them to walk away perplexed (dismissing anomalies of signification as functionally insignificant).[112] By outmanoeuvring the analogizing habits of thought (which 'contain potential within resemblance'),[113] the *Quasi-cinemas* draw attention to expression as co-poietic interaction which exceeds commanding (active) and controlled (passive) polarities. Expression operates in the dynamic, transformative in-between of affect, which contains much more than perception apprehends — Peirce's monadic qualities of feeling (change); it belongs both to signs and their interpreters. The installations and their audiences end up expanding indistinction between passivity and activity, between subjects and objects, which are intensively distributed across plural elements, levels and matters. If each synaesthetic affective hit momentarily suspends the organized subject, it can also be said that Oiticica's art 'produces subjectivity-effects as a residue of its own self-expressive emergence'.[114] As affective hits translate into habitual, recognizable feelings linked to recognizable symbolic-discursive systems of reference, the subject re-emerges but altered: if the affective is what Massumi calls a generative matrix for subjective variation, then at each instance of conjunction the subject returns and 're-returns [...] because it withdraws, with feeling, between. [...] The return of the subject is not of the same. Following the snowballing of severalled feeling,

---

[110] Brian Massumi, 'Painting: The Voice of the Grain', in Bracha L. Ettinger, *The Matrixal Borderspace*, ed. by Brian Massumi (Minneapolis: University of Minnesota Press, 2006), pp. 201–13 (p. 209).
[111] Hélio Oiticica, 'O aparecimento do suprasensorial na arte brasileira', p. 39. Oiticica's theorizing draws on Gullar's 'Teoria do não-objeto', pp. 85–94, and on Pedrosa's 'Arte ambiental, arte pós-moderna, Hélio Oiticica', pp. 205–09.
[112] See Karl Heinz Bohrer on the 'confusion of feelings' caused by innovative — 'criminal' — artworks' 'pure presentness' in *Suddenness: On the Moment of Aesthetic Appearance*, trans. by Ruth Crowley (New York: Columbia University Press, 1994), p. 72, p. 83.
[113] Brian Massumi, 'Introduction: Like a Thought', in *A Shock to Thought: Expression after Deleuze and Guattari*, ed. by Brian Massumi (London and New York: Routledge, 2002), pp. xiii–xxxix (p. xxxi).
[114] Massumi, 'Painting: The Voice of the Grain', p. 210.

it returns displaced, redistributed, and artistically augmented'.[115] Inasmuch as the subject is 'augmented' by an art which hinders resemblance — thereby forcing the perceptive body to think — Oiticica's *Quasi-cinemas* may be said to have an 'agapastic' or ethical mission of their own. Here though, augmenting subjects is not synonymous with improving them (changing them in relation to specific values bound to a transcendent ideal of 'the good'); it is merely a case of increasing subjects' powers to think and act. For Peirce would have surely balked at the idea of a coke-caked actress and basins of tepid water as an agapastic means of conferring 'upon men a life broader than their narrow personalities'.[116] Spinoza, however, and Deleuze after him, would not have hesitated in agreeing with Oiticica's decision to call this ethical enhancement of subjects' powers to think and act 'joyful'.[117]

Coda: *Geléia geral*, Ethics of Affection

Through the simultaneous use of different media, the *Quasi-cinemas* facilitate the perception of the work of art as a process of 'being in relation'; each element in the installation-projection is pulled beyond its specificity 'by way of its relation to, indeed its composition through, the forces of encounter' with other components and with spectator-participants, which effectively means each of these elements is 'as much outside itself as in itself — webbed in its relations — until ultimately such firm distinctions cease to matter'.[118] It seems apposite to add here that in terms of Tropicália's aesthetics, which Oiticica is famously credited with articulating, this observation goes some way to defining the elusive common ground of all Tropicalist cultural production: affective relationality. Tropicália is after all about art sweeping away the identities of individuated bodies or concepts and seeing culture's affectual doings and undoings, its forces of encounter. With the *Quasi-cinemas*, as in Oiticica's *Tropicália* before them, the oppositional manifestly collapses through anthropophagic incorporation, everything hovers between categories; these works' privileging of relationality affects suspension. Affecting suspension, bringing everything together to force it to become-other, became the heart of a Tropicalist ethics in which representation accordingly bowed to impelling sensation. By cultivating an art of togetherness, of evanescent identities — of 'geléia geral', to cite Décio Pignatari's phrase made famous in Torquato Neto and Gilberto Gil's song — Oiticica innerved aesthetics with ethics. His is a suspensive art of ethical affection.

---

[115] Ibid.
[116] Peirce, *The Collected Papers of Charles Sanders Peirce*, VI, 451.
[117] Baruch Spinoza, *Ethics*, ed. and trans. by G. H. R. Parkinson (Oxford: Oxford University Press, 2000), pp. 173-74 (III: 11); Gilles Deleuze, *Spinoza: Practical Philosophy*, trans. by Robert Hurley (San Francisco: City Lights Books, 1988), p. 50.
[118] Gregory J. Seigworth and Melissa Gregg, 'An Inventory of Shimmers', in *The Affect Theory Reader*, ed. by Melissa Gregg and Gregory J. Seigworth (Durham, NC: Duke University Press, 2010), pp. 1-25 (p. 3).

Afro-Brazilian Culture in London: Images and Discourses in Transnational Movements

Simone Frangella

Universidade de Lisboa, Instituto de Ciências Sociais

Afro-Brazilian culture is a fundamental political and historical point of reference in the creation of Afro-descendent identities in Brazil, and constitutes an arena of debate where racial perceptions undergo constant criticism and transformation, and in which the heterogeneities of contexts, agencies and classifications regarding racial relations and blackness are highlighted.[1] Concepts such as ethnicity and race are often entangled in different and diffuse contexts of racial debate and political discourses. This arena has recently gained renewed strength with newly affirmative positions and in a wider sense challenging the hegemonic Brazilian project of racial conviviality and *mestiçagem*.[2] This furthermore remains a complex political and social picture.

We would thus expect to find such complexity in Afro-Brazilian manifestations outside national boundaries. Brazilian cultural production brought to and produced in London over the last decade encompasses many images and discourses of Afro-Brazilian reference, re-inserted in a different social and racial context, and as part of a cultural transposition strongly connected to transnational consumption and national migration movements.[3] The purpose of this article is to examine the visibility of Afro-Brazilian culture and the articulation of its component elements in transnational dynamics, thereby hoping to grasp the plurality of images and movements that arise from these encounters.[4]

---

[1] Osmundo Pinho, 'As Etnografias do Brau: Corpo, masculinidade e raça na reafricanização em Salvador', *Estudos Feministas* (Florianópolis), 13.1 (2005), 127–45; Olivia Maria Gomes da Cunha, 'Black Movements and the "Politics of Identity" in Brazil', in *Cultures of Politics, Politics of Culture: Re-visioning Latin American Social Movements*, ed. by Sonia E. Alvarez, Evelina Dagnino and Arturo Escobar (Boulder, CO: Westview Press, 1998), pp. 220–51; Livio Sansone, *Blackness without Ethnicity: Constructing Race in Brazil* (New York: Palgrave Macmillan, 2003).

[2] Patricia de Santana Pinho, *Mama Africa: Reinventing Blackness in Bahia* (Durham, NC: Duke University Press, 2010).

[3] Steven Vertovec, 'Conceiving and Researching Transnationalism', *Ethnic and Racial Studies*, 22.2 (1999), 447–62.

[4] This text forms part of a three-year project, funded by the AHRC, on *Cultures of the Lusophone Black Atlantic*, hosted by the Centre for the Study of Brazilian Culture and Society, King's College London. I would thank Nancy Naro, David Treece, Roger Sansi-Roca, Daniel Stone and Liv Sovik for their generous suggestions and comments on this work.

The article intends to demonstrate how, on the one hand, narratives of Brazilianness tend to overlap the signs of the Afro-Brazilian diasporic cultural circulation, neutralizing its political content and repositioning it in a national representation that has always drawn heavily from black culture,[5] subsumed in the idea of hybridism. On the other hand, however, the diversity of these cultural forms experienced in London opens up glimpses of traits of black identities that emerge in confrontation or consonance with the plural and intricate universe of blackness existent in the city. Such experience alludes to incipient and possible diasporic dialogues and exchanges, instigating different political meanings to these cultural productions.

The present deliberations were drawn mostly from an intensive one-year research project, undertaken in 2006–07, along with additional empirical observations made over the following years. The research included interviews with members of cultural organizations, media producers, Brazilian and other local cultural promoters, the Brazilian Embassy, magazine publishers, artists and Brazilians who have lived in the city for a long time (one or two decades). The research also included observations of events and places, and analysis of advertising and texts. The article provides a description of this cultural universe, as well as some analytical insights into the effects of the transit of meanings of blackness that emerge from it.

Brazilian culture — understood here as a set of transnational flows of events, commodities, images and discourses that compose the entertainment and consumer environment regarding Brazil — emerged on the London scene with remarkable visibility over the last decade. This new fashion is due to two movements that eventually intersect. On the one hand, there is the increasing cultural and financial demand for Brazilian images as a cultural product by entrepreneurs and cultural actors in the city. Prompted by the international promotion of Brazil through recent images in the media world that highlight the country, as well as a marketing selection of 'cheerful' images of the country as a potential source of profit, many businessmen have been led to invest in Brazilian-themed music, dance and food outlets in London. *Havaianas* flip-flops have become the shoes of summer. Brazilian music is played in stores, in streets, in films, while fashionable Brazilian music and art trends have taken over various London pubs and cultural clubs. Recent Brazilian films are to be found in Blockbusters. Brazilian artists perform or exhibit their arts in sophisticated venues across the city and to audiences composed mostly of other Londoners. Brazilian plays have been performed by British theatre groups in recent years with great success. Brazil has become stylish and attracted significant cultural and financial interest. The images in this universe highlight both the 'traditions' and the trendy 'innovations' of the nation's culture.

However, another factor that has contributed fundamentally to this cultural boom is the inward Brazilian migration flow to the UK (particularly London).

---

[5] P. Pinho, *Mama Africa*, p. 183.

By taking part in commercial dynamics and sharing cultural experiences, Brazilians play an important part in feeding the flow of representations and goods. In previous decades, Brazilians were a very slight presence, with only occasional or intermittent arrivals into Britain.[6] From 2001, a significant migratory flow began, and migrant workers joined the existing population of temporary students and professionals, intensifying transnational social networks and creating local businesses, places of religious worship, magazines, etcetera. Thus, Brazilians have collectively been a growing movement in the UK, although with only incipient forms of structural or political organization, and their presence is still often undetected and lower in profile than other migrant communities in the country.[7] However, despite their low visibility, this increasing flow has brought with it a whole network of services, goods, educational courses and entertainment in order to help the newcomers in their arrival and adaptation.[8]

These two concomitant movements create diverse images, which are received and produced by Brazilians and other London residents. Brazilian culture, on the one hand, is celebrated and experienced far beyond the community itself, since the cultural references through which Brazil becomes visible are not necessarily provided or consumed by Brazilians. Whilst some cultural manifestations are organized to meet Brazilian community demands, most are more commonly directed at other Londoners interested in an imaginary about Brazil that has its sources in the facility of commodity circulation in global terms. On the other hand, the cultural field both feeds and is fed by the Brazilians who work in the clubs and stores, or run boutiques and market stalls, even when not directed specifically or restrictively at them. While magazines and websites focus more directly on the community, some provide a bilingual edition to reach out to non-Brazilian audiences. Above all, culture is the field in which relations between Brazilian and other London residents seem to be more tangibly constructed. References to the country were incorporated and then reinforced with the concrete presence of Brazilians and their respective expressive forms. All these aspects have contributed to building a diversity of images of this culture and of its forms of experience and consumerism.

---

[6] Ângela Torresan, 'Quem Parte, Quem Fica: Uma etnografia sobre imigrantes brasileiros em Londres, Inglaterra' (unpublished Master's thesis, Federal University of Rio de Janeiro, 1994).
[7] In the UK, Brazilians are hardly ethnically identifiable, particularly as regards their physical appearance. There has been a recent attempt to create a sense of 'community', and a process of self-definition of identity has cautiously begun.
[8] For more details on this emerging community, see Simone Frangella, 'O "Made in Brasil" em Londres: Migração e os bens culturais', *Revista Travessia*, 66 (Jan–Jun 2010), 33–44; and Simone Frangella, '"Brazilianness" in London: National Goods and Images in Transnational Mobility', in *Brazilian Subjectivity Today: Migration, Identity and Xenophobia*, ed. by Szilvia Simai and Derek Hook (Villa María, Argentina: Eduvim, 2011), pp. 149–70.

The Brazilian Cultural Scene in London

From the mid-1980s and throughout the 1990s, Brazilian culture in London meant only sporadic events. They were mainly produced by cultural institutions, such as Brazilian Contemporary Arts (BCA) and the Embassy. In this period, certain genres of Brazilian culture were brought to show to Londoners,[9] featuring renowned names such as Caetano Veloso, Gilberto Gil, Gal Costa, Jorge Amado, Alceu Valença and Grupo Corpo. Apart from these events, though, Brazilian residents shared spaces of sociability with other Latin American immigrants in *salsa* and *lambada* clubs,[10] meaning that although well attended and popular they remained out of broader public view.

This situation started to change from the beginning of 2000. As a result of the expansion of the community, many activities and products were facilitated to alleviate Brazilian 'nostalgia'. DJs and musicians brought *forró*, *sertaneja*, *pagode*, and *samba* as entertainment for the immigrants. Brazilian food came alongside it. English language courses targeting Brazilian students increased significantly. Brazilian artists residing in London, such as photographers, dancers, and painters, found many more professional possibilities. Many of these events and products also spilled over into the Portuguese community in London.

Concomitantly, prominent events have promoted Brazil in very central and iconic venues in London, such as the Barbican Centre and the Royal Albert Hall, organized by the Embassy, whether in partnership with Brazilian organizations or supported by London entrepreneurs. Furthermore, the main commercial cinemas of London have shown Brazilian films, with a tremendous public response.[11] And some physical landmarks, such as the Gallery Pavilion in Hyde Park, designed by Oscar Niemeyer, have increased the Brazilian presence. For many of my interviewees, the turning point in Brazil's visibility was a remarkable event in 2004, at Selfridges, the famous department store. *Brazil 40 degrees* was a whole month dedicated to Brazil, creating an environment based on Brazil's images and commodities. The Selfridges' event — a proper blend of culture and commerce — attracted strong interest from the public by its representations of themes that composed an imaginary of Brazil.

Carnival and samba also came under the spotlight when, in 2005, the Paraíso Samba School, one of three long-established samba schools in London, won awards at the Notting Hill Carnival, an event staged by mostly black Caribbean and black African groups. The victory was repeated in subsequent

---

[9] The criteria adopted by the BCA — an institution, now defunct, directed at a British audience interested in Brazilian culture — and the Embassy favoured the selection of musicians and artists who were well known and well regarded by the Brazilian media. Interviews with Felipe Fortuna (Embassy Cultural Section, 20 June 2006) and Edna Crepaldi (BCA, 22 April 2006).
[10] Mailis Valentim, 'L'Immigration latino-américaine, et plus particulièrement brésilienne, à Londres des années 1970 à nos jours' (Mémoire de Maitrise, Université Sorbonne-Paris IV, 2005).
[11] Films such as *City of God*, followed subsequently by *Lower City*, *Carandiru* and *Elite Squad*.

years. Marketing images also spread throughout the city: the 2006 World Cup campaign for Brazil, in Nike's Oxford Circus store; the celebration of *caipirinha*,[12] in clubs, rapidly increasing imports of *cachaça*. Lastly, the beer brand Brahma entered the European market, using an advertising campaign based on Brazilian *grafiteiro* (graffiti art), seen on billboards and buses all over London. These are some illustrations of the emerging and ongoing state of Brazilian cultural production in London. Within this universe three different contexts of production nurturing and re-articulating a diversity of representations are observable. These three contexts promote the plurality of representations and discourses produced in the flow between Brazil and London.

The first context concerns short-term events and exhibitions coming from Brazil; they are very effective in feeding diverse images from the country. The artists performing depend on London-based promoters and advertising sponsors, who invest a lot of money in contacting, bringing over and paying artists or producers from Brazil. Some major events with renowned Brazilian artists are backed by a combination of sponsors.[13] For artists coming to meet community-level demand, unknown to other Londoners and with a more restricted audience on a tighter budget, money becomes correspondingly more difficult to raise. Promoters then, usually Brazilian, explore many avenues, usually putting up their own money as well as finding investment partners, such as money transfer businesses.[14] Finally, private British investors are an important source of investment, either bringing artists from Brazil or inaugurating venues with Brazilian decorative themes, events, music or food. This is the case of famous clubs in Central London, for example, Guanabara and Favela Chic.

The second cultural development regarding Brazilian culture is what may be called the transmission/reinvention of cultural repertoires, fomented by both Brazilians and non-Brazilians living in London, who make a living out of consumerism or entertainment culture. Primarily this involves teachers of *capoeira*, samba, *maracatu*, and Afro-Brazilian dance. It also includes artists based in London who perform their work while not necessarily reproducing traditional representations. This form of production creates interesting effects and innovations, embodying diverse repertoires and trends, while challenging the traditional discourses usually imprinted on these activities. These courses are not usually frequented by Brazilians, but mainly by people from many different countries — especially, British citizens interested either in this exotic and curious type of art, or seeking deeper knowledge about a foreign country. In this sense, one may also say it is a culture for export. This phenomenon is

---

[12] A cocktail made of sugar-cane spirit, mixed with sugar, ice and lemon. It is Brazil's most famous drink.

[13] Such as the Brazilian Embassy, the Arts Council, the British Council, Varig, Petrobras, Banco do Brasil and money transfer businesses.

[14] This is the case of Brazilian producers, such as DJ Marcus and DJ Tubarão, two promoters who often appear in Brazilian magazines.

remarkably distinct from the experience of other national/ethnic groups in London, whose performance of cultural manifestations is directed only at the group itself, as a means of keeping memory alive after crossing national borders.

The third interesting context of cultural production developed in the city is that of culture applied as part of educational or community projects for vulnerable and problematic environments, or even projects of cultural exchange. It is not a new issue in London or in many parts of the world; but what seems to be new and increasingly expressive is the use of Brazilian cultural manifestations to work with problematic social contexts in London, such as schools with serious disciplinary problems, or poorer communities in the boroughs. Many samba schools and *capoeira* groups based in the city, and Brazilian artists coming for short periods, are constantly requested to hold workshops and long-term courses within these circles. Such events are normally financed by the local governments of each borough, and run as extra-curricular activities. Some of them are private classes welcomed by parents seeking free-time activities for their children.

In all contexts, stereotyped ideas of Brazil still dominate the portrayals, advertising discourses and selection criteria of events and products. Samba, soccer, beautiful women and 'genuine joy' remain the mainstream portrait of Brazilians. However, two important references have been feeding such an imaginary with other attributes.

The first is an emphasis on the idea of diversity in Brazil (ethnic/racial, cultural, geographical), addressed by the media and accessed through contemporary commercial, information and migration flows. This diversity has opened up new channels of information about the country while making the previous stereotypes more nuanced. In other words, music is not just samba and *bossa nova*; soccer is not the only activity in Brazil; the country is not just Amazonia and Rio/Salvador; and Brazil becomes more clearly distinguished from other Latin American countries, as evidenced by catchphrases such as 'we clearly don't speak Spanish!'

The second reference may generally be called the aesthetics of poverty and violence, a different and transgressive reality, surrounded by features related to an urban Brazil: shanty-town houses and streets, *cachaça*, popular saints, Christ the Redeemer, street vendors on *carioca* beaches, *feijoada*, *botecos*, *capoeiristas*. This portrait acquired particular visibility with the film *City of God*, and became reinforced by other films, by the names of stores and venues such as Barraco, Favela Chic and Favela Shop.[15] The artistic inspiration of urban landscapes associated with the outskirts of big cities is the most identifiable among the very high quality advertising of Brazilian events and products.[16] This trend also brought forward famous Brazilian artists that in some way

---

[15] Favela Chic, for example, has its entire interior decorated in 'favela' style, its walls covered with pieces of rotten or broken wood, in a kind of a simulacrum of a slum dwelling.
[16] 'Dos muros para as galerias', *Jungle Drums*, 33 (March 2006), p. 27.

address subjects such as shanty towns, drug dealing and resistance (MV Bill, AfroReggae, Rappa). Funk carioca (a rhythm created in the slums of Rio de Janeiro) became part of DJ collections (especially British DJs).

Traditional stereotypes of Brazil emerge in parallel with all these cultural manifestations, promoting other symbolic and material repertoires and contributing towards reinventions and inclusions of new discourses on Brazilianness. The selection criteria of events and performances relate to either traditional representations of Brazil or the innovations that circle around a wider and more challenging imaginary about the country. Brazil is less distant now, less exotic, but more dangerous and 'creative'.

Nevertheless, these narratives of Brazil generally emerge as a cultural style, rarely associated with political connotations or statements. Even poverty emerges as an indistinct characteristic of Brazilian society, fashioned in the colours of the shanty towns or glamorized in a particular cinematic interpretation. Political issues regarding ethnic or racial boundaries, for instance, were not a concern in their production. The marketing coordinator of Selfridges made very clear the company did not take into account any political or socio-economic connotations in representing Brazil. Even the Guanabara club, a plausible arena for debates and proposals on Brazilian culture, either at an artistic performance or organizational level, seems unable to effectively respond to these suggestions.

What place does Afro-Brazilian culture hold within this cultural universe? How are forms and representations of black culture articulated — or disarticulated — in this transnational dislocation? Marked by historical processes of struggle for social and political acknowledgement, as well as transnational and local references,[17] black Brazilian culture faces new articulations under contingent and negotiated reinterpretations in this new environment. In Brazil, the process of political and cultural re-Africanization has comprised diverse perspectives during the last decades. From the weight of the inheritance of African tradition, to cultural reinventions of African repertoires, politics and race have all been constantly re-articulated in culture.[18]

Blackness has adjusted to regional contexts, class and generational differences. As a reference, while Bahia is the major producer of blackness, appealing to a common thread of African traditions in the routes of the Black Atlantic, essentialized in the body,[19] Rio reinforces the emphasis on the political relations between blackness and poverty, bringing out another kind of racial construction. Black culture enabled the emergence of plural black Brazilian discourses and experiences, as well as the entanglement between the idea of tradition and of invention.[20]

[17] Osmundo A. Pinho, 'O Mundo Negro: Sócio-antropologia da reafricanização em Salvador' (unpublished PhD dissertation, State University of Campinas, 2003), p. 17; Sansone, p. 14.
[18] Cunha, p. 235.
[19] P. Pinho, *Mama Africa*, p. 8.
[20] Cunha; O. Pinho, 'As Etnografias do Brau'; Sansone.

Looking at Afro-Brazilian culture in London leads to an intricate picture. Facets of blackness have different weightings and produce different experiences in London. And this varies according to the contexts of production. On the one hand, this circulation of cultural goods for export fosters a recognition of black culture as representational of an Africa in Brazil. On the other hand, in daily relations in the city where culture is involved, frictions with diverse ethnic and national boundaries and within the Brazilian community itself defy Brazilian blackness in its potentiality as an ethnic and racial discourse. This seems repositioned or at least challenged within the context of multiculturalism — alongside its fragilities — in London.

Afro-Brazilian Culture in London

Within the scope of the short-term events and transmission of repertoires, Afro-Brazilian artists and cultural expressions have been brought to the London cultural arena since the mid-1980s by the organization Brazilian Contemporary Arts. It promoted the first Gilberto Gil concert in London in 1985, and the Afro-Brazilian Fair plus a Grand Carnival in the African Centre, in Central London, at the end of the 1980s.[21] Three times in the 1990s it brought Mãe Stella de Oxossi, a renowned *mãe-de-santo* of Bahia, to the city to deliver lectures. In 1994, she joined a seminar called *Sincretismo e Miscigenação na BAHIA*, together with other renowned guests of Bahia, such as Jorge Amado, António Olinto and Pierre Verger. BCA also promoted the first performances and workshops of *capoeira*, *gafieira* and samba groups.

The Embassy of Brazil has replicated such efforts with many other events, including black artists in other fields besides music, such as a big exhibition in 2006 of photographs by the London-based photo-journalist Luis Santos, portraying aspects of 'sincretismo religioso' [religious syncretism] in Bahia. Other black artists visit, often with the sponsorship of Brazilian cultural institutions, or British supporters, such as the Barbican Centre, the Arts Council and the British Council. There have also been some other shared support projects run by community organizations and individuals, as in the case of the magazine *Jungle Drums* and Tubarão productions.

Events promoted by BCA and the Embassy brought to London artistic expressions that have been praised as authentic, and representative of cultural expressions derived from ideas of the Afro-Brazilian 'tradition', particularly those associated with Bahia-ness.[22] As part of this re-Africanization movement in Brazil, tradition appears as a source of power and legitimacy of an African

---

[21] BCA had good contacts with the African Centre, promoting events in it during the 1990s, with a significant participation of artists of African descent. Musicians also used to perform at the African Centre. This fact, unknown to most Brazilian residents, suggests that Brazilian culture has been raising some interest in African communities, as much as Brazilians use African 'inheritance' in this cultural commodity. These relations seem to be at an early stage, but ongoing.
[22] P. Pinho, *Mama Africa*, p. 184.

inheritance.[23] The performances attract significant attention from the city's public due to their quality, and also due to the attraction that this specific 'authentic' portrait of Afro-Brazilian culture brings to foreign eyes, as well as to those Brazilian residents who can afford entrance to the venues.[24]

Other artists under the spotlight recently in Brazil such as Seu Jorge, Elza Soares, MV Bill, Gilberto Gil, Jorge Ben and TrioMocoto have been presenting shows and lectures in London quite regularly in recent years. They have brought diverse styles of music, updating Brazilian traditional and regional styles to make new blends of musical genres, mixing contemporary beats with popular music. However, in spite of the strong statements of racial identity reflected in these artists' works and interviews, their presentations are appreciated rather as part of a broader national picture. Blackness is again understood and appreciated as a diluted component of the hybridism of Brazilian culture.

Among the recent tendencies, funk, rap, and hip-hop emerge on this scene as a set of important black references. Being 'powerful new musical and cultural phenomena',[25] associated with cultural movements of the 1980s and 1990s in big Brazilian cities, they were updated in the following decade through the mixing with other Brazilian popular music genres.[26] They are a set of cultural practices and representations that tie the aesthetic forms directly to a reference to community (geographical and political),[27] with the manifestation of social resistance, and racial issues embraced by this. This articulation can be found in movements such as the theatre and cinema group Nós do Morro, from Vidigal, a shanty town in Rio; they performed in the UK for the first time in 2006, and returned, when other opportunities presented themselves, to perform Shakespeare in London.[28]

These movements are created as a critical response to a dominant consensual culture that dissimulated social and racial inequality, resulting in heterogeneous and malleable interconnections between black representations, community identities and class issues. These cultural trends traced a specific path in an Afro-descendent identity, in which slums, black people and resistance are in a necessary relationship, thereby compounding this particular imaginary. They became one instance in which blackness remains as an open-ended meaning allowing other political articulations.[29] However, many of these movements

[23] O. Pinho, *O Mundo Negro*, p. 185; P. Pinho, *Mama Africa*.
[24] Many of these shows in famous London clubs are quite expensive, meaning that migrant workers usually cannot afford the tickets. Also the artists featured are not necessarily of interest to them. These factors reinforce differences in lifestyle within the so-called community.
[25] David Treece. 'Rhythm and Poetry: Politics, Aesthetics and Popular Music in Brazil since 1960', in *Cultural Politics in Latin America*, ed. by Anny Brooksbank Jones and Ronaldo Munck (London: Macmillan, 2000), pp. 29–42; Cunha, p. 240.
[26] The first decade of the new century witnessed a profuse blending of Brazilian rhythms and electronic beats on the one hand, and reinforcements of mass culture on the other.
[27] Cunha, p. 243.
[28] The group presented *The Two Gentleman of Verona* at the Complete Works Festival in Stratford-upon-Avon, in 2006, and again at the Barbican, in 2008.
[29] P. Pinho, *Mama Africa*, p. 21.

have been gradually absorbed by national mainstream media and also became a genre consumed mostly (though by no means exclusively) by middle-class Brazil.[30] As a result, the potential critical content of such expressions risks dilution in the mass consumption style.

Thus, this cultural production highlights the Afro-Brazilian universe; but, in a more general imaginary, its expressions are diluted in the outline of social hybridism, of a 'nation building' enterprise,[31] which has been so ingrained in official, intellectual and popular discourses in Brazil. The issue of racism and ethnicity, particularly Brazilian, remains vague, with a reluctance to discuss them or to acknowledge them as problematic. There are no direct references to black culture, with the exception of occasional texts in Brazilian magazines. In my interviews, especially with Brazilian producers, questions about the visibility of Afro-Brazilian culture in the city were answered hesitantly. Very few people related to the idea. Most, after some thought, could not identify black Brazilian culture in London, with the exception of *capoeira* as the one single obvious expression.

In a general sense, Brazilian cultural production and the national narratives that underline them became a currency, a fundamental aspect of the imagination produced as a social practice in this broad process of relocation or, in other words, deterritorialization.[32] Diversity is reinforced, but under a single 'ethnic' entity, the Brazilian.[33] This production aggregates institutional agendas and the mobility of other actors, in which the idea of Brazilianness becomes of central commercial and mediatic interest on the one hand, and a necessary form of self-representation (by migrants) on the other hand. And, whilst in Brazil the expressive culture and set of values and sentiments reproduced by black people have been helping construct an Afro-Brazilian identity,[34] they seem once again to attenuate their political and historical mobilization when transported to this specific transnational flow. Blackness in this context remains partly essentialized as a traditional myth. There is a potential space for cultural reinventions and agency in this cultural market, of which producers do not always avail themselves.

Such emptiness in the socio-political contextualization or ethnic recognition is also strongly existent among Brazilian residents in London. This void is partly explained by the small number of self-declared Afro-Brazilian descendants in

---

[30] *Funk carioca*, originated in black 'bailes funk' [funk balls] in the suburbs of Rio, gaining a remarkable space in the national and mass media. The same had happened to funk, rap and hip-hop, although there is still strong use of these styles as a form of 'counter-culture'.
[31] O. Pinho, *O Mundo Negro*, p. 195.
[32] Arjun Appadurai, 'Global Ethnoscapes: Notes and Queries for a Transnational Anthropology', in *Recapturing Anthropology: Working in the Present*, ed. by Richard G. Fox (Santa Fé, NM: School of American Research Press, 1991), pp. 191–210.
[33] Frangella, '"Brazilianness" in London', p. 155.
[34] Miguel V. de Almeida, 'The Brown Atlantic: Anthropology, Postcolonialism, and the Portuguese-speaking World', paper presented at the Seminar on *Cultures of the Lusophone Black Atlantic* (King's College London, 11 March 2005); O. Pinho, *O Mundo Negro*, p. 194.

London, less than five per cent of Brazilian migrants, according to informal figures. And it alludes to the fact that this black culture is transmitted and produced with a certain detachment from subjects otherwise usually part of this social construct. Added to this is the denial of racial distinctions, with the emphasis on hybridism a seemingly comfortable position. Interestingly enough, issues regarding colour and race sometimes emerge when Brazilian migrants face the very visible black presence in London. Their remarks about 'how black these people are', caught in very informal and fragmented conversations, point to a certain dislocation, a perception of ethnic and racial models other than those of their homeland.

For the Afro-Brazilian men I interviewed, all of whom had arrived in London around ten or more years ago, there was a new experience of blackness in London.[35] They were firmly convinced of the absence of an authentic black Brazilian culture in the city. Cicero, who had lived there for fifteen years and used to run a restaurant in south London, saw the Brazilian cultural environment slowly growing with no particular visible Afro-Brazilian cultural manifestation. According to Luis Santos, a photographer, expressions normally attributed in the city to the Afro-Brazilian culture are just shallow presentations, within a tourist framework. The same is affirmed by Alberto, a musician from Salvador, whose musical production is totally based on the idea of African roots and shared with other African musicians in a band. Alberto, as much as Luis Santos, sees an absence of initiative from the Brazilian community.

Reconfiguring Blackness in the Multi-ethnic Arena

However, there is another side to this picture. The men interviewed claimed to feel very comfortable living in London — and, mostly, more comfortable than in Brazil — feeling that their presence, as black people, fitted in there. They felt part of a plurality where black people, despite the difficulties, experienced social and personal mobility and were not subjected to everyday hostility. This however does not mean an absence of confrontation. Cicero, for example, complained about the suspicious attitude of the border authorities every time he returns to the country. Even though he holds a European passport, he is kept back while his credentials are checked — which he attributes in part to his long black hair. But Luis, on the other hand, affirmed that in the city he could get many jobs that would still allow him to keep his long black hair. Cicero reported occasional frictions with other African or Caribbean descendants. In Brixton, the fact that he had white friends bothered some black people, who came to complain to him. To Cicero, it felt like prejudice. But they all felt less discriminated against in London than in Brazil or in other countries of Europe.

Thus, there seems to be a detachment between the Brazilian black presence and black production. Hence, while the absence of Afro-Brazilian manifestations

---

[35] Interviews with Cicero Souza (13 March 2006), Luis Santos (15 December 2006), and Alberto Jashie (21 August 2006).

or their alienation into a hybrid culture bothers these men, their presence in the capital city makes them better acknowledged as Afro-Brazilian and provides a recognition they do not get in its Brazilian community, even when Afro-Brazilian discourses are expressed. Their experiences suggest their condition of blackness finds a fertile field in this environment. One might expect that the multicultural experiences of the city, built up under a history of harsh adjustments and enabling various forms of black experiences, from the affirmation of traditional black identities to new forms of adaptation in the British social order,[36] establishes the grounds for these men to locate themselves in an appreciation of diversity, looking for a place guaranteed by the constant diaspora flows that circulate within it.

The issue is that London seems to be a place where the emergence of new ethnicities, or the repositioning of old identities, is constant, with cross currents of different fields, and the creation of dynamic strategies to tackle the racism and harsh conditions experienced by black people. British multi-ethnic society raises a lot of issues about its unfolding progress, still struggling to fight discrimination and racism, and to redefine what it means to be British.[37] At the same time, however, its own cultural and social diversity, with the emergence of new ethnicities fomented either by the constant global flows or by the emergence of second-generation immigrants, enables some cultural encounters and open-ended modes of identity.

Regarding the London cultural arena, how does this happen in practice? It is true that the 'Brazilian blend' tends to be fed by consumer expectations. The stress on a hybrid culture seems to be really attractive to the London public, normally used to facing constant ethnic and racial boundary issues in everyday life. The idea of a blend — and a joyful blend — seems to be a counterpart to problems the British population faces nowadays in terms of 'multicultural' dynamics, due to their complicated management and probably also related to the legacy of a model of ethnic segregation.[38] The attractiveness of this image of Brazilianness also tends to obscure the socio-economic disruptions of Brazilian society and their concrete consequences for Afro-Brazilians. Thus, black images come without great contextualization, or as an amalgam of juxtaposed meanings.

A depiction of one of my observation evenings in the Guanabara Club is very illustrative of this consumption environment. At an event to choose the Paraíso Samba School queen drummer, the club quickly filled up; there were many Brazilians, but most were other Londoners relaxing after work. Before the competition, a DJ played a mixture of samba and other percussion rhythms and electronic beats. Two videos about Brazil showing images of Pelé, of Olodum

[36] Steven Vertovec, *The Hindu Diaspora: Comparative Patterns* (London: Routledge, 2000).
[37] Peter Kivisto, *Multiculturalism in a Global Society* (London: Wiley-Blackwell, 2002).
[38] Peter Fry, 'Undoing Brazil: Hybridity versus Multiculturalism', in *Cultures of the Lusophone Black Atlantic*, ed. by Nancy Naro, Roger Sansi-Roca and David Treece (New York: Palgrave Macmillan, 2007), pp. 233–49 (p. 237).

(an Afro-Brazilian group), and of Rio de Janeiro, were projected onto the stage and walls. At the front of the stage, a black man was playing some drums that enriched the sound. When the percussionist stopped, the DJ changed to other very different genres. Some *funk carioca* beats began, to which the dancers reacted very cheerfully. Many white, Asian and black British people were part of the audience, absorbing those references of Brazilian culture. This was purely recreational consumption of an exotic culture.

However, when it comes to two other contexts of production, the transmission of repertoires in courses and schools, blackness is more incisively targeted. There are a number of courses and workshops addressing the subject. At the time of my research, I noted one Afro-Brazilian dance course teaching *orixá* dance; three samba schools, which run workshops; more than thirty-five *capoeira* schools; and a *maracatu* group. Most have references to Black History in Brazil in their advertising texts, in this way justifying the roots of their arts. It is similarly a fact that only a few go any deeper into such issues. Eventually, for many of these teachers, black roots become more of an attractive background. The subjection to a more indistinct national Brazilian identity may also be explained by the fact that, in many of these places, as already stated, the public is more interested in the fitness dimension such courses provide rather than their sources of inspiration.

Nevertheless, some groups do rely more heavily on the African heritage in their arts to attract an audience more interested in the flows of the diaspora. Such proves the case with many different ethnic groups, and including black British and black and white Portuguese speakers. What is at stake here is the celebration of Brazilian blackness as a source of empowerment and knowledge, a narrative relocated in the transnational flows. It is through this kind of work that one can see more nuanced discourses and representations of Afro-Brazilian culture that grows slowly but firmly. Such a factor definitively contributes towards new interactions among Afro-Brazilian cultures and other black cultures in London as well as enabling Brazilian blackness to be fully respected in a wider audience. This may be a slow and hesitant movement, very incipient, but it is under formation.

Furthermore, although these performances take Brazil as their original source, their performers/masters/teachers are from diverse countries (Brazil, Britain, Portugal, Angola, Mozambique to name but a few). These arts, therefore, enable the addition of different cultural experiences, enhanced in this transnational context. *Capoeira*, and its variations in international contexts, makes a good illustration of this process. They also allow for a closer approach by London's spectators/audiences to Brazilian culture while opening up new possibilities for knowledge and the deconstruction of stereotyped images, even if unable to eliminate them. In this sense, factors such as language, musical instruments and their history, different styles of music and dance, and Brazilian history help convey nuanced contexts not just from black Brazil, but also from the Lusophone universe.

Regarding the application of culture in the city's social projects, they show interesting and dynamic articulations and frictions between two different ways of dealing with ethnicity, discrimination and poverty. Afro-Brazilian culture in this context indicates a means of 're-integrating' segregated or vulnerable groups. It does so out of a double assumption: the empowerment of the African heritage and the allegedly similar conditions of social and economic vulnerability experienced in Brazil. The case of the AfroReggae group is paradigmatic. Formed as both a band and a social project in Vigário Geral, a big shanty town in Rio de Janeiro, in 1993, the group works with multiple artistic expressions such as music, dance, acting and *capoeira*. Besides performances, they manage cultural centres inside Rio's shanty towns, using art as a social project to combat the recruitment of children and adolescents into drug dealing. They have gained the support of renowned artists such as Caetano Veloso, Regina Case, Gilberto Gil, and the late Wally Salomão.[39] The aesthetics of poverty have inspired cultural productivity applied as part of educational or community projects in cities.

In London, AfroReggae has run various workshops in so-called problematic schools, with students coming from diverse ethnic backgrounds and vulnerable conditions. The results were excellent according to Paul Heritage (who managed the project).[40] Students at problematic London schools responded well to the cultural propositions put forward by AfroReggae; and it would seem that the appeal of percussion instruments and dance/fight movements receives good feedback from such student groups. It is furthermore clear that this is the main purpose. However, interestingly enough, AfroReggae members became deeply bothered by the fact that the children did not 'mix'; that is, they maintained the same ethnic boundaries during workshop intervals, which AfroReggae indicated as one of their main problems and difficulties. The children, when asked why they did this, were surprised at such an unfamiliar question.

This conflict underlines the 'localization' of blackness experiences. The AfroReggae experience, marked by racial and social inequality, but also by ethnic indistinctness, is confronted by another logic, where ethnic boundaries meet social relations, not necessarily with inequality, but constituting a problem concerning issues of social interaction. They perform and sell rhythms that are part of a current 'global memory' of identity references, which in some way feed the black diaspora.[41] AfroReggae belongs to these more recent movements, in which a black culture existent within the younger working-class generation gains prominence at a national level. This reinforces their connection to African roots and their political struggle, as well as facilitating their international recognition. Locating themselves in specific, poor urban environments (the 'community') in large Brazilian cities, they perceive racial

---

[39] 'From the Favela to the World: In conversation with AfroReggae', lecture given at the Barbican, 1 March 2006.
[40] Interview with Paul Heritage, 3 April 2006.
[41] Sansone, p. 14.

inequality, but through a kind of indistinct ethnicity — 'we are all black in the *favelas*'.[42] The *favela* becomes the central locus of transformation.[43] Whilst this makes sense in the confusing debate surrounding terms such as race and ethnicity in Brazil, it takes on other shades when transported to a multiracial environment as strongly marked by ethnic discourses as London. In this sense, the interesting presence of Afro-Brazilian culture as knowledge to be shared brings forth relational and frictional discourses on ethnicity. Nevertheless, it is still a movement whose local experiences also reposition local black identity. We might conceive of such a fact as two local references of ethnicity and race that, within the framework of the globalized movement of objects and ideas, commodities such as black culture are necessarily likely to be somewhat frictional.

One friction resides in an issue important to the debate on the black diaspora: the embodiment of black culture as a narrative of blackness.[44] Manipulating the body, allegedly an inheritance of African movements, objects and traces are one of the main supports of blackness discourses within the black diaspora and the Afro-Brazilian movements. While in Bahia, Africanness was centred on the body,[45] producing some essentialist notion of blackness, groups like AfroReggae claim they invest in the potential of black movements to transform them into emancipating performances that challenge and go beyond tradition. Both perspectives are present and operational in this cultural production brought to London, whether to meet the demands of commercial/aesthetic desires or more political aspirations.

However, in any case, Afro-Brazilian culture in London is basically taught or introduced by white Brazilian people or white British people. The majority of their public is white, and/or middle class. Samba schools are a particularly good illustration of this. Although they attract people from many different backgrounds, including black people, the majority of students are white. This fact has a definitive impact when one observes Notting Hill Carnival, founded at the end of the 1950s as a response to the bad race relations then prevailing. Most of the groups participating are of either Caribbean or African origin. The Carnival depicts the efforts of black British citizens to reinforce African traits present in their or their parents' homelands. Brazil brings the cheerful Brazilian image to the street. Many lyrics, such as the last samba *enredo* by the group Quilombo, make reference to black people in Brazil. Yet, it is white people — and the majority non-Brazilians — who consume these fantasies.

The same contrast occurs in *capoeira* courses and other dance classes.

---

[42] Remark made by a member of AfroReggae in a show recorded in the documentary *Favela Rising*, dir. by Matt Mochary and Jeff Zimbalist (Paris Filmes, 2005).
[43] Cunha, p. 242.
[44] Paul Gilroy, *The Black Atlantic: Modernity and Double Consciousness* (London: Verso, 1993); P. Pinho, *Mama Africa*, p. 101.
[45] P. Pinho, *Mama Africa*, p. 8.

This situation seems comparable with the *candomblé* and *umbanda terreiros* in Portugal, where the *pais de santo* (priests) are either white Brazilians or Portuguese and the clientele belongs to the white Portuguese middle class.[46] However, unlike the Portuguese case, where there is simultaneously both a cultural and linguistic affinity due to the historical context, this entire Brazilian framework is brought to London anew, with no common references, and therefore there is no cultural bond giving meaning to this relationship between white people and black knowledge.

Such a contrast is an aspect that confounds the strong ethnic boundaries of black people in London and in a certain way makes them curious, but reserved. Furthermore, these courses above all attract people who are interested in the innovative (exotic) and hybrid aspect of black Brazilian manifestations. Thus, the *capoeira* groups and samba schools, described as representation of Afro-Brazilian culture in the city, are the bearers of these contradictions. On the one hand, it is interesting to evaluate how strong African roots and memories do subsist, despite the continuous reconstruction of culture. On the other hand, this also demonstrates the perverse historical, economic and social course that ends up defining migration routes and reinstating racial inequalities.

Final Remarks

I have attempted to provide a brief account of the dynamics and the visibility of the Afro-Brazilian aspects prevailing, and suggested two simultaneous movements in such a transnational process. On the one hand, the relocation of Brazilian culture into London tended to present the profile of a mixed country, guaranteeing 'novelty' in the field of ethnic concerns, and fostering the better commercialization of events and products. These cultural transpositions are complex as this deterritorialization opens up the space in these flows[47] for partial transpositions, often marked by commercial interests and neutralizing any underlying political statements.

However, just as the constant reinvention of these cultural expressions in the city allows for gaps, there is also the corresponding and constant updating of Afro-diaspora experiences. In these gaps, the confrontation of narratives of blackness and racial conviviality not only creates amazement and estrangement but also permits an incipient dialogue from which blackness in Brazil might profit, as it reflects upon new models of black experience. As regards the British environment of consumption and the cultural sharing experience, black culture representations articulated in this cultural imaginary in London do display the potential to reverse this loose articulation between aesthetic expression and social meaning.

[46] Clara Saraiva, 'African and Brazilian Altars in Lisbon: Some Considerations on the Reconfigurations of the Portuguese Religious Field', in *Cultures of the Lusophone Black Atlantic*, ed. by Naro, Sansi-Roca, and Treece, pp. 175–96.
[47] Appadurai, p. 194.

Courting Death in Hélia Correia's *Adoecer*

Isabel Fernandes

Universidade de Lisboa, Centro de Estudos Anglísticos

> Storytellers are Death's secretaries. It is Death who hands them the file. The file is full of sheets of uniformly black paper but they have the eyes for reading them and from this file they construct a story for the living.
>
> John Berger, 'The Secretary of Death'[1]

> Como Rossetti resgatando a dádiva de amor
> Verso a verso ao corrupto corpo
> De Elizabeth Eleanor, o escritor
> É um ladrão de túmulos...
>
> [Just like Rossetti rescuing the gift of love
> Line by line from Elizabeth Eleanor's
> Corrupted body, so the writer
> Is a robber of tombs...]
>
> Manuel António Pina, 'The House of Life'[2]

It is my purpose here to give an overview of Hélia Correia's latest novel, *Adoecer* (published in April 2010 and, to my knowledge, not yet translated into English) by concentrating on some of the aspects that characterize it as a novel that simultaneously courts death and defies it. Death is at the centre of this novel, where most characters seem to be in love with it and where the authorial narrator is intent on unearthing a love story marked by the excessive feelings of two doomed lovers, thus bringing it to light and making it relevant for the living.

It is different from all previous narrative works by the author, in that it deals with a real person about whom there is a fair amount of historical documentation.[3] We may therefore classify it as a biographical novel about Elizabeth

---

[1] In *The Sense of Sight* (London: Vintage, 1994), pp. 238–42.
[2] In *Os livros* (Lisbon: Assírio & Alvim, 2003), p. 49. In the present article all translations from Portuguese are my own.
[3] In the case of her previous novel, *Lillias Fraser* (2001), the protagonist, although based on a real person, is much more a figment of Correia's imagination, since there is not much information available and the author was not much interested in such sources. She goes as far as repudiating the idea of considering it a historical novel. Cf. her interview with Marisa Torres da Silva at: <http://static.publico.

Eleanor Siddal,[4] well known as the model for John Everett Millais's famous painting *Ophelia* (1851–52) and as Dante Gabriel Rossetti's favourite model and muse — and eventually his wife. The mystery that Correia addresses in her fiction, and invites the reader to share in, is related to the subterranean force of the inevitable attraction that linked her to Rossetti in a disturbing relationship that defied well-established Victorian social conventions and which had a tragic outcome.

From History to Fiction with a Vengeance

As in other instances of Correia's fiction, here we are faced again with a to-and-fro movement between past historical events and a fictional recreation of them by an authorial narrator deeply engaged by their significance for herself and for our own present. Totally enticed by the feminine figure at the heart of this story and deeply sympathetic with a love affair with all the necessary ingredients to engage her Brontëan predilection for lost causes, the author is somehow convinced that fiction is the only appropriate means of deciphering this mystery, of penetrating the darkness enveloping this doomed pair of lovers. According to the authorial narrator: '[o]s escritores de biografias redigem com os pulsos amarrados' [biographers write with their hands tied].[5] For her part, the writer refuses the mere accuracy of yet another biographical account and prefers to consider her work as an 'autobiography' — a fictional autobiography, one would add. As she surprisingly declared in an interview, shortly after the novel was published: '[d]e alguma maneira é a minha autobiografia' [to a certain extent it is my autobiography].[6] This statement comes from her belief that she is writing about an artist whom she felt she knew intimately ('sentia que a conhecia por dentro').[7] Correia clearly identifies closely with Lizzie (as Elizabeth Siddal was known among her acquaintances), going so far as to say: '[é] quase um alter-ego. Se tivesse vivido naquele tempo, naquelas circunstâncias, a minha história seria assim' [she is almost an alter ego. Had I lived in that period, in those circumstances, my story would be similar].[8]

Hélia Correia's work often deals with women who are characterized as being outside the conventions and expectations of their time, as somehow marginal

---

clix.pt/docs/cmf2/ficheiros/21HeliaCorreia/Apaixonei.htm> [accessed 12 August 2011].
[4] Her family name was Siddall, but it was later altered by Rossetti and his circle to Siddal, a spelling adopted by many biographers and by Correia. For consistency the latter spelling is used here.
[5] Hélia Correia, *Adoecer* (Lisbon: Relógio D'Água, 2010), p. 119 — henceforth referred to as *A*.
[6] Maria Leonor Nunes, 'Hélia Correia: Uma paixão inglesa', *Jornal de Letras, Artes e Ideias*, 24 March–6 April 2010, pp. 10–16 (p. 12).
[7] Nunes, p. 12.
[8] Ibid.

and rebellious,[9] whether they be historical figures such as Emily Brontë,[10] Florbela Espanca,[11] Lillias Fraser, and Lizzie Siddal, for instance, or fictional characters (Antigone is a case in point).[12] It is this fascination that very often determines a movement of empathy towards these characters and generates in her fictional texts the appearance of a surrogate author, acting almost as a sort of double to these figures, intent on reconstructing and/or vindicating their inner world and hidden motives. And the theme of the double, according to the author, together with that of the eternal return of passionate lovers who refuse to vanish once and for all after death, but come back to look for their counterparts even after centuries have elapsed, is the key to the mystery enveloping Rossetti's and Lizzie's lives.[13]

The most interesting feature of Correia's text is the way in which it occupies a liminal space between on the one hand historical facts (as can be found in the various biographies, letters, diaries, etc., which the author has thoroughly researched and from which she quotes extensively)[14] and on the other hand fictional and psychological conjecture (very often based on poems and other writing by the protagonists, but also on a claimed instinctive knowledge of their predicament on the author's part). These two ingredients are intertwined in a palimpsestic prose densely charged with a maze of historical allusions and historical characters, well known to all those familiar with British literary history and the Victorian period in particular, which the author cherishes.[15] Except that, a bit like José Saramago — and unlike the regular history text-book

[9] This predilection for figures with such attributes is admitted by the author: 'para mim, a única possibilidade de criação é a afirmação da diferença. As duas possibilidades de afirmação da diferença são a marginalidade ou a loucura. São os grandes temas dos meus livros' [for me the only possibility for creation is the affirmation of difference. The two possible ways of affirming difference are marginality or madness. These are the main themes of my books]. Ernesto Rodrigues, 'Hélia Correia: Insânia', in *Verso e Prosa de Novecentos* (Lisbon: Instituto Piaget, 2000), pp. 249–55 (p. 253).

[10] Correia often refers to Emily Brontë as 'my Emily' (a minha Emily) both in this very novel (*A* 27) and in interviews or when speaking in public. She even wrote the preface to a Portuguese edition of *Wuthering Heights: O Monte dos Vendavais*, trans. by Maria Franco and Cabral do Nascimento (Lisbon: Relógio D'Água, 2001).

[11] Florbela Espanca appears, for instance, in a play included in the volume *Perdição. Exercício sobre Antígona. Florbela. Teatro* (Lisbon: Publicações D. Quixote, 1991). Even though Correia's relationship to Florbela is ambiguous and not straightforwardly reverent, she succumbs nevertheless to the poet's strangeness and heterodoxy. Cf. Isabel Cristina Rodrigues, 'Florbela Mínima: Exercício sobre Hélia Correia' <http://revistas.ua.pt/index.php/formabreve/article/view/235> [accessed 8 August 2012].

[12] Antigone is the central character in the play *Perdição* (1991).

[13] 'Essa ideia do reencontro e do duplo sempre me fascinou. E essa é a chave do mistério' [the idea of re-meeting and the double has always fascinated me. And that is the key to the mystery]. Nunes, p. 12.

[14] In the 'Note' immediately following the narrative, Correia refers to some of her sources, emphasizing the contribution of Jan Marsh's works on the Pre-Raphaelites and Lucinda Hawksley's biography of Lizzie Siddal (2004) — see note 28. From her quotations it is easy for a reader familiar with the Pre-Raphaelite Brotherhood to recognize the amount of research done by the author and her familiarity with her various sources.

[15] In more than one interview she refers to her 'anglophilia'. See, for instance, Raquel Ribeiro, 'Hélia Correia é o gato da casa nesta história de amor', *Público*, 26 March 2010, section *Ípsilon*, pp. 7–11 (p. 8), also at <http://ipsilon.publico.pt/livros/entrevista.aspx?id=253200> [accessed 20 November 2012] and Ana Raquel Fernandes, 'Interview with Hélia Correia', *Anglo-Saxonica: Revista do Centro de Estudos Anglísticos da Universidade de Lisboa*, 25 (2007), 259–74 (p. 264).

— 'Hélia embrenha-se em digressões biográficas minuciosas e nem sempre compreensíveis' [Hélia plunges into minute biographical digressions not always easy to understand].[16] Such great and diverse names as Darwin, Ruskin, Marx, Engels, Turner, Queen Victoria, Walter Scott, Lord Byron and Mary Shelley, to mention but a few, are here juxtaposed and put on a level with less dignified and more obscure characters such as James Greenacre, a murderer who lived next to Lizzie's parental home and was hanged when she was eight years old. This taste for the lurid detail, recognizable as one of Correia's characteristic features,[17] is joined with an evocation of the social and material conditions of the lives of Londoners in the second half of the nineteenth century. Thus the reader becomes immersed in the smells, noises and generally insalubrious atmosphere of the Victorian period, in a way slightly reminiscent of Dickens's universe. This contextual dispersion also serves to tone down the impact of a sickly and passionate love affair whose indomitable strength has behind it the compulsion of a predestined fate, threatening to disrupt the surface of the text.[18] On the other hand, the physical context echoes metaphorically the idea of illness that dominates the novel, from the title to the choice of its female human figure, so that the environment itself is seen as sickly: London streets are insalubrious, for instance, and the Thames is seen as pestilent.[19]

But there are other factors that justify the choice of fiction to address the mystery inherent in the lives of this pair of lovers, and it has to do with the way in which their lives and their relationship were so entirely seen through the distorting lens of literary texts and literary characters, which gave them a mythical dimension. For Rossetti, immersed as he was in literature from early childhood, Lizzie was perceived as reliving the tragic destiny of Dante's Beatrice. Casting her in the role of Beatrice, moreover, was a way of building himself as the great Italian poet's alter ego and rewriting his magnum opus through an existential re-enactment. Therefore he saw her not as she actually was, but as he imagined her or wished her to be. His sister, Christina Rossetti, in one of her poems (first published in 1856), recognizes this mental projection on her brother's part:

> Not wan with waiting, not with sorrow dim;
> Not as she is, but was when hope shone bright;
> Not as she is, but as she fills his dream.[20]

---

[16] Pedro Mexia 'Vitorianos Eminentes', *Público*, 26 March 2010, section *Ípsilon*, p. 41, also available at <http://ipsilon.publico.pt/livros/critica.aspx?id=253213> [accessed 10 April 2010].
[17] I have in mind here her taste for allusions to the violently physical, the telluric, the bodily functions, and the repulsive, often verging on the grotesque, which resurfaces time and time again in her work in general, as recognized by some critics.
[18] On the striking balance achieved between formal contention and the intensity of the feelings depicted in the novel, see Isabel Fernandes's review essay 'Adoecer de Hélia Correia ou um "conhecimento por dentro"', *Colóquio/Letras: Revista Quadrimensal*, 175 (2010), 145-55 (pp. 150-51).
[19] For a brief discussion of the use of illness as a metaphor in the novel, see Fernandes, p. 152.
[20] Christina Rossetti, 'In an Artist's Studio', in *An Anthology of Pre-Raphaelite Writings*, ed. by Carolyn Hares-Stryker (Sheffield: Sheffield Academic Press, 1997), p. 365.

Besides being unable to see her as the living woman that she was, he preferred to see her rather as the potential dead lover. As Correia puts it:

> Ele não queria Lizzie entre os humanos, não a queria com carne de mortal. [...] Gabriel prendera-a em folhas de desenho como quem prega alfinetes em borboletas. Mas ela continuava a agitar-se, incomodando. Já esquecera o seu papel. (A 277)

> [He did not want Lizzie among the living, did not want her with mortal flesh. [...] Gabriel had pinned her to sheets of drawing paper, as one pins down butterflies. But she kept on squirming, disturbingly. She had already forgotten her role.]

Her resistance notwithstanding, however, both in terms of the type of beauty that she exhibits and the illness she experiences — two things that go together in the novel as they did in the corresponding historical period — Lizzie lends herself to a personification of the Romantic feminine ideal of the Pre-Raphaelites:

> O ideal feminino dos românticos, que Lizzie encarnou sem qualquer esforço, devia muito às chaminés mal ventiladas das lareiras dos quartos, aos espartilhos, a pesadas toxinas do ambiente [...]. Estava a adoecer com elegância, e o seu talento para a passividade construía uma imagem sedutora, a de alguém que se inclina para o chão, da folha que se deita para o Outono. (A 105–06)

> [The feminine ideal of the Romantics that Lizzie personified without any effort owed a lot to ill-ventilated chimneys in bedroom fireplaces, to corsets, to a heavily toxic environment [...]. She was wasting away with elegance, and her talent for passivity was building a seductive image, the image of someone who stoops to the ground, of the leaf that lays down for the autumn.]

The effect of this contamination, of the cultural atmosphere and of the material conditions of life, turns Lizzie (both the person that she was and the character that Hélia Correia recreates for us) into a literary figment of the period's imagination.

So one could discern here a triple movement: from the historicity of biographical facts Correia salvages Lizzie and turns her into the fictional character that she and those around her had built, especially Gabriel, but, by informing this fiction with the intimacy of a long-standing subliminal knowledge of shared motives and predispositions, she accurately diagnoses her case and gives it in turn the truth and poignancy of a *true* autobiography. By reliving for us Lizzie's life story, by means of narrative strategies and devices, Correia is able to rightly diagnose a case that, at the time, left doctors puzzled.

The Art of Dying

The exploration of the importance of feminine images of illness and death for *fin-de-siècle* culture has been the subject of several books, such as Elizabeth Bronfen's *Over her Dead Body: Death, Femininity and the Aesthetic*,[21] and Bram Dijkstra's *Idols of Perversity: Fantasies of Feminine Evil in Fin-de-siècle Culture*.[22] In both books the Pre-Raphaelites figure as a case in point. In Bronfen's work the relationship between Lizzie and Rossetti is itself taken literally as a 'Case Study' that illustrates the chapter entitled *'Noli me videri'* which addresses the problem of women's (in)visibility in suicide. Dijkstra's work, on the other hand, describes how the image of the female invalid emerges and becomes a pervasive icon in late nineteenth-century culture:

> Throughout the second half of the nineteenth century, parents, sisters, daughters, and loving friends were kept busy on canvases everywhere, anxiously nursing wan, hollow-eyed beauties who were on the verge of death. For many a Victorian husband his wife's physical weakness came to be evidence to the world and to God of her physical and mental purity [...].[23]

This cult of invalidism and death is closely linked to women's dependency on their male counterparts and to their passive role in Victorian society. It is also considered a sign of docility, purity and childlike vulnerability, conveniently placing women in a subaltern position.

Moreover it gave rise to a morbid and erotic fascination on the artists' part for the 'consumptive sublime', characterized by images of slightly under-developed women, marked by pallor, in languid and recumbent attitudes, and suggestive of decline or impending death.[24] However, this victimization of women, seen as passive objects, was not the exclusive choice of male artists since 'many of the fine women painters of the period were as adept at depicting "the sensuously dead heroine" as their male colleagues'.[25] And moreover, and more importantly, as Dijkstra has justly pointed out: 'women attempted to transform their passive position in this society as manipulated objects into the illusion of an active participation in their domination through a supposedly self-elected ideal of physical invalidism and consumptive fragility'.[26]

It is remarkable how this ideal and the attendant ideology seem to have entered the life of Elizabeth Siddal. According to Correia, posing as the dying Ophelia for Millais in the early 1850s somehow seemed to determine her fate

---

[21] Elizabeth Bronfen, *Over her Dead Body: Death, Femininity and the Aesthetic* (Manchester: Manchester University Press, 1992).
[22] Bram Dijkstra, *Idols of Perversity: Fantasies of Feminine Evil in Fin-de-siècle Culture* (Oxford and New York: Oxford University Press, 1986).
[23] Dijkstra, p. 25.
[24] Dijkstra, p. 29.
[25] Dijkstra, p. 58.
[26] Dijkstra, p. 53.

and predispose her to tragedy. As the authorial narrator recognizes:

> [q]ualquer coisa de Ofélia se alojara definitivamente no seu corpo, essa tristeza de uma personagem que nasce com a única função de comover as audiências e ajudá-las a ver na morte um corolário da beleza. (A 72)
>
> [something of Ophelia had got permanently lodged in her body: that sadness of a character who is born with the sole function of moving audiences and helping them recognize death as a corollary of beauty.]

The Pre-Raphaelites' attraction to death, and for dying women in particular, somehow determined Lizzie's adoption of a stance of invalidism throughout her life, something that she must have felt to be in accordance with the group's expectations and its aesthetic predilections.

The actual state of Lizzie's health has been a matter of debate and it remains to a certain extent enigmatic.[27] While addicted to laudanum, at least in the final stages of her life, her illness seems nevertheless to have been much more of the heart (and determined also by her love of art) than of the body.[28] The author of the novel has no great doubts about this:

> [e]ssa doença que intrigou os médicos, levando-os à suspeita de tratar-se de um fenómeno de auto-indução e acabou, no entanto, por matá-la, chamou-se Dante Gabriel Rossetti (A 72).
>
> [that illness that puzzled the doctors, making them suspect they were dealing with a case of self-induction, but which, however, ended up by killing her, was called Dante Gabriel Rossetti.]

Bronfen's opinion converges with this, when she hypothesizes: 'She may have staged her life as a prolonged illness, always short of impending death, to gain Rossetti's attention, otherwise diverted by his own amorous fickleness'.[29]

As is apparent from many of Rossetti's poems, the recurrent theme of the dead beloved woman suggests the extent to which his poetic imagination was obsessed with and erotically drawn to this image, even before he had met Lizzie.[30] No wonder then that by envisioning their meeting as a repetition of past encounters he would conceive of her as his dead Beatrice: the theme of the double introduces a disturbing necrophilia into the universe of both paintings and poems, and inevitably had implications in their relationship. I refer in particular to the poem 'Sudden Light' and to the drawing *How They*

---

[27] See, for instance, the chapter on E. Siddal's life, entitled 'Lizzie's Mysterious Illness', in Lucinda Hawksley, *Lizzie Siddal: The Tragedy of a Pre-Raphaelite Supermodel*, 2nd edn (London: André Deutsch, 2008), pp. 69–93.

[28] The love of art is seen in the novel as literally another type of illness (Cf. A 49).

[29] Bronfen, pp. 171–72.

[30] 'Dante Gabriel Rossetti was only 18 when he wrote "The Blessed Damozel" in 1847, well before he met Lizzie. The poem went through many subsequent revisions, and it was not until 1871 that Rossetti began to work on a visual rendering of the poem.' See Hae-in Kim, 'The Spiritual Depths of the Feminine Soul in Rossetti's "The Blessed Damozel"', in *Syllabus for English / History of Art 151: Pre-Raphaelites, Aesthetes, and Decadents* (Brown University, 2004), available at <http://www.victorianweb.org/authors/dgr/hikim5.html> [accessed 6 September 2011].

Met Themselves, also known as *Bogie drawing*,[31] which significantly occupies one of the few sections of Correia's novel staged in our own time. It registers the impact on the authorial narrator of being able to see the drawing and to touch one manuscript page of the actual volume confided by a remorseful Rossetti to the corpse of Elizabeth Siddal: the drawing and manuscript are both held at the Fitzwilliam Museum, in Cambridge, which Correia visited in 2005. Rossetti's lines are unequivocal, and are somehow even more disturbingly echoed by the drawing, where instead of a renewal of 'delight' the feminine figure of 'reality' (as opposed to the spectral doubles facing her and her lover) faints as she realizes the uncanny and ominous nature of their encounter:

> I have been here before,
> But when or how I cannot tell:
> I know the grass beyond the door,
> The sweet keen smell,
> The sighing sound, the lights around the shore.
> You have been mine before —
> How long ago I may not know:
> But just when at that swallow's soar
> Your neck turned so,
> Some veil did fall, — I knew it all of yore.
> Has this been thus before?
> And shall not thus time's eddying flight
> Still with our lives our love restore
> In death's despite,
> And day and night yield one delight once more?[32]

In the fictional universe created by Hélia Correia, this mythical compound of literary and metapsychological elements gave rise to what we could call a choreography of death, appropriately marking the rhythms of the narrative: alternate moments of withdrawal and reunion between the lovers, where the magnetic attraction exerted by Lizzie's failing health or impending death would inexorably draw Rossetti to her side, after periods of unfaithful wanderings on his part. The novel stages the impulses that determine these successive movements and structurally takes advantage of their juxtaposition, as in the following passage:

> O chamamento da cidade agia como um atenuar de circunstâncias e Gabriel procurava os grandes ventos de Newcastle em Londres. [...] Lizzie acompanhava-o, enfrentando os temporais para visitar as Howitt, e via-o desprender-se devagar, como um batel que puxa pelas amarras. Ele queria duas vidas separadas, uma com Lizzie, no pequeno mundo ao qual presença alguma era bem vinda, e outra sem ela, entre os homens, no exterior. E ela, que detestava o tempo quente e se entusiasmava com as chuvas, começou nesse Outono a adoecer. (*A* 105)

---

[31] This is a pen-and-ink and brush drawing begun by Rossetti in 1851 and finished during their honeymoon in Paris in 1860.
[32] Hares-Stryker, p. 225.

[The call of the town acted like attenuating circumstances and Gabriel would look for the strong winds of Newcastle in London. [...] Lizzie would accompany him, facing storms, to visit the Howitts, and she witnessed his slow withdrawal like a skiff pulling at its mooring. He wanted two separate lives, one with Lizzie, in the small world where no other presence was welcome, and another without her, among men, outside. And she, who hated warm weather and was thrilled by the rains, that autumn gradually started to fall ill.]

The need on Gabriel's part to break away from her and affirm his masculine independence in the outside world in turn determines in Lizzie a waning health that she 'knows' will draw Rossetti back to her side. These moments of reunion have a restorative or invigorating effect on both partners. As Bronfen rightly signalled: 'they repeatedly enacted a deanimation of the feminine body as engendering an animation of the artist, a production of images and poems, resurrecting the deanimated body as source and theme of these representations'.[33]

Creative as it might have been, in the long term this dynamic, extensively explored in the text, had an exhausting effect both on their relationship (torn by conflicting impulses and intense feelings of possessiveness, betrayal, deprivation and guilt) and on Lizzie's body. And there was no way out of this vicious circle, except death. The reader is faced with this realization in the final stages of the novel, even though the fatal outcome has been anticipated from the outset of the text:

> Lizzie sabia o quanto Gabriel dependia do seu bem-estar para viver sem ela. Fora-lhe dado um único poder que era o de afectar. Era o poder dos grandes suicidas. Ele acorria a um aceno mais convulso, à notícia de lágrimas. Não queria que ela determinasse o seu caminho, procurava afastá-la como a um vício de cujos prejuízos dava conta. Mas o espaço que Lizzie ocupava estava por todo o lado e dentro dele. (*A* 219)

> [Lizzie knew how Gabriel depended on her wellbeing for living apart from her. A sole power had been granted her, the power of affecting him. It was the power of great suicides. He would run to assist her if she waved her hand more convulsively, if the news of tears reached him. He did not want her to determine his path; he tried to keep her at bay as though she were an addiction, of whose pernicious effects he was aware. But the space occupied by Lizzie was pervasive and it was inside him.]

Out of place in this world, Lizzie is slowly drawn to progressive physical decline and gradually more extreme signs of failing health, until she is left with no further resource but to die. Her apparently self-inflicted death, due to an overdose of laudanum, is the end of this self-destructive path.

What the legend had told us, and which the novelist's imagination confirms, thus comes as no surprise: that immediately after Lizzie's death, and before

---

[33] Bronfen, p. 177.

calling in the undertakers, Rossetti allegedly painted her dead face in what is now known as *Beata Beatrix*. An apt epigraph for this painting would be Sylvia Plath's lines:

> The woman is perfected.
> Her dead
> Body wears the smile of accomplishment.[34]

Death, Doubles and Liminal Spaces

Inhabiting a liminal space between life and death during most of her lifetime, Lizzie's character plays out the role of an Ophelia: 'Ela condensa todo o devastamento do amor, a vocação do feminino para a perda, o erotismo sacrificial' [She epitomizes all love's devastation, the feminine vocation for loss, for sacrificial eroticism] (*A* 200).

In this novel, the authorial narrator, as the double of her female character, also moves in the interstitial space between life and death, the living and the dead, the present and the past.[35] As in other works by Correia, notably *A casa eterna*,[36] the writer is intent on bridging these gaps by creating a character (in the present case, an authorial narrator) who follows closely in the footsteps of her chosen figure, 'breathing [her] air, visiting the places where [her] physical presence would have walked', so as better to be with her and recreate the 'spirit of place' inherent in her life.[37] The writer figure that appears in the opening section, entitled 'Highgate Cemetery, 2005', presents herself as a go-between, wishing to establish an exchange between the living and the dead, to abolish the convenient space separating the two realms. But in her labour of reconstructing Siddal's life she is also — and somewhat ironically — duplicating the sacrilegious gesture of another Portuguese, Charles Augustus Howell, who, in 1869, seven years after Lizzie's death, exhumed her coffin to recover the manuscript of poems that Rossetti had impulsively hidden in his lover's auburn hair. Likewise Correia, not content with the superficial facts of biography, plunges imaginatively into the inner lives and secret motivations of these long-dead historical figures, intent on finding a hidden pattern both in

---

[34] Sylvia Plath, 'Edge', in *Selected Poems*, ed. by Ted Hughes (London and Boston: Faber & Faber, 1985), p. 85.
[35] This characteristic movement on the surrogate author's part has also been acknowledged by Isabel Capeloa Gil in her essay on Correia's play, *Perdição*, where she qualifies Tiresias as the author's surrogate and a mediator across borders, in between the mythic past and the present of history, the living and the dead, etc. Cf. Gil 'Espectros Literários: *Perdição* de Hélia Correia', in *Furor: Ensaios sobre a obra dramática de Hélia Correia*, ed. by Maria de Fátima Sousa e Silva (Coimbra: Imprensa da Universidade de Coimbra, 2006), pp. 61–76 (p. 65).
[36] Hélia Correia, *A casa eterna* (Lisbon: Publicações D. Quixote, 1991).
[37] I am adapting this quotation from a passage on *A casa eterna* in: 'Giving up Whose Ghost in the Works of Hélia Correia?', in Hilary Owen and Cláudia Pazos Alonso, *Antigone's Daughters? Gender, Genealogy, and the Politics of Authorship in 20th-Century Portuguese Women's Writing* (Lewisburg, PA: Bucknell University Press, 2011), pp. 158–77 (p. 161).

the psychological depths of her characters' inner lives and in their path through life, a path evocative both of previous and of later passionate lovers. In order to 'tocar no coração desta história' [touch the heart of this story], she chooses to 'ouvir a voz' [listen to the voice], to give voice to the unsaid, because, as Ribeiro puts it, '[s]ão muitos não-ditos. E são não-ditos porque nem sequer há palavras para os dizer' [there are many things unsaid. And they are unsaid because there are not even words to say them].[38] Again she is exploring a threshold space between consciousness and language, on the one side, and the unconscious and the unsaid, on the other. The idea of the novelist as a listener and recorder of voices/languages, both audible and inaudible, underlies Correia's entire work, where intonation, prosody, patterns of sound and rhythm are paramount, giving this novel a markedly polyphonic character.[39]

The ironic doubling strategy consisting of juxtaposing the figure of the authorial narrator with that of Charles Augustus Howell (obliquely evoking the idea of the author as Lizzie's double), which is explored in the first two sections of the novel, is just one of a series of doubling gestures pointing to similarities and dissimilarities between characters, spaces and groups, but mostly determined by the guiding aim of having from the start intimations of death and of the tragedy that will follow. The third section, for instance, 'Hatton Garden, Holborn, London, 1833' introduces Lizzie's family background, but at the same time alludes to certain elements in the Rossetti household which hint at a predisposition to decay, suicidal tendencies, and the attraction of the dangerous and the unruly — features which are shared by the two groups and thus prepare the encounter of the two doomed lovers. Another example occurs in the section 'Red Lion Square, 1850', addressing the theme of the female painter's model in Victorian England, and where Lizzie's refusal to abide by the pervasive rules in the artistic milieu of the period is contrasted to the much more pragmatic if morally questionable attitude of that other Pre-Raphaelite model, Annie Miller, much to Lizzie's disadvantage in the long run.

Gestures of duplication are, after all, of the essence in a novel dealing centrally with doubles, a novel that duplicates the past in search of meaningful moments of revelation for those living in the present. Not content, however, with replicating the past, it reinvents it, conferring upon it the hues and depths of a fictional dimension capable of recreating history, and making sense of and redeeming rebellious gestures and iconoclastic attitudes for our own neo-Victorian and preordained social order.

Hélia Correia is addressing, questioning and moving beyond the established categories of past and present, good and evil, conscious and unconscious, life and death, as well as simultaneously suggesting their provisional nature and

---

[38] Ribeiro, p. 8.
[39] Even her prose is determined by a surprisingly regular prosody, lending itself to scansion. This happens, for instance, in the first paragraph of the novel, made up of thirteen lines of ten syllables each; many other similar examples can be found throughout the text.

artificial boundaries. And through her deep understanding of the two figures at the heart of her novel, she invites us to attune ourselves to the pulsating rhythm of their passion that verges on death.

The Novels of Valter Hugo Mãe

Carlos Nogueira

Universidade Nova de Lisboa

The poet, novelist, columnist and author of books for children and young people, Valter Hugo Mãe (born Saurimo, Angola, 1971) is one of the most important writers on the contemporary Portuguese literary scene. However, his work, while read both in Portugal and abroad and recognized by specialist criticism, is insufficiently studied; rich and complex, it calls for an overarching examination. In this article we are concerned with his fiction published to date: *O nosso reino* (2004), *O remorso de Baltazar Serapião* (2006), *O apocalipse dos trabalhadores* (2008), *A máquina de fazer espanhóis* (2010), and *O filho de mil homens* (2011).

In his novels Valter Hugo Mãe presents us with characters in extreme situations who have in common an intense relationship with love — in the various acceptances of the word. But while in the first three books the search for love is overwhelmingly tragic, in the latter two we find a celebration of life through love, after tough challenges without which it would not be so well deserved and intensely enjoyed. In *A máquina de fazer espanhóis* António Jorge da Silva, despite the anguish from which he never frees himself, learns to live with the death of his wife. In the cemetery, now more tranquil and rational, he confesses that 'o pior ainda é ter de a ver nessa imagem oval, encolhida aí nessa fotografia cravada na mármore. chegar aqui e vê-la reduzida a esse ponto, uma coisa tão pequena para quem explodia nos lugares como uma aparição' [the worst thing is having to see her in that oval picture, huddled there in that photograph set in the marble. coming here and seeing her so diminished, reduced to something so small for one who used to erupt into places, like an apparition].[1] In *O filho de mil homens*, as in no other work, there is an 'epiphany of love', and the celebration of the non-standard family.[2] The invention of a family united by love takes as its starting point a man, Crisóstomo, who takes his wife to be the centre of creation and the human world. In a long passage that is one of the most intensely lyrical in all of Valter Hugo Mãe's work, the narrator starts by telling us that Crisóstomo, contrary to the common tendency to exalt man, 'pensava que o corpo dos homens estava condenado a uma tristeza maior, como se fosse o corpo fraco da humanidade, o corpo menor. O corpo

---

[1] Valter Hugo Mãe, *A máquina de fazer espanhóis* (Carnaxide: Editora Objectiva, 2010), p. 232.
[2] Miguel Real, 'A epifania do amor', *JL — Jornal de Letras, Artes e Ideias*, 1070, 5 October 2011, p. 13.

triste' [thought that a man's body was condemned to a greater unhappiness, as if it were the weak body of humanity, the lesser body. The sad body].[3] Human plenitude exists in women, whom Crisóstomo 'sonhava que haviam de ser perfeitas [...] por serem escolhidas para a maternidade, a construírem pessoas dentro de si [dreamed that they must be perfect [...] because they were chosen for motherhood, to create people inside themselves].[4] Crisóstomo's thinking is, in a surreal way, both intuitive and subjective, free and omnipotent, magic and oneiric:

> O Crisóstomo pensava que a construção acontecia como no mar profundo e que as mulheres eram profundas e os filhos seres de água. Ele sonhava que sob o barco vogavam na água escura da noite milhões de filhos enroscados sobre si mesmos à espera do milagre do chamamento das mulheres. Sonhava que os peixes passavam pelos filhos e os adoravam como deuses, não entendendo que eram apenas gente.[5]
>
> [Crisóstomo thought that their construction took place as if in the deep sea, and that women were deep and their children beings of water. He dreamt that under the boat there were drifting in the dark waters of the night millions of children curled up and waiting for the miracle of the women's call. He dreamt that the fish swam past the children and worshipped them as gods, not understanding that they were simply people.]

His novels give an impression of imminent desolation and disintegration, and a coexistence of love and hate which, with the exception of *O filho de mil homens*, persists to the end. That sensation, very obvious in his early novels, is relatively attenuated in *O apocalipse dos trabalhadores* and *A máquina de fazer espanhóis*, but only in *O filho de mil homens* is there an real overcoming of it through love. In this novel there is an individual and broader movement toward resolving conflicts that is consumed in spiritual fulfilment and a celebration of life. To be aware of the suffering experienced is essential to this process of spiritual enrichment and human growth. Crisóstomo, 'the fisherman' who 'crescia para ser homem tremendo' [grew up to be a fine man], as the narrator defines him, well understands the significance of the learning process that love brings.

In his other novels — with the exception of Quitéria, in *O apocalipse dos trabalhadores*, who could live happily with a Ukrainian man — love results in unhappiness and tragedy. The protagonist and narrator of *O remorso de Baltazar Serapião* feels a powerful love for his beautiful and devoted wife, but that does not stop him from subjecting her to constant and violent physical punishments that disfigure her. At the end of the novel, when Ermesinda is raped over several nights by a brother and a friend of Baltazar (who does nothing to prevent it), and she dies, he notes: 'e a minha ermesinda mais se tentou debater e mais lhe custava a respirar, mais eles se afligiam para controlá-la para, mais que não

---

[3] Valter Hugo Mãe, *O filho de mil homens* (Carnaxide: Editora Objectiva, 2011), p. 228.
[4] Ibid.
[5] Ibid.

fosse, voltarem aos seus lugares e esperarem que se acalmassem, as duas, ela e a vaca' [and the more my ermesinda tried to fight back and the more she struggled to breathe, the more concerned they were to control her if only so that they could get back to their places and wait for the two of them to calm down, her and the cow].[6]

The characters in the other novels do not react to adversity the way Crisóstomo does. They all have their worries, but they seem to accept that they are irredeemably condemned to bad luck, suffering and unhappiness. In *O nosso reino*, ideas of finality, despair and death haunt Benjamin and all the community to which he belongs, and the same can be said of Baltazar and his family, who are victims of an unjust society, an obscurantist religiosity, and various kinds of prejudice. The two cleaning women and the Ukrainian in *O apocalipse dos trabalhadores* live in a different society, but they too find themselves deprived of their freedom in a social context that is, for the most part, unequal and discriminatory. But the novel does not just highlight the Portuguese context. By following the young Ukrainian in Portugal who is fleeing the tragic effects of Soviet communism and also his family back in the Ukraine, where 'esconde-se [...] o reino da exploração dos trabalhadores ucranianos' [the exploitative world of Ukrainian workers is hidden], he shows a wider picture. In western Europe they can earn some money and avoid penury, but they encounter a 'nova exploração económica' [new economic exploitation].[7]

The realities of control, caused by ideology and social and religious structures, are sometimes so pronounced that they imply the complete annulment of the person who has to submit to another's power. Ermesinda, in *O remorso de Baltazar Serapião*, gives herself up wholly to Baltazar, who loves her, but at the same time assaults her physically, in the most brutal manner. Confronted by her husband's power, there is nothing left to her but silence and physical and spiritual suffering. In this novel, the feudal lord, his wife, and the king deprive Baltazar and his family of any rights, and prevent them from reconstituting themselves in freedom; they impose on them an arbitrary power and terror that traps them in a constant fear of death.

O remorso de Baltazar Serapião is a novel about love and death that is not restricted to a matter situated in space and time, to be resolved by way of its ideological and cultural implications. The reader faces the problem of male violence as proper to the Middle Ages, kings and feudal lords, but also understands its contemporary relevance and social ambit. In Baltazar, who treats Ermesinda with both tenderness and brutality, is concentrated a whole culture of the subordination and exploitation of women.

In his three most recent novels, the relationship between those who hold power and those who have to submit is not predetermined or rigid. Socio-

---

[6] Valter Hugo Mãe, *O remorso de Baltazar Serapião* (Matosinhos: QuidNovi, 2007), p. 174.
[7] Miguel Real, '"Sem tecto, entre ruínas"', *JL — Jornal de Letras, Artes e Ideias*, 1026, 27 January 2010, p. 10.

cultural and economic conditions, along with the biological condition of man as a being who grows old, create rich and poor, strong and weak, but they do not deprive the less favoured of all sovereignty. The problem of interpersonal relations is very different. Maria da Graça, the cleaning woman in *O apocalipse dos trabalhadores*, is not locked into a fixed social transaction with her employer, as Ermesinda is with her feudal lord, whose wishes she must obey. Maria da Graça can, despite everything, make choices, react, change her life.

In discussing these relations of power we should also consider the question of old age. António Jorge da Silva and all the other residents of the old people's home in *A máquina de fazer espanhóis* have largely lost their self-determination; they are excluded from a socio-economic and moral system that privileges youth, and the so-called active life, grounded in services, production, and the exchange of material goods. There is a sense of social and metaphysical orphanhood, a heightened awareness of the tragic nature of life, and of physical and mental degradation which António Jorge da Silva comments on, without euphemisms:

> passamos a ser cidadãos terrivelmente antipáticos, mesmo que façamos uma gestão inteligente desse desprezo que alimentamos crescendo. e só não nos tornamos perigosos porque envelhecer é tornarmo-nos vulneráveis e nada valentes, pelo que enlouquecemos um bocado e somos só como feras muito grandes sem ossos, metidas dentro de sacos de pele imprestáveis que já não servem para nos impor verticalidade nem nas mais pequenas batalhas.[8]

> [we turn into terribly unpleasant citizens, even if we take an intelligent approach to the disdain that we increasingly nurture. and if we don't become dangerous it's because to grow old is to become vulnerable and not at all brave, so we go a bit crazy and we are just like great wild beasts with no bones, stuck inside sacks of useless skin that are no use to keep us upright even in the smallest battles.]

The concept of death and its concrete form, which occurs suddenly or at the end of a long process of suffering, is, in Valter Hugo Mãe, a cause for anxiety and terror, but it also constitutes a space for freedom and the prolongation of an ambiguous notion of love. Maria da Graça surrenders to death by leaping off the building where she lives, 'porque o amor não cabia quieto no espaço tão pequeno que era o corpo de uma mulher' [because love didn't fit so easily in such a small space as the body of a woman].[9]

The conflicted consciousness, torn by the totalitarian force of the other (a person, a social or moral system), manages to overcome it by way of insults, curses, or satire. In Maria, melancholy, suffering and a desire to die for love alternate with moments of rage and satirical humour. When faced with her anguish at the death of Senhor Ferreira, with solitude, and with the disdain

---

[8] *A máquina de fazer espanhóis*, p. 28.
[9] Valter Hugo Mãe, *O apocalipse dos trabalhadores* (Matosinhos: QuidNovi, 2008), p. 182.

of the police officer, she unleashes a curse of her own creation. Her outburst imagines intentions whose symbolic and curative value lies in its aesthetic of violence and punishment (justified, and therefore just, in the eyes of the speaker):

> [...] desejando honestamente que a agente Quental pagasse por ser desumana. queria que ela sofresse, ficasse sem pernas, descabelada, que fosse esfolada, lhe arrancassem os dedos, abrissem cortes no peito, furassem os olhos, secassem o sangue com morcegos muito pequeninos, lhe chamassem puta, lhe metessem muitas agulhas sob as unhas dos pés e a deixassem de boca fechada no fundo de um poço escuro onde vivessem organismos esdrúxulos dentados e esfaimados. (86)

> [honestly wanting that the policewoman, Quental, should pay for her inhumanity. she wanted her to suffer, to lose her legs, to go bald, to be flayed, have her fingers torn off, be slashed in the chest, have her eyes gouged out, have her blood sucked by tiny bats, be called a whore, have needles stuck under her toenails and be left gagged at the bottom of a dark well where fantastic famished sharp-toothed beings lived.]

Distressed by the absurd death of his wife, feeling forgotten by his daughter and by society, the protagonist of *A máquina de fazer espanóis* also takes refuge in violent sarcasm and in tears. Bitterness and sadness turn into hatred and satire against others and against life. This rebellion and imprecation do not arise from mere resentments or from a passing exhaustion. In agony, but quite lucid, António Jorge da Silva analyses himself and confesses to feelings that are generally hidden or repressed:

> fica-se muito zangado como pessoa. não se criem dúvidas acerca disso. fica-se zangado e deseja-se aos outros pouco bem, e o mal que lhes pode acontecer é-nos indiferente ou, mais sinceramente, até nos reconforta, isso sim, como um abraço de embalo, para que não se ponham por aí a arder como o sol e, sobretudo, não nos falem com uma alegriazinha ingénua, de tempo contado, e nos façam perceber o quanto éramos também ingénuos e nunca nos preparámos para a derrocada de todas as coisas.[10]

> [he gets quite angry as a person. there is no doubt about that. he gets angry and has little good will for others, and the harm they can come to is of no concern to us, or to be frank, it even comforts us, yes really, like a soothing cuddle, so they don't put themselves there to burn like the sun and, above all, they don't talk to us with a naive, hurried cheerfulness, and make us understand how much we were ingenuous too and never prepared ourselves for a defeat on all fronts.]

Old age comes as a brutal and sudden experience, of being deprived of basic rights (identity, autonomy, freedom of choice): 'A Laura morreu, pegaram em mim e puseram-me no lar com dois sacos de roupa e um álbum de fotografias' [Laura died, they seized me and put me in an old people's home with two bags

---

[10] *A máquina de fazer espanhóis*, p. 28.

of clothes and a photo-album].[11] The very evening he arrived at the home, they took away his album, arguing that it would only 'cultivasse a dor de perder a minha mulher' [heighten the pain of losing my wife], and they put in his room an image of our Lady of Fatima (a religious symbol which, along with Christianity in general, is to be the object of subversion throughout the novel). António Jorge da Silva reacts violently, unable to accept his new situation of marginality, the artificial transition between life and death, and above all the hypocrisy and aloofness of others:

> que se fodam os discursos de falsa preocupação dessa gente que sorri diante de nós mas que pensa que é assim mesmo, afinal, estamos velhos e temos de morrer, um primeiro e o outro depois e está tudo muito bem. sorriem, umas palmadinhas nas costas, devagar que é velhinho, e depois vão-se embora para casa a esquecerem as coisas mais aborrecidas dos dias.[12]

> [fuck them and their expressions of false concern, these people who smile at us but think that's the way it is, we're old and we have to die, first one then the other and that's just fine. they smile, a few pats on the back, gently because he's an old man, and then they go off home to forget the most annoying parts of the day.]

Sex and Sexuality

Sex as a physiological drive and a manifestation of power is another major theme explored in the novels of Valter Hugo Mãe. *O remorso de Baltazar Serapião* addresses, like none other of his books, sex that wells up as an uncontrollable force and takes the form of a devouring energy that takes no account of the physical or emotional needs of the woman. The moral and social implications of sex are also weighed up in his work. Benjamin, the protagonist of *O nosso reino*, tells us that his mother not only censures the anti-social behaviour of his sister but also has expectations about what she ought to do: 'a irmã em actos sexuais, sem a bênção do casamento, sem a comunhão da igreja, de onde viria aquele mal. e supostamente teriam de casar-se, remediar o que haviam feito para provarem a deus o amor e o respeito pelas carnes um do outro' [his sister having sexual relations, without the sanction of marriage, or the involvement of the church, what's to blame for that. and supposedly they would have to get married, put right what they've done to prove to god the love and respect for one another's flesh].[13]

In Valter Hugo Mãe's first two novels society is regulated by a strict religious code that has a lot in common with medieval Christianity. In *O remorso de Baltazar Serapião* this religious thinking determines every action of the characters. The woman is not only imperfect and impure and therefore obliged

---

[11] Ibid. p. 29.
[12] Ibid, p. 29.
[13] Valter Hugo Mãe, *O nosso reino*, 2nd edn (Matosinhos: QuidNovi, 2009), p. 52.

to remain in the home practically as a slave; she is also the source of evil and perdition for her husband, unless he knows how to protect himself. Only the woman who imitates the model of the Virgin Mary (as mother, protector, saviour) can aspire to a life without sin. Man and woman cannot be joined except by a marriage approved by the community, which demands proof of the woman's purity: 'e o lençol sujou-se de sangue e assim o apresentámos aos meus pais para que surdamente se espalhasse o orgulho de toda a família' [the sheet was stained with blood and we presented it like that to my parents so that the pride of the whole family could be silently shared around].[14]

Feminine sexuality outside marriage is repressed, and the woman who falls into lust, like Teresa Diaba in *O remorso de Baltazar Serapião*, is reduced to a sub-human or animal condition: '[...] era como um animal que fizesse lembrar uma mulher, servia assim como melhoria de uma vez que tivéssemos de fazer com a mão' [she was like an animal that resembled a woman, she was an improvement on the time we had to do it with our hand].[15] In a cultural environment in which the man determines the forms that love and sexuality take, only male sexuality and desire are valued and understood: 'disse à minha ermesinda que se estendesse nua na cama. que eu a queria ver à luz da vela, muito próxima de cada pedaço da sua pele. ela pareceu acalmar quando lhe pus a mão suave no contorno da anca' [I told my ermesinda to stretch out naked on the bed. that I wanted to see her by the light of the candle, very close to every scrap of her skin. she seemed to calm down when I put my smooth hand on the curve of her hip].[16]

For those who will not integrate into this one type of pairing there is no salvation. In *O nosso reino*, Benjamin, who believes he was born of an adulterous relationship on the part of his mother, regards himself as lost, a 'fruto do mal' [fruit of evil].[17] In *O apocalipse dos trabalhadores* an approximation is established between masculine and feminine sexuality. The love between Quitéria and Andriy, first carnal and later spiritual too, is one of several cases where sex without sin is represented. The desire of Quitéria, who can give herself without any shame, is equal to that of Andriy; and despite the conflicts that always plague her, the same can be said of Maria da Graça, who maintains a loving and sexual (if unsatisfactory) relationship outside marriage.

The body frequently appears in Valter Hugo Mãe as the arena of sexual drives and needs which have to be met, either through a connection with another body or through masturbation. But it is in *O filho de mil homens* that the sublimation of the human being through love as a mental and physical energy reaches its clearest expression. Crisóstomo and Isaura can live out their sex lives free of prejudices or feelings of sin. The intimate moment that the two

---

[14] *O remorso de Baltazar Serapião*, p. 39.
[15] Ibid, p. 25.
[16] Ibid. p. 39.
[17] *O nosso reino*, p. 130.

characters share after the party in Crisóstomo's house is, in its discretion and economy, the representation of a love in which the spiritual and the physical melt into a single plenitude. At this point Crisóstomo and Isaura are ready for a love without limits, simultaneously platonic and physical, a love fully realized in the spirit and the body of the other:

> Estendido o Crisóstomo sobre a cama, via nele a Isaura uma beleza indescritível. A imensidão, pensava, a imensidão de um homem, como hábil alastrando por todas as evidências, todas as manifestações, todos os instintos dela. Cada ínfimo segundo tornava-se um efeito da existência dele, cada ínfimo gesto tinha por moldura a existência dele, cada ímpeto era sempre a direcção do caminho para chegar a ele. Despiu a camisa de noite, e o peito caía-lhe pequeno à luz quente.[18]

> [As he stretched out over the bed, Isaura saw in Crisóstomo an indescribable beauty. The immensity, she thought, the immensity of a man, skilfully spreading himself over all the proofs, all manifestations, all her instincts. Each tiny moment became the result of his existence, each tiny gesture was shaped by his existence, each impulse was directed towards reaching him. She took off her nightdress, and her breasts struck her as small by the warm light.]

Homosexuality and Homoeroticism

The novelistic output of Valter Hugo Mãe is still relatively small, but it has given us highly memorable characters and an imaginary that deals with the most pressing problems of Portuguese society. Central, and interrelated, are the power relations between husband and wife, between bosses and workers (or, in *O remorso*, between subjects, feudal lords and the king), and the hypocrisies of communities whose apparent tendency to mutual aid hides less obvious moral fragilities and wretchedness. *O filho de mil homens* takes up a theme that first appears in *O nosso reino*, that of homosexuality and homoeroticism. That earlier novel had dealt with the subject of the arse and attention to the body and its trappings, seen through the eyes of the protagonist and narrator who evokes his childhood:

> e os meus tios, pensava eu, eram maricas, como aqueles de que falava o Carlos, mas eu não sabia dessas coisas do cu. eram maricas de parecer, delicados como a Germana achava que eram os maricas, lavam-se muito e têm perfume como as senhoras, e depois não falam alto nem são parecidos com homens, parecem mais crianças como se fossem grandes, abanam-se, não param quietos. e eu até via a luz acender-se no cu deles muito periclitante, como uma luzinha muita tímida e sensível. ficava perplexo e parecia-me algo tão errado.[19]

> [and my uncles, I thought, were queers, like the ones Carlos used to talk

[18] *O filho de mil homens*, p. 212.
[19] *O nosso reino*, pp. 108–09.

about, but I knew nothing of stuff about the arse. they looked like queers, delicate like Germana thought queers were, they keep themselves very clean and use perfume like women, and then they don't talk loudly or behave like men, they are more like big children, they shake their heads, they don't keep still. and I even saw their arses light up perilously, with a shy, sensitive little glimmer. I was puzzled and it seemed to me something quite wrong.]

In this book, Benjamin and Michael's relationship with homosexuality is sparked off by the religious and cultural prejudices of Michael's older brother, Carlos. He speaks to them, with disgust, of men who 'fazem amor pelo cu' [make love up the arse], and also refers in offensive terms to Benjamin's aunt, 'uma mulher tão porca que fode com todos os homens e mesmo que tenha racha para foder deixa que lhe ponham a pila no cu' [such a filthy woman that she fucks all the men and even though she's got a cunt for fucking she lets them stick their dick in her arse].[20] These images immediately influence both boys, who start to associate 'arse' and being 'queer' with some evil that could afflict anyone: 'havia um modo de toda a gente ser maricas [...], um modo porco de toda a gente querer enfiar coisas pelo cu, como se devêssemos lembrar durante o dia, e para coisas práticas de bem, que havia aquele lugar horrível no nosso corpo' [there was a way for everyone to be queer [...], a filthy way in which everyone wanted to stick things up their arse, as we should remember by day, and for good practical purposes, that there was that horrible place in our body].[21]

But as previously stated, it is in O filho de mil homens, in the character Antonino, Matilde's son, that the topic of the 'queer man' emerges. In this novel homosexuality and homoeroticism form one of the major elements of the plot, and are often referred to by the third-person narrator. There are frequent references to the ferocity of a reactionary and perverse society that sees in homosexuality an unacceptable deviation, punishable by death:

> Uma vizinha dizia à Matilde: se deus quis que o fizesse, também há-de querer que o desfaça, se assim tiver de ser. Mate-o. É um mando de deus. [...] A outra perguntava: e não lhe dá nojo, a lavar-lhe as roupas e as louças. Ainda apanha doenças com isso de mexer nas porcarias do corpo dele. [...] Mate-o, como se faz aos escaravelhos que nos assustam.[22]
>
> [A neighbour said to Matilde: if god meant him to do it he must want him to undo it, if he has to be like that. Kill him. It's god's commandment. [...] The other neighbour asked: doesn't it make you sick, washing his clothes and his dishes. And you can catch diseases touching the filth from his body. [...] Kill him, like you would the beetles that scare us.]

We can see from this passage, which starts a chapter dedicated to Antonino, how other themes and topics that run through the writings of Valter Hugo Mãe are intertwined with the problematization of (male) homosexuality. We see the intellectual poverty of a mean-spirited people, given over to intrigue and

---

[20] Ibid, p. 57.
[21] Ibid, p. 58.
[22] O filho de mil homens, p. 107.

jealousy, ideology, the conventional family, machismo and religious hypocrisy. This section is entitled 'Devorar os filhos' [Devour your children], while the following one, also dealing with Antonino, is called 'Esbagoados' [Harvested].

Matilde lives the tragedy of someone who oscillates between maternal love and her prejudices. She too punishes and humiliates Antonino, to the point of wanting to kill him, or hoping that he will leave the house and never return, but the hope that her son will change his behaviour never leaves her. Her neighbour makes things harder by saying to Matilde: 'pelas redondezas os poucos casos daqueles tinham sido tratados em modos' [around here the few cases like these had been dealt with].[23] 'Uns racharam os filhos ao meio, outros mandaram-nos embora espancados e sem ordens para voltar, e um homem até subiu pelo cu acima do filho uma vara grossa e pô-lo ao dependuro para todos verem' [Some split their children down the middle, others beat them and told them to go away and never come back, and one man even stuck a thick stick up his son's arse and left him swinging for everyone to see].[24]

In Antonino the sexual impulses and the enigmas of Eros and Love converge realistically. The problem that he has with his body and spirit emerges dramatically when, at the age of seventeen, he masturbates. Antonino does not find himself alone with his body and his mind; after the act, which the narrator describes crudely and objectively, he is afflicted by the perception he has of himself, which is the same as the perception that others have of him. The moralism of the community he lives in imposes a tragic view of life of which he will only free himself many years later, thanks to the company of Crisóstomo and a rejuvenated Isaura:

> Estava estupefacto com o seu gesto, assustado, os olhos, abertos numa vergonha sozinha, íntima, uma vergonha de si mesmo. Metera o dedo. Como se o dedo fosse algo que não podia ser, autonomizando-se, servindo de amor. Um dedo a fazer do amor de outrem. A servir de amor. Cauteloso, carinhoso, lascivo. Pensou que estava louco e zangou-se consigo mesmo repugnado e recusando aceitar ser assim, repetir tal vergonha. Uma bágoa rosto abaixo laminou-lhe a pele a ferver.[25]

> [He was astonished by his act, frightened, his eyes opened at a solitary, intimate shame, a shame at himself. He had put his finger in. As if his finger were something that it couldn't be, becoming autonomous, standing in for love. A finger making someone else's love. Standing in for love. Cautious, caressing, lascivious. He thought he was crazy and was angry with himself, revolted and refusing to accept being like that, to repeat such a shameful thing. A berry of a tear spread like a scalding film over his face.]

Antonino feels guilty, vile and unhappy knowing that he knows nothing about love, and so he rejects his sexuality: 'Além de ter medo de ficar sozinho, não

---

[23] Ibid.
[24] Ibid. pp. 107–08.
[25] Ibid. p. 112.

sabia rigorosamente nada sobre o amor' [As well as being afraid of being alone, he knew absolutely nothing about love].[26] But the character cannot do as he will to negate or hide his identity. His attempts to suppress his desires and hide his sexual orientation by marrying Isaura fail; his self-marginalization and violation of his most basic rights continue, as he is not only rejected by society but beaten up, and so deprived of his moral and physical integrity:

> O primeiro homem jurou que ele estava de calças arriadas a tocar-se. Dizia: estava a comer-se de nós, a pensar em nós. [...] Quando o primeiro o esbofeteou, já um segundo lhe levava o pé ao peito. Pela raiva, tanto lhe pediam explicações como o esganavam.[27]
>
> [The first man swore that he had his trousers down and was playing with himself. He said: he was wanking off on us, thinking about us. [...] When the first man hit him, the second kicked him in the chest. In their rage, they were demanding explanations as much as they were choking him.]

In this novel, Valter Hugo Mãe constructs an anatomy of homosexuality. Antonino and the other characters do not simply comment, with disdain and disgust, on his feminine mannerisms and feelings; the sensuality that runs through him is also portrayed, via a mixture of internal focalization and the narrator's translations, in terms of an incontrollable human force. The alienation that characterizes his thoughts and behaviours does not deprive him of an intimate and fleeting erotic impulse, which emerges against the idea of abnormality and sin supported by Judaio-Christian morality (or religion in general). The intellectual resistance that Antonino offers to his natural impulses, and his momentary conviction that men are 'animais perigosos que nunca poderia, ou deveria, amar' [dangerous animals that he never could, or should, love],[28] carry no weight with his body, which demands its instinctive and vital celebration:

> Depois, na distracção, a certa confiança de estar bem agachado entre os arbustos permitiu-lhe ver como os corpos dos trabalhadores eram moldados à força de muita virilidade. Eram homens como árvores maciças a abrir as águas em jogos brutos, espaventando tudo com os braços e mergulhando vezes sem conta de rabo para o ar. Ficavam depois boiando como impossivelmente leves, ágeis, inertes de só beleza na superfície da água. O Antonino pôde ver como os homens eram belos na sua rudeza, como pareciam fortes para tudo, com braços largos para abraços esmagadores. E o amor parecia tão esmagador e criado pela robustez.[29]
>
> [Then, at recreation, his confidence at being well hunkered down amongst the bushes let him see how the workmen's bodies were moulded by dint of much virility. They were like huge trees, parting the waters with their rough games, making a show with their arms and diving over and again with their

[26] Ibid.
[27] Ibid., p. 114.
[28] Ibid, p. 113.
[29] Ibid, pp. 113–14.

buttocks in the air. They ended up floating, as if impossibly light, agile, inert with mere beauty on the surface of the water. Antonino could see that the men were handsome in their coarseness, that they seemed strong enough for anything, with broad arms for crushing embraces. And love seemed just as crushing, and created by their robustness.]

The account that the narrator offers us of Antonino's erotic and sensuous energies as a sublimation of homosexual desire is rare in Portuguese literature. In a brief delirium of senses and images, Antonino sees an instinctive, human conception of love, disconnected from the feeling of guilt that a puritanical society inculcates in him. In the following chapter the eroticism of this character is again presented straightforwardly.

Antonino's sexual desire is channelled into an imaginary into which enter 'os sentimentos mais delicados' [the most delicate feelings],[30] and parts of the male bodies that populate his daily life. The narrator lists these parts along with the owner of each: 'mascarando o desejo, coleccionando numa mudez absoluta os braços do senhor do autocarro, os lábios e os dentes brancos do filho da senhora da farmácia, o rabo generoso do padre [...]' [concealing his desire, cataloguing in complete silence the arms of the bus driver, the lips and white teeth of the son of the woman at the pharmacy, the priest's generous backside].[31] He immediately recovers these parts, integrating them in a series of erotic scenes that he imagines while he masturbates: 'Com o tempo, Antonino aprendeu a tocar-se recolhido, compondo na cabeça um abraço ao senhor do autocarro com um beijo no rapaz da farmácia, a mão no rabo do padre e uma declaração de amor murmurada pela voz do homem da rádio diante do azul intenso dos olhos do adolescente' [With time, Antonino learnt to play with himself discreetly, combining in his head an embrace from the bus driver with a kiss from the boy at the pharmacy, a hand on the priest's behind and a declaration of love murmured by the man on the radio to the intense blue eyes of the adolescent].[32] But this idealized scene rapidly dissolves, and in its place appears crude existence and existential questions that Antonino cannot resolve. The sensual and sexual impulse allowed him to think that 'poderia estar apaixonado por um desses homens' [he could be loved by one of those men], but that hope for a fuller life is replaced by the idea that 'destituíra o coração de sentimentos' [he had drained his heart of feelings]. Feeling 'que se amava sozinho' [that he loved alone], Antonino also hates himself, and sees the 'gloria' [splendour] of the pleasure that playing with himself brought is dissipated.

We see Antonino's suffering, but we also witness his redemption and a reconciliation to sexual difference by at least a part of society. It is Crisóstomo who shapes a new status for Antonino, with a life on a level (almost) with that of heterosexuals:

---

[30] Ibid, p. 120.
[31] Ibid.
[32] Ibid.

Crisóstomo dizia que talvez para os campos as pessoas fossem mais atrasadas, porque ali ao pé da água já se via de tudo e os maricas não tinham novidade nem ofereciam qualquer ameaça. Os maricas eram como gente mais colorida a alegrar os passeios. O povo podia rir-se mas não queria fazer grande caso. Só era necessário isso, não lhes fazer caso.[33]

[Crisóstomo said that maybe people were more backward in the countryside, because here on the coast they'd seen everything and the queers were nothing new and posed no threat. The queers were like more colourful people to cheer things up. The common folk might laugh but they didn't make a big deal of it. That's all you needed, for them not to make a fuss.]

But the celebration of Antonino's difference, and his qualities, is not summed up by this remark about the people on the coast. Isaura singles out his emotions and his behaviour, his involvement with people around him, his ability to cry for himself and for others: 'A Isaura, que mudara o mundo com o seu entusiasmo, disse que não concordava. Disse que o Antonino era o melhor ser humano de todos porque chorava e se magoava com as coisas e disse que era essencial aprender a prestar-lhe atenção' [Isaura, who had put the world to rights with her enthusiasm, said she didn't agree. She said Antonino was the best human being because he cried and was distressed by things and said they needed to learn to pay attention to him].[34] According to Isaura, his integration into his new life does not depend on just ignoring or respecting his homosexuality; it works because he stands out from all the others by his sensitivity and dedication to everything and everybody.

Antonino does not find himself excluded from this reconciliation with life through the love and companionship of others; he is welcomed unconditionally by Isaura and her mother, who 'sabiam que precisavam uma da outra para serem melhores. Sabiam, já tão claramente, que juntas podiam ser muito mais felizes': 'Dizia: dona Matilde, conte sempre comigo. Conte sempre comigo para si e para a Mininha, que ao Antonino já nem que me batam o deixo na mão. É meu' [knew they needed one another to be better. They knew so clearly now that together they could be much happier': 'She said: dona Matilde, you can always count on me. Count on me for yourself and Mininha, and as for Antonino, I wouldn't abandon him even if they beat me. He's mine].[35] Then Antonino can enjoy life and the love that until then he had only glimpsed, and from which he felt irremediably separated.

Nor is Antonino separated from love as a spiritual and carnal attachment to one person. We see that in his new life an unknown person, who later on we find out is a 'queer', suddenly appears and makes a big impression on Antonino, whose thoughts and emotions are made available to us by the narrator's free indirect narration that is emotional and picturesque (in common parlance,

---

[33] Ibid, p. 207.
[34] Ibid.
[35] Ibid, p. 245.

'effeminate', but not in a pejorative sense here). Antonino did not know that the man was there to help him to carry the dead body of Gemúndio, and so surmises: 'Se fosse por ele, pelas alminhas, podia pegar. Não tinha preço ou tinha o preço de um pardal. Pode comprar-me pelo preço de um pardal, pensou' [If it was him, by heavens, he could have me. I had no price, or only that of a song. He could buy me for a song, he thought].[36]

Though at first violently marginalized by everyone, including his own mother, and himself, by the end of the novel Antonino takes his place amongst those able to fight for a full and redemptory love. Reconciled with himself and others, he can finally be who he is, say what he thinks about love and be moved without being criticized. In the closing paragraphs of the novel, the narrator tells us of this transformation. The boy Camilo, the orphaned son of a dwarf-woman and an unknown father, whom Crisóstomo adopts as his son, embraces Antonino, who is touched and sees 'entre tantos rostos, o do homem desconhecido' [amongst so many faces, that of the unknown man].[37]

This treatment of male homosexuality is unique in Portuguese literature. In *O filho de mil homens* the aim is not to treat homosexual feelings and behaviour from the point of view of characters who rise above their time, free of social prejudices and taboos, nor to ignore or underplay the weight of social moralizing and its negative effects on people like Antonino, nor again to show only the marginalization he is driven to by the group. It aims not only to show internal and interpersonal conflicts and dramas that are relevant to the construction of a sexual and emotional identity but also to portray the character's redemption through the relationship with a family and a man.

The great originality in the handling of this theme in *O filho de mil homens* rests in this articulation: we do not have only, or mainly, the display of homosexual (auto)eroticism, which in any case is not as crudely described as in some other Portuguese novelists, notably Luiz Pacheco and Rui Nunes;[38] nor do we have only, or mainly, the insistence on the prejudice and rage of communities towards homosexuals. The narrator is not a participant, but the attention he devotes to Antonino, from discovering his physical and emotional nature to his final emancipation as a person, not neglecting the different types of violence to which he is subjected by society, surpasses the range of other perspectives of Portuguese novelists writing about homosexuality and homoeroticism, such as Eduardo Pitta, Frederico Lourenço, Henrique Levy and Joaquim Almeida Lima.[39] There is nothing coy or evasive about his writing, either in the narration

[36] Ibid, pp. 241–42.
[37] Ibid, p. 252.
[38] Luiz Pacheco, *O libertino passeia por Braga, a idolátrica, o seu esplendor*, 6th edn (Lisbon: Edições Colibri, 1992); Rui Nunes, *O mensageiro diferido*, 2nd edn (Lisbon: Relógio d'Água, 2004).
[39] Eduardo Pitta, *Persona* (Matosinhos: QuidNovi, 2000) and *Cidade proibida* (Matosinhos: QuidNovi, 2007); Frederico Lourenço, *O curso das estrelas* (Lisbon: Cotovia, 2002), *Pode um desejo imenso* (Lisbon: Cotovia, 2002), and *À beira do mundo* (Lisbon: Cotovia, 2003); Henrique Levy, *Praia Lisboa* (Lisbon: Livros de seda, 2010); Joaquim Almeida Lima, *Ensaiao sobre a angústia* (Lisbon: Gradiva, 2012).

and description of Antonino's eroticism or even less in the physical and moral repugnance of the community towards male homosexuality.

The Fantastic and the Grotesque

The introduction of extraordinary elements of a fantastic nature is common in the novels of Valter Hugo Mãe. In his first three books, the strange and negative atmosphere is there from the start, and in the first two it increases as the story advances. In *O nosso reino*, the 'homen mais triste do mundo' [the saddest man in the world] is the first to cause unease. Named in the novel's first sentence, and described in its first pages, this mysterious character is an obsessive presence in the first-person narration by Benjamin, a child who concentrates the fears, anxieties and religious conflicts of a people in daily contact with both God and the Devil. These disturbing references, expressive of good or evil, to the 'saddest man in the world' heighten an uncertainty between empirical reality and the supernatural: 'era o homem mais triste do mundo, como numa lenda, diziam, dele as pessoas da terra, impressionadas com a sua expressão e com o modo como partia as pedras na cabeça ou abria bichos com os dentes tão caninos de fome' [he was the saddest man in the world, like in a fairy story, the local people said of him, impressed by his expression, and by the way he broke stones on his head or tore open animals with his hungry canine teeth].[40]

The origin of these elements that disturb the empirical order remains to be explained. We do not know if the events are shown to us as they really occurred, or if they result from some sort of illusion on the part of the narrator (who has no doubt of their veracity). The fantastic element, therefore, lies in what Todorov calls the hesitation of the reader,[41] and not in the perplexity of the characters. We find precisely one of the criteria of the fantastic set out by Todorov, for whom the most common is a coincidence of reactions between the reader and the protagonist (who may be connected to other characters). But the author also emphasizes that the hesitation may not exist inside the text, which is the case in *O nosso reino*, where the fantastic is present, rather, in the way the reader deals with the events described. What for the reader is a manifestation of the fantastic, and therefore odd and ambiguous, is the norm for Benjamin and other members of his community.

In *O nosso reino* we encounter the defamiliarization of bodies and landscapes in dark and surreal and terrifying scenarios. The evil, the devilish and death take on a living presence that never fades away. The death and suffering of people close to Benjamin, feelings of sin and expiation of guilt, visions of the devil and the 'saddest man in the world', storms and natural disasters — these all appear in the everyday world, and give the reader an impression of unintelligibility and

---

[40] *O nosso reino*, p. 9.
[41] Tzvetan Todorov, *Introdução à literatura fantástica*, trans. by Maria Clara Correa Castello, 4th edn (São Paulo: Perspectiva, 2010), p. 37.

unreality: 'vi como o carlos morreu, vi como foi, os animais reunidos ao seu pé, a escavarem covas uns, de chegarem, não de partirem, e outros a pairarem no ar. pareciam animais de revolver tudo, a destruírem e a reordenarem' [I saw how Carlos died, I saw how it was, the animals gathered around him, some digging graves, arriving, not departing, and others hovering in the air. they seemed like animals that would overturn everything, destroying and reordering].[42]

But the auodiegetic narrator never shares the reader's hesitation when confronted with elements of undecidability in the plot. Like the community, Benjamin is convinced that the 'saddest man in the world' is real and supernatural: 'e eu juro que o vi voar por sobre o casario numa noite de inverno' [and I swear that I saw him fly over the houses one winter's night].[43] Right at the start of the novel, to his own 'diziam' [they were saying] (two occurrences at the beginning, in the first two paragraphs), the protagonist adds his own testimony about the 'saddest man in the world', who 'recolhia os mortos, juntava-os um a um nos braços, e dava-lhes terra e silêncio para comerem' [collected the dead, gathered them one by one in his arms, and gave them soil and silence to eat].[44] The emphatic communicative act marked by 'eu juro' [I swear] suggests that the narrator is in no doubt about what he has seen; but above all, such narrative techniques show that the narrator sees the need to persuade the reader not to dismiss what s/he is being told.

The main theme of this novel is human existence and its mysterious, unsettling and traumatic relationship with the supernatural. Benjamin is continuously confronted with his condition as a mortal being in the face of life's mysteries. This character, who reveals his inner life, his anxieties and his fears, tries to unveil the truth of the world by means of the aura of sanctity with which he invests himself. Benjamin's existence is marked by a heightened subjectivity, by awareness of things other people do not see, and an ability to see into the future: 'e eu garanti-lhe, ainda que assim seja, serás santo, Manuel, alarás num cavalo e não terás mortes. deus espera de ti coisas importantes sem que tenhas de fazer mais nada' [and I assured him, even if it's like that, you'll be a saint, Manuel, you'll lay on a horse's back and not experience death. god expects great things of you without your having to do anything more].[45]

The reader is assailed by an unease as s/he witnesses a succession of events mixing or alternating the realistic and the grotesque, the verisimilar and the surreal. The reader may be inclined to believe there are natural explanations for such ambiguous strange phenomena, or simply attribute them to errors and delusions on the part of Benjamin; but s/he cannot fail to confront the existential problem of the narrator, who forces him or her to think of the complexities of life, of human fragility, and the significance of death.

---

[42] *O nosso reino*, p. 87.
[43] Ibid. p. 10.
[44] Ibid.
[45] Ibid, p. 151.

Benjamin (the name is biblical) says he is predestined to a life of miracles and divine blessings, and, thus qualified, reveals to us visions of the supernatural world, of dialogues with the dead, predictions of death, and contacts with the divine and the demonic. His life and his metaphysical visions are marked by the fear of death and apocalyptic terror, on the one hand, and a belief in salvation through faith, on the other. The irreducibility of death and the notion of sin are the laws that underlie the tragic sense of life for Benjamin, and for the community he belongs to, but it is there that is to be found the character's ability to ask questions of himself, and of the world.

It is the Christian context within which the narrator and his characters live, particularly the popular religiosity linked to the 'pobreza como condição julgada milenar' [poverty as a condition judged age-old],[46] to superstition, magic, and ideas of evil and sin that explain the expressionist pathos of *O nosso reino*. Benjamin starts by placing us in a strange everyday environment occupied by the 'saddest man in the world', whose very presence forces the local people to confront their mortality and the anguish that comes from it. But the novel does not dwell only upon metaphysical sorrow, which only exists in relation to the known and familiar. The narrator shows us situations and behaviour that demonstrate the tendency, individual and social, towards prejudice and cruelty (the priest's physical and moral aggression toward Benjamin, the attitude towards Tia Cândida's life and pregnancy, the sense of shame after masturbation).

Grotesque disfigurement, which appears in the novel as an indestructible force and condemnation which Benjamin is unable to avoid, contributes to this expressionist feel. Life is confused with death, order gives way to disaggregation, the human draws closer to repugnant life-forms and becomes abject, and a cruel and painful truth appears below the lie.

The fantastic, as we have seen, is in dialogue with aspects of existentialist, surrealist and expressionist aesthetics, which are in constant articulation in this first novel, a novel in which we find the favourite themes and topics of Valter Hugo Mãe. *O remorso de Baltazar Serapião* too has this alternation and mixture of elements that also form part of the novel's syntax. There are actions that connect with one another, and which are immediately taken by the reader to be strange, repugnant, fantastic, grotesque or surreal. The degradation of Ermesinde's body, repeatedly beaten by Baltazar, who repeats what his own father had practised on his wife, the description of the infanticides (filicides, even) practised by the two, who cannot accept the idea of being deceived by their wives, or the effects of sorcery on the landscape and the people — these produce an effect that is both strange and truthful, both distancing and problematizing.

---

[46] Luís Mourão, 'Valter Hugo Mãe: A lei menor dos temas maiores', in *Pensar a literatura no século XXI*, ed. by João Amadeu Silva, José Cândido Martins and Miguel Gonçalves (Braga: Publicações da Faculdade de Filosofia / Universidade Católica Portuguesa, 2011), pp. 479–85 (p. 481).

The repugnant in this novel is often associated with the appalling. The crude and remarkable visuality of the scenes of male violence shows us to what extremes the irrational and destructive energy can go, and underlines the physicality of human life and death. The extreme behaviour, which Baltazar will repeat, evokes the visceral behaviour of a certain kind of Portuguese man and a culture than marginalizes women:

> e foi no dia em que o povo se preparava para queimar a mulher que o meu pai rebentou braço dentro o ventre de minha mãe e arrancou mão própria o que alguém deixara ali. e gritou, serás amaldiçoado para sempre. depois estalou-o no chão e pôs-lhe pé nu em cima, sentindo-lhe carnes e sangues esguicharem de morte tão esmagada.[47]
>
> [and it was on the day the people were preparing to burn the woman that my father thrust his arm into my mother's belly and dragged out with his own hand what someone had left there. and he shouted, you'll be cursed forever. then he smashed it on the ground and put his bare foot on top, feeling its flesh and blood gushing out as he crushed it to death.]

The fantastic, in this second novel by Valter Hugo Mãe, lies in the spell that the burnt woman casts over Baltazar, Dagoberto's brother, and in the consequences for the landscape and the characters. The reader will question the phenomena that Baltazar repeatedly refers to, and which often structure the narrative, but even if they are inscribed in its ethnographic realism (which also exists in *O nosso reino*) uncertainty persists. The bodies of Baltazar and his companions, who are obliged to travel together when they have to leave their village, become desiccated, as does everything around them. Baltazar assumes that there are women capable of joining the real and the supernatural, he believes in supernatural laws, and so he does not ask if what is happening to them is real. The explanation can only be of a supernatural kind. It falls to the reader to question the reality of these phenomena.

The comic, the tragic, the grotesque and the surreal are forms of perception and expression also found in the dreams described in the works of Valter Hugo Mãe. In *O nosso reino*, the dream is a way of escaping the terror the narrator lives through. Benjamin dreams because he wants to see whether the future will bring freedom to him and the others: 'deitei-me convicto de que sonharia naquela noite com algo revelador, cobri-me até à cabeça [...]'; 'esta noite sonhei com o futuro e pude imaginar todas as coisas, Manuel' [I went to bed convinced I would dream that night of something revealing, I covered myself up to the head [...]; that night I dreamt about the future and I could imagine everything, Manuel].[48] It is in this prophetic dream that this character's subjectivity, which always implies an other, finds one of its most surprising expressions. The limits of the present and the real disappear, and in their place emerges a reality we can associate with the surrealist imagination, which constantly surpasses itself:

[47] *O remorso de Baltazar Serapião*, p. 67.
[48] *O nosso reino*, p. 64.

poderemos ter uma existência infinita, reanimando as células do cérebro, e se quisermos estaremos a nadar na praia todo o ano, a comer coisas doces, a conversar com amigos ou a ler livros, porque a nossa cabeça estará preparada para criar essa sugestão infinitamente, reinventando eternamente todas as coisas para nos parecerem novas.[49]

[we can have an infinite existence, renewing our brain cells, and if we want we'll be on the beach swimming all the year, eating sweet things, chatting with friends or reading books, because our minds will be ready to create that proposition indefinitely, eternally reinventing everything so as to seem new to us.]

Language and Story-Telling

Valter Hugo Mãe is an author whose absorbing and suggestive language has spontaneity and naturalism, but also alertness and rigour. Awareness of language is very much present in his writing, firmly linked to the themes and motifs of each novel, and drawing on different tendencies and tonalities. *O remorso de Baltazar Serapião* is the novel in which we see how he conciliates lesser cadences with broader movements, imposes ruptures and dissonances, makes major changes of register, changes from melancholy to satire, from a solemn expression to a rougher and more familiar word.

Each new book by this author has been a synthesis of these aspects, but it is undoubtedly in *O remorso de Baltazar Serapião* that we find the clearest evidence of these balances. In this book, the medieval themes are accompanied, from start to finish, by a language that combines the mannerisms and solemnity of pre-Fernão Lopes prose with the familiarity of modern speech. This free and agile idiolect, with its underlying archaic musicality, discreet but noticeable, lends itself to the flowing and resonant expression of environments and emotional states that the reader sees as sometimes distant and sometimes close:

> partimos imediato el-rei nos expulsou. desgraça tão grande, nosso pai, e nada nos consolava. nem que a mulher queimada nos desdenhasse presa em ferros, onde el-rei a deixaria perecer para juízo depois de morta. nem que o dagoberto nos acompanhasse como irmão, dizia dele el-rei, levai-o, infestado por noites de vossa companhia [...]. e partimos imediato nos amaldiçoou mais ainda e nos quis tão longe, como mortos abaixo da terra enfiados e esquecidos.[50]

> [we left as soon as the king expelled us. so great a disgrace, dear father, and nothing consoled us. even that the burnt woman who disdained us was clapped in irons, where the king would leave her to perish to be judged after death. even that dagoberto accompanied us like a brother, the king said of him, take him, infested by nights of your company [...] and we left

---

[49] Ibid, p. 64-65.
[50] *O remorso de Baltazar Serapião*, p. 125.

immediately he cursed us more still and wanted us as far away as if pushed dead under the earth and forgotten.]

In his novels there are phrases and expressions that evoke one another, and create the effect of a lexical and semantic echo to which the reader will associate patterns of meaning. For example, there are gendered notions that Baltazar insists on from the beginning of the novel, and from the first sentence we find the majority of words and semes later repeated, such as 'voz' [voice], 'mulheres' [women], 'diabo' [devil], 'arder' [burn], 'perigosa' [dangerous (feminine)], 'burra' [mule (female)], 'abaixo' [down].[51] The narration asserts the intellectual inferiority of woman, her tiny place in the divine creation, her need to be educated through the violence of her father and her husband, her tendency to adultery and evil, and the absolute rights of the man over the woman.

The linguistic and literary (or artistic) awareness in these novels, notable in their style, receives significant expression at the level of the storytelling. The themes of music, painting, cinema and literature appear explicitly in some of the novels as sublime fields, to which the characters attribute the function of saving, or at least improving, the world. The defence of art is made through the characters in programmatic and metaliterary terms. In *O apocalipse dos trabalhadores*, Sr Ferreira constantly tells Maria da Graça of his fascination for art, regarding it as surpassing the divine: 'este é um livro sobre o trabalho de goya, dizia-lhe o homem, um génio, veja. são coisas como já não há e nem deus havia de estar consciente da maravilha que vinha ao mundo quando este homem nasceu' [this is a book about goya's work, the man said to her, a genius, look. there's nothing like them anymore, and not even god could have been aware of the miracle that came into the world when this man was born].[52]

In *A máquina de fazer espanhóis*, the idea of literature 'como incrível epifania' [as an incredible epiphany] is formulated by the 'esteves sem metafísica' [Esteves lacking metaphysics][53] from the poem 'Tabacaria', by Fernando Pessoa. As a resident in an old people's home and a figure of national and international literary importance, this Esteves evokes Pessoa through the phrase 'come chocolates, marmajona, come chocolates' [eat chocolates, you rogue, eat chocolates], directed at a 'dona Leopoldina', who 'estava a comer uns chocolates minúsculos' [was eating some tiny chocolates].[54] This connection allows him to link 'literatura' and 'a nossa impressionante vida real' [our impressive real life]. This Esteves appears in the narrative to confirm his own notion that literature can manifest itself as a real miracle: '[...] come chocolates, come chocolates. caramba, era mesmo verdade que não havia mais metafísica no mundo que chegasse ao brilhante elementar daquela ideia' [eat chocolates, eat chocolates. heavens, it was true that there was no other metaphysics in the world that could

[51] Ibid, p. 9.
[52] *O apocalipse dos trabalhadores*, p. 11.
[53] *A máquina de fazer espanhóis*, p. 88.
[54] Ibid.

match the simple brilliance of that idea].⁵⁵

From being an Esteves without metaphysics this character passes, in his 'own' chapter ('o esteves a transbordar de metafísica' [esteves overflowing with metaphysics]), to being 'o nosso esteves cheio de metafísica' [our esteves full of metaphysics].⁵⁶ Valter Hugo Mãe does this because, contrary to what happens in Pessoa's poem, he reflects on life and death, ageing and the body: 'porque é o corpo que nos ataca. estamos finalmente perante o mais terrível dos animais, o nosso próprio bicho, o bicho que somos' [because it is the body that attacks us. we are finally facing the most terrible of the animals, our own worm, the worm we are].⁵⁷

Realism, magical realism and ethnography, the fantastic, the tragic, the comic, the grotesque, burlesque, satire, lyricism: here are some of the terms we have recourse to, with a greater or lesser degree of rigour, in defining a novel or the whole prose of this author. But any approach would be incomplete if we failed to refer to the construction, in Valter Hugo Mãe, of a poetics of testimony, in the sense that Jorge de Sena has used the term:

> [...] o testemunho é, na sua expectação, na sua discrição, na sua vigilância, a mais alta forma de transformação do mundo, porque nele, com ele e através dele, que é antes de mais linguagem, se processa a remodelação dos esquemas feitos, das ideias aceites, dos hábitos sociais inscientemente vividos, dos sentimentos convencionalmente aferidos.⁵⁸

> [testimony is, by its expectation, its discretion, its vigilance, the highest form of transformation in the world, because in it, with it, and through it — which is above all language — proceeds the remodelling of schemes achieved, of ideas accepted, of social habits unwittingly lived, of sentiments conventionally gauged.]

---

⁵⁵ Ibid.
⁵⁶ Ibid, p. 149.
⁵⁷ Ibid.
⁵⁸ Jorge de Sena, *Poesia — I* (Lisbon: Moraes Editores, 1961), pp. 11–12.

Abstracts

Revisiting the Anglo-Norman Crusaders' Failed Attempt to Conquer Lisbon c. 1142

LUCAS VILLEGAS-ARISTIZÁBAL

ABSTRACT. This article revisits the failed attempt to conquer Lisbon by a combined host of Anglo-Norman and Portuguese crusaders in 1142 within the wider context of both the crusader movement to the Holy Land and the Iberian Reconquista. Focusing on the *Historia Gothorum*, *De expugnatione Lyxbonensi* and other sources, it endeavours to demonstrate the degree of involvement of the Anglo-Norman contingents in maritime adventures at a time when no other crusades had been declared. Finally, it illustrates the consequence of this undertaking for the final conquest of Lisbon, as part of the Second Crusade, in 1147.

KEYWORDS. Afonso Henriques of Portugal, Anglo-Normans, *De expugnatione Lyxbonensi*, Jerusalem, *Historia Gothorum*, Lisbon, Second Crusade, King Stephen, Reconquest, William Vitalus.

RESUMO. Este artigo revisita a tentativa falhada de conquista de Lisboa em 1142 por uma força combinada de cruzados anglo-normandos e portugueses no contexto simultâneo da reconquista ibérica e do movimento cruzadístico para a Terra Santa. Centrado na *Historia Gothorum*, *De expugnatione Lyxbonensi* e outras fontes, o artigo procura demonstrar a escala de envolvimento dos contingentes anglo-normandos em aventuras marítimas numa altura em que não tinham sido lançadas outras cruzadas. Finalmente, o artigo ilustra as consequências deste empreendimento na conquista de Lisboa pela segunda cruzada em 1147.

PALAVRAS CHAVE. D. Afonso Henriques, anglo-normandos, *De expugnatione Lyxbonensi*, Jerusalém, *Historia Gothorum*, Lisboa, segunda cruzada, Stephen de Inglaterra, *Reconquista*, William Vitalus.

'The lyceums work in silence, they do not advertise, and have no time for envy or rivalry': A Case Study of the 'Liceu Rodrigues de Freitas/D. Manuel II' during the Portuguese Estado Novo

LUÍS GROSSO CORREIA

ABSTRACT. During the Estado Novo in Portugal, the ethos of the *liceus* in secondary education, and particularly those operating in the public sector, enjoyed wide support from political and social authorities. However, the fact that the *liceu* provided a post-primary education that was voluntary, with admission exams, restricted places, and high fees, made it particularly selective with respect to the social background of pupils. The present study analyses the educational market for *liceu* education at two different levels, the national and the case-specific. The case study deals with the continuous process of selection, the predominance of a highly academic curriculum, the examination results of pupils, and their drop-out rate, at the Liceu Rodrigues de Freitas/D. Manuel II in Porto, one of the most prestigious boys' schools in Portugal.

KEYWORDS. Estado Novo, New State, liceu education, Liceu Rodrigues de Freitas/D. Manuel II, Porto.

RESUMO. A missão do ensino secundário liceal e, em especial, as escolas da rede pública concitaram uma grande unanimidade junto das autoridades políticas e sociais, durante o período do Estado Novo em Portugal. O facto de se tratar de um ensino pós-primário de frequência facultativa, com exames de admissão, numerus clausus e propinas elevadas, tornavam-no particularmente seletivo do ponto de vista do recrutamento social dos alunos. O presente estudo tem por foco a análise do mercado educacional do ensino liceal em dois níveis diferenciados: nacional e micro-contextualizado. O estudo de caso será operado sobre o processo contínuo de seleção, domínio de um currículo muito académico, avaliação e drop-out dos alunos do Liceu Rodrigues de Freitas/D. Manuel II, uma das mais prestigiadas escolas de ensino masculino em Portugal situada na cidade do Porto.

PALAVRAS CHAVE. Estado Novo, ensino liceal, Liceu Rodrigues de Freitas/D. Manuel II, Porto.

An Ethics of Displaying Affection: Hélio Oiticica's Expressions of Joy and Togetherness

KARL POSSO

ABSTRACT. Experimental artist Hélio Oiticica (1937–80), whose neo-avant-garde or 'conceptual' work became increasingly engaged with popular culture, is often cited as a key influence on the aesthetics of Tropicália, the Brazilian countercultural movement of the late 1960s. Focusing on his *Parangolé* series and *Quasi-cinema* slide sequences, this paper aims to show how Oiticica's aesthetic practices from the mid 1960s to mid 1970s make sensation or affective quality the domain of politics and ethics. It argues that by engaging with ideals, but suspending coherent representation, Oiticica interrupts audiences' action-reaction circuits as a means of hindering habits of judgement and producing what might be termed 'ethical intensity'.

KEYWORDS. Hélio Oiticica, *Parangolés*, *Quasi-cinemas*, ethics, affect, sensation.

RESUMO. O artista experimental Hélio Oiticica (1937–80) — não só neovanguardista ou 'conceitual', mas também comprometido com a cultura popular — teve uma influência decisiva sobre a Tropicália, o movimento contracultural brasileiro do final dos anos 60. Esta análise, enfocada nos *Parangolés* e nas

sequências de slides conhecidas como *Quasi-cinemas*, pretende mostrar como as práticas estéticas de Oiticica de meados dos anos 60 até os anos 70 transformam a sensação, ou qualidade afetiva, numa proposta ética e política. Argumenta-se aqui que, ao lidar com ideais e ao mesmo tempo suspender a representação coerente, Oiticica interrompe os circuitos de ação–reação do público a fim de dessolidificar os hábitos de julgamento e produzir o que se poderia chamar de 'intensidade ética'.
PALAVRAS CHAVE. Hélio Oiticica, *Parangolés*, *Quasi-cinemas*, ética, afeto, sensação.

Afro-Brazilian Culture in London: Images and Discourses in Transnational Movements

SIMONE FRANGELLA

ABSTRACT. In the context of the production and dissemination of Brazilian culture in London over the last decade, Afro-Brazilian references inform many cultural events, being articulated in the transnational dynamics involved both in the consumption of cultural goods exported from Brazil to the UK and in the diverse cultural experiences brought about by migration movements. The aim of this article, the result of ethnographic research conducted in London, is to show how this creates a complex web from which emerges a plurality of images and practices relating to the Afro-Brazilian experience. Whether that is swallowed by a national narrative of Brazilianness or counterposed to new racial encounters and cultural transpositions, such analysis can contribute to the debate on Brazilian racial representation and its unfolding in the context of globalization.
KEYWORDS. Cultural production, Afro-Brazilian culture, migration, multiculturalism.

RESUMO. No contexto da produção e divulgação da cultura brasileira em Londres desde a última década, referências afro-brasileiras atravessam uma série de eventos, articuladas nas dinâmicas transnacionais tanto do consumo dos bens culturais exportados do Brasil para o Reino Unido, quanto das diversas experiências culturais trazidas pelos movimentos dos migrantes. O objetivo deste artigo, um resultado de pesquisa etnográfica feita em Londres, é mostrar como se constrói um quadro complexo no qual emerge uma pluralidade de imagens e práticas sobre o universo afro-brasileiro. Seja diluído em uma narrativa nacional de brasilidade, ou contraposto a novos encontros raciais e transposições culturais, este contexto contribui para pensar o debate sobre a dinâmica das representações raciais e seus desdobramentos em contextos de globalização.
PALAVRAS CHAVE. Produção cultural, cultura Afro-brasileira, migração, multiculturalismo.

Courting Death in Hélia Correia's 'Adoecer' (2010)

ISABEL FERNANDES

ABSTRACT. *Adoecer* (2010), Hélia Correia's latest novel, is her first of a truly biographical genre, based on the life of the famous Pre-Raphaelite model, Elizabeth Siddal. The aim of the article is to give an overview of the text, concentrating on aspects that characterize it as a novel that simultaneously courts death and defies it, by annulling the divide between past and present, thus replicating the gesture of the pair of lovers at the centre of its story who see themselves as doubles of Dante and Beatrice. Following closely in the footsteps of Correia's textual strategy and language, it explores the way in which Elizabeth Siddal uses her precarious state of health as a seduction strategy which culminates in her premature death, thus echoing the Pre-Raphaelite fascination with death and lethargic conditions, apparent in both their poetry and their paintings.

KEYWORDS. Hélia Correia, Pre-Raphaelites, illness, death, doubles, Elizabeth Siddal.

RESUMO: *Adoecer* (2010), último romance de Hélia Correia, é o primeiro de caráter verdadeiramente biográfico, já que se debruça sobre a vida do famoso modelo dos Pré-rafaelitas, Elizabeth Siddal. É meu objetivo dar uma visão do texto como um todo, centrando-me nos aspetos que o caracterizam como um romance que simultaneamente corteja e desafia a morte, ao anular a fronteira entre passado e presente, assim replicando o gesto do par amoroso no centro da história que eles a si próprios se viam como duplos de Dante e Beatriz. Seguindo de perto as marcas da estratégia textual e da linguagem de Hélia Correia, explorarei o modo como Elizabeth Siddal usa a sua saúde precária como artifício de sedução que culmina na sua morte prematura, assim se fazendo eco do fascínio dos Pré-rafaelitas pela morte e pelas condições letárgicas, tal como transparece tanto na respetiva poesia como na pintura.

PALAVRAS CHAVE. Hélia Correia, Pré-rafaelitas, doença, morte, duplos, Elizabeth Siddal.

The Novels of Valter Hugo Mãe

CARLOS NOGUEIRA

ABSTRACT. This article takes an overview of the five novels published to date by Valter Hugo Mãe, whose work has been distinguished with a number of prizes, most recently the *Grande Prémio Portugal Telecom* (2012). It identifies the themes and motifs that are specific to this author's novels, namely love and hate, life and death, Portugal, youth and old age, desire and sexuality, freedom, power and oppression, rebellion, debate and satire. At the same time it traces the narrative and stylistic elements, and the shadings of the fantastic, the grotesque, the supernatural, the existential, the surreal, and the expressionist that Valter Hugo Mãe has explored from his very first novel.

KEYWORDS. Valter Hugo Mãe, novel, Portugal, twenty-first century.

RESUMO. Fazemos neste artigo uma leitura global dos cinco romances publicados até ao momento por Valter Hugo Mãe, cujo trabalho é já distinguido com vários prémios, inclusive, mais recentemente, o Grande Prémio Portugal Telecom (2012). Destacamos os temas e os motivos que fazem a especificidade da escrita romanesca deste autor: o amor e o ódio, a vida e a morte, Portugal, a juventude e a velhice, o desejo e o sexo, a liberdade, o poder e a opressão, a revolta, a contestação e a sátira. Ao mesmo tempo, salientamos os elementos narrativos e estilísticos e as tonalidades do âmbito do fantástico, do grotesco, do sobrenatural, do existencialismo, do surrealismo e do expressionismo que Valter Hugo Mãe explora já desde o seu primeiro romance.

PALAVRAS-CHAVE. Valter Hugo Mãe, romance, Portugal, século XXI.

www.ingramcontent.com/pod-product-compliance
Lightning Source LLC
Chambersburg PA
CBHW050558300426
44112CB00013B/1983